SIR
DAVID JASON

A Life of Laughter

SIR
DAVID JASON
A Life of Laughter

STAFFORD HILDRED AND TIM EWBANK

JOHN BLAKE

Published by John Blake Publishing Ltd,
3 Bramber Court, 2 Bramber Road,
London W14 9PB, England

www.johnblakepublishing.co.uk

www.facebook.com/Johnblakepub   facebook

twitter.com/johnblakepub   twitter

First published in paperback in 2007 and subsequently hardback in 2009
This edition published in hardback 2012

ISBN: 978 1 85782 803 0

British Library Cataloguing-in-Publication Data:

A catalogue record for this book is available from the British Library.

Design by www.envydesign.co.uk

Printed and bound in Great Britain by CPI Group (UK) Ltd

1 3 5 7 9 10 8 6 4 2

Papers used by John Blake Publishing are natural, recyclable products
made from wood grown in sustainable forests. The manufacturing processes
conform to the environmental regulations of the country of origin.

Pictures reproduced by kind permission of The Hornsey Journal,
PA Photos, Pearson TV, Channel 4, LWT, Alpha, Rex Features,
Universal Pictorial Press, All Action and People in Pictures.

Every attempt has been made to contact the relevant copyright-holders,
but some were unobtainable. We would be grateful if the
appropriate people could contact us.

DEDICATION

Stafford: To Janet, Claire and Rebecca.
Tim: To my mother Joy, and my children
Emma, Oliver and Carole Anne.

The authors would like to extend a huge personal thank you to all those who have helped in the preparation of this book. We are very grateful to the many people who shared their memories of David Jason but preferred to keep their identities confidential, and also to Perry Aghajanoff, Stuart Allen, Michael Aspel, Brian Babb, Paul Barber, Humphrey Barclay, Ronnie Barker, Lynda Baron, Sue Bond, Ray Butt, John Challis, Shane Chapman, Steve Clark, Vivienne Clore, Brian Cosgrove, Ann Croft, Barbara Dunks, Mark Eden, Terence Frisby, Bill Gelder, Cheryl Hall, Richard Harris, Julie Horton, Sue Holderness, Robert Knights, Vernon Lawrence, Hugh Lloyd, Roger Lloyd-Pack, Sydney Lotterby, Nicholas Lyndhurst, Ken MacDonald, Buster Merryfield, Bob Monkhouse, Margaret Morrison, Patrick Murray, Vera Neck, David Nobbs, Simon Oates, Garth Pearce, Vince Powell, Ernie Pressland, Dave Prowse, Jane Rossington, Enn Reitel, Anne Rutter, Ray Selfe, Virginia Stride, Gwyneth Strong, John Sullivan, Malcolm Taylor, Maureen Wanders, Christopher Webb, Douglas Wetherhead, Mike Weedon, Arthur White, Olwen White, Colin Williams and Joan Woodward. And most of all to David Jason for being Britain's most popular actor. Whilst he has not authorised this biography, he has always been generous with his time and helpful to the authors.

For their support and practical help we would also like to thank Corinna, Chris, Charmian and Malcolm Cowie, Arethusa, Corinne, Henri and Isabelle Plouidy, Geoffrey and Norma Barrett, Sara Cywinski, Jackie Finch, Kathryn Holcombe, Moira Marr, Beth Gibson, Jane Ennis, Rod and Joy Gilchrist, Richard Johnston, Janet Johnstone, Yvonne Partridge, Jonathon Jagger. Ella and Nesta Blundell, Clare Dillon, Simon Kinnersley, Anne Landon, Alan Rawes, Rosie Riley, Rosalind Sack, Michale and Miles Shevrin, Jack White, Francis White, Jane White and the remarkable Walter Robson. And a big thank you to all the cheerful slaves at Blake Publishing for their co-operation and kindness.

CONTENTS

PROLOGUE

David Jason was absolutely delighted by the prospect of going to Buckingham Palace in June 2005 to be knighted by Her Majesty The Queen. He was certainly surprised by the award, but without any false modesty he recognised it as a reward for a long and successful career for which he was extremely grateful. But he also knew it was a personal award to him alone and quickly came up with a perfect way to transform the personal honour into a real family celebration – by getting married to long-time partner Gill Hinchcliffe, the mother of the couple's adored five-year-old daughter Sophie Mae.

'I'd been with Gill for eight or nine years so getting married wasn't really an enormous change,' said David afterwards, anxious as usual to play down any emotions, but the smiles on their faces told a different story. Because it meant devoted Gill and little Sophie were all the more part of his joy.

Close friends said later that finally taking the plunge into matrimony the day before going to the Palace pleased him every bit as much as being elevated to a knight of the realm.

'It was all great fun,' says David. 'My daughter was very amusing as usual. She said to her teacher before the knighthood, "I'm going to the palace with my daddy because he is being reunited with the Queen".'

David's wife and daughter are far and away the two most important people in his life and he flatly refuses to get carried away by being 'Sir David'.

Months after he was honoured, David said, 'I still find it difficult to comprehend and get a handle on my title. If people want to use it they can, but I feel a bit guilty about it. I think that is because of my background.'

The actor remains fiercely proud of his working class roots in north London and still retains many friends from the days before he was famous.

And the knighthood certainly did not signal any let-up in Sir David Jason's busy work schedule. He starred in ITV's highly successful epic two-parter *Ghostboat*, screened in April 2006. It was a remarkable project that began when David found himself thumbing through a book he was handed as a prop while filming an episode of his detective series *Frost*. The 1972 novel, by George Simpson and Neal Burger, told a supernatural submarine story that was not like anything that had been seen on television before. David was intrigued by the originality of the tale and full of respect for all the brave, real-life wartime submariners. 'The Germans called subs "Iron coffins,"' noted the actor, 'because so many people died down there.' It was one of the most expensive dramas ever made by ITV and it took all of David Jason's persuasive talents and popular appeal to get it made, but both ratings and reviews were excellent. David said quietly he was simply pleased to have provided a much-needed alternative to TV's usual diet of soaps, reality shows and police and hospital dramas.

He was just as pleased to sign up to appear in the first live-action treatment of Terry Pratchett's *Discworld*. The writer has watched *Harry Potter*, *Narnia* and *The Lord of the Rings* films break box-office records but for a long time resisted all attempts to transform his own best-selling series into the promised goldmine. He agreed to turn *Hogfather*, the twentieth book in the series into one of the most expensive films made for TV, by starring as Albert, 'Death's two thousand-year-old manservant,' in a £6million, four-hour film, for screening in two parts at Christmas 2006.

Pratchett's 'Discworld' is a parallel universe that drifts through space, perched on top of four elephants which stand on the shell of a giant turtle. The *Hogfather* story takes place on the alternate universe's version of Christmas, called Hogwatch. It's a time when the Hogfather delivers gifts to children but, when he mysteriously disappears, it is Death and his manservant Albert who take over the duties.

Hogfather was premiered at the Curzon cinema in Mayfair in London towards the end of November 2006 and was greeted with general approval and critical acclaim. David said of his role: 'It was a great opportunity to get back into doing funny characters, because I started my career playing mainly funny ones – and I thought I was missing that a bit. I'd been playing all sorts of serious roles, that I'd enjoyed – though you can't say that Frost is totally serious. But when this came along I thought well here's an opportunity to get back playing a funny character. I liked the idea of playing a silly loony really, that's what attracted me.'

At the premiere David was at pains to congratulate the makers for 'breaking down the barriers' to produce *Hogfather* on a limited budget, adding: 'I think you've achieved what the Americans would have thrown money at.'

The successful adaptation of Terry Pratchett's *Hogfather* for the screen prompted Sky TV to plan a follow-up and this time the production team went back to the beginning of the Discworld series to bring to life the first two novels, *The Colour of Magic* and *Light Fantastic*. The first task for writer and director Vadim Jean was to merge the two books together to create one screenplay. It was a lengthy process, but once it had been fine-tuned it became apparent it would be the perfect vehicle for David Jason's talents – especially as it transpired that the pivotal role of Rincewind, an incompetent wizard, was a role he had always wanted to play.

David said: 'I remember reading *The Colour Of Magic* when it first came out years ago. The central character was this failed wizard who'd got a spell from the famous Octavo in his head. He was just such an amusing, endearing character. He was the sort of driving force behind the book, and I remember thinking to myself that this would make a great movie. It never came to pass, but I always kept this idea in my head that one day I would play Rincewind. I don't know why I had that belief in it. I never really thought that television could make it. I thought it was only something that big budgets could afford.'

Buoyed by the success of *Hogfather*, Sky TV were prepared to fund the project and ambitiously sanctioned the production team – largely the same as behind *Hogfather* – to build their own sets for filming at Pinewood studios. David slipped smoothly into his role of Rincewind with the help of a beard, which took 30 minutes to affix each morning, and a full-length purple wizard's gown adorned with 1200 stars and a matching purple pointed hat with a floppy brim.

And there was no doubting David's enthusiasm for his character. 'Rincewind is a failure,' he explained, 'having had a lengthy and troubled time at Unseen University, where the wizards and scholars describe him as "the magical equivalent to the number zero." Rincewind spends much of his time running away from trouble and the failed wizard is reputed for being able to solve minor problems by turning them into major disasters.'

The Colour Of Magic turned out, however, to be anything but a simple shoot with David prepared, as ever, to perform as many of his own stunts as possible. A scene on the edge of Discworld proved to be the biggest challenge for both David and for Vadim and his team. It called for Rincewind and Twoflower to be swept towards the edge of the world and potentially to watery deaths. To create this nail-biting scene, the world's biggest water tank on Pinewood's back lot, containing 806,000 gallons of water, was brought into play with wave machines and pumps employed to produce the necessary effects.

With extensive experience as a diver, the freezing water held no fears for David but it proved to be one of the hardest scenes he had filmed in his long career. He said: 'I happen to be quite adept in water because I spent many years diving, so when this idea came up, getting in the tank was no problem for me. But what they didn't tell you was that not only will you be in four feet of water, but you will have a rubber dinghy behind you with very powerful outboard motors. They didn't tell you that there would be huge pumps creating a current and waves. In the movie it will look very good and dramatic, as it should be, but to have to do it was probably one of the worst things that I've had to do. Remember you don't do this once, you do this at least a half-dozen times or more and you've got your costume on that is now full of water and weighs a ton.'

No less difficult for David to film was an upside-down sword fight. 'It's fantastic in the book.' said David, 'and I thought in my innocence, "We'll do it standing up, have a sword fight, and they'll comb your hair back and make your hair stand on end and then they'll reverse the film. Then it'll look like you're upside-down." No. That's not what happened.

'One day we were starting to film and some guy, a stunt co-ordinator, came round and said: "David, have you got ten minutes? We'll try the harness on you." And I thought: "What does he want me to try a harness on for?" We went round to one of the stages and there hanging from the roof were these two wires and he produces this harness, something that looked like it was out of an asylum to stop the lunatics going mad. And that was the first that I knew of it.

'They got me into this harness, pulled me up and then he said: "Tilt backwards. Put your legs up and wrap them round the wires." There's supposed to be stunt men who earn a fortune to do this. They pulled me up to the top of the studio to spin over, put my feet on the ceiling and I and this very attractive girl have this sword fight.

'But one of the things that you don't realise is that all the weight of your body is now on two places – on your shoulders and on your crotch. When they pull you up, everything's on the crotch, when you spin upside-down everything is on your shoulders. It's not a nice experience.

'I thought it was bad enough nearly getting drowned, but being hung upside-down like the last chicken at Sainsbury's, I wouldn't do that again in a hurry!'

For the premiere of *The Colour Of Magic*, David took along his daughter Sophie Mae on a rare public outing. Sophie by now was seven years old and David and Gill felt she was old enough to be taken out to experience an event where good behaviour was required. Their confidence in their little girl was not misplaced. 'She certainly did behave beautifully,' David said proudly of Sophie. In recent years David has paced himself in order to spend more time with Gill and watching little Sophie Mae growing up. He has now entered his 70th year but he shows no sign of retirement or of bringing to an end the long David Jason success story. 'I love entertaining people,' says David. 'But I also love trying new things and it's not easy to do both.'

Fans of Inspector Frost were enthralled to see David Jason

stepping onto the wrong side of the law on television in a highly entertaining crime series *Diamond Geezer*. He played an imprisoned jewel thief and conman Des Parker, a lovable rogue had more than a hint of Del Boy about him as he put together his teams of oddball villains to assist with ambitious heists. With high quality supporting stars like George Cole and Jenny Agutter the initial pilot and three follow up episodes were hugely enjoyable. Parker was a master of disguise, a talent that helped him to avoid the law, and David was delighted to find some excellent writing which lifted the inventive series.

Parker took on many different identities, from professor to photocopy repairman and from art lecturer to businessman, and Jason insisted, as usual, on doing as many of his own stunts as possible. *Diamond Geezer* was impressive and it had many viewers wondering if its star would ever return to upholding law and order in murderous Denton.

'I wanted to go back to Frost,' he said. 'I really did, but I have to admit that I thought the old chap had finally come to the end of the line about five years ago.

'Then I was persuaded to give it another go, purely because there were three scripts that I thought were truly five-star.'

David Jason was in his late 60s and clearly past police pensionable age but he decided to give Frost fans what they wanted, more high quality crime stories. The three new *A Touch of Frost* films were screened in 2008 and the formula proved as successful as ever. 'I was really pleased by the reaction,' said David. 'I think one of the reasons they went down so well was that we had some really excellent guest stars.

'It was a delight to discover high profile actors of the calibre of Cherie Lunghi and Keith Barron were available. We were very lucky. It's good to know *A Touch of Frost* has this reputation within the business as well as with the viewers.' And, not surprisingly, the talented Mr Jason did not take long to fit into the role.

'It happens overnight really,' he said. 'As soon as I begin to go through the script, I read it as Frost. I'd say that reading a Frost script was like putting on a warm, comfortable pair of slippers that fit perfectly.'

The three films – *In The Public Interest*, *Mind Games* and *Dead End* – went down very well and David Jason spoke frankly about the age factor. 'As an actor, it is my job to entertain people,' he said simply. 'I enjoy the whole process from beginning to end. Fortunately, Frost won the hearts and minds of the public.

'Of course, it has been noted that Frost would be retired by now, but because we're in entertainment and not real life, we're able to ignore that. We love Frost and as long as he can solve the crime and punish the villain we can ignore that fact.'

Even so, he at last finally decided enough was enough. After agreeing, to the relief of ITV bosses, to make two final Frost adventures in 2009 he announced they would be the last we would see of the crumpled, yet charismatic, copper.

'I don't want to go down the Dixon of Dock Green route, where George Dixon was apparently still in the police force when he was in his 80s, leaning on the cop shop counter for support and wearing his carpet slippers out of view of the camera.'

But fortunately, no more Inspector Jack Frost does not mean no more David Jason. The actor remains in remarkable demand. Even Marks and Spencer called on his voice as they decided to re-vamp their award-winning ads. And also for screening in 2009 is the remarkable television film *Albert's Memorial*. It is the moving story of three World War Two veterans, Albert, Harry and Frank. As Albert lies dying in hospital his old comrades decide to make his last wish, to be buried on one of their old German battlefields, come true. The last time Albert, played by Michael Jayston, felt really alive was in the closing stages of the taking of Berlin so Harry (David Jason) and Frank (David Warner) take his body and attempt to take it to Germany. The plot unfolds as Harry and Frank eventually kidnap Albert's body from the hospital mortuary and begin a journey that will change their lives forever, as they explore dark events, hardly mentioned since 1945. With Albert's coffin tied to the roof rack of Harry's black cab, they set off on their adventure to honour their friend's last wish and create Albert's memorial. The journey will see Frank and Harry coming to terms with the trauma and emotion of what happened all those years ago, when as soldiers fighting for their survival, they joined forces with the Russians to encircle Berlin. Throughout their voyage of adventure, each skates on dangerously thin emotional ice, as the events of 1945 continue to haunt them. It's a brilliant black comedy about friendship that provides yet another enthralling platform for the sublime and enduring acting talents of Sir David Jason.

One great sadness was the death of David Jason's great friend and mentor Ronnie Barker. The memories are very precious. David Jason said, 'I will always feel very, very, very lucky to have been able to work with Ronnie. I'll always remember one particularly wonderful line that Ronnie said to me one day. We were rehearsing *Open All Hours* and all the cast were laughing their heads off about something. Ronnie turned to me with this big grin and he said, "Isn't this marvelous – we're getting paid to make ourselves laugh!" That's how I remember him.'

But with his young family and his energy for work Sir David Jason spends much more time looking forwards than backwards. Aged 69, he is still going up in the world, having swapped his bus pass for a helicopter pilot's licence. He said, 'It's taken me quite a long time to achieve, but I finally got it at the end of last year, just at the age when most people are retiring. You've got to have something to aim at if you want to get off the ground and go places, haven't you?'

Stafford Hildred and Tim Ewbank

CHILDHOOD

The tidy, terraced houses in Lodge Lane, Finchley, were built more than 200 years ago. They were first built as farm cottages for workers on the agricultural estates that swept right down into the edges of north London which have long since been swallowed up by suburbia. On 2 February 1940, as the Second World War raged bitterly across Europe, one of the coldest winters in years had encouraged most residents to stoke up the fires and stay indoors. But Billingsgate fish porter Arthur White and his sprightly little Welsh wife Olwen, who lived at 26 Lodge Lane, were otherwise occupied at the nearby North Middlesex Hospital bringing twin baby boys into the world.

They already had a seven-year-old son, also called Arthur, and they were delighted to increase the size of their young family two-fold. Four days later, a neighbour generously used some of Arthur's precious petrol ration to ferry Olwen and the baby boys home and, for a few days, their joy at their domestic bliss was undimmed, even by the horrors of war. But one of the boys was weak and ailing. His breathing was failing as a massive infection took hold of his fragile frame. Olwen did everything she could to try to breathe life into her sickening son but, tragically, he died after just two short weeks of life.

'I was in such despair,' said Olwen bleakly, years later. 'We had decided to call the twins David and Jason. David was healthy but Jason was so sickly he never had a chance and I felt so helpless. I just had to watch him go. I don't even know what was really wrong with him. I buried the tiny body myself, out the back. I didn't know what else to do. We didn't tell anybody. We had no money for a proper burial. It was war and I had to do it.'

The healthy twin thrived and his birth was registered a month afterwards when Arthur and Olwen later trudged to Edmonton Register Office on 19 March 1940 to record, sadly, a single addition to the family. David John White was a lively baby with a powerful set of lungs which he was always eager to demonstrate to his grieving parents. Olwen and Arthur were devastated by their loss, but they were also determined that their tiny son should not be forgotten, and would often quietly wonder together what might have become of Jason had he been strong enough to survive. Olwen was naturally especially delighted when her surviving twin eventually went on to make the two names so well loved and famous throughout the land.

Yet, in fact, it was not until David was 14 that he discovered the stunning truth that he was a twin and that his baby brother had died soon after birth. It was an enormous shock to the teenager. To outsiders, David has always tried hard to look deeply unimpressed by the revelation but, in reality, it had a shattering effect on the young man. When asked by the authors about his lost brother, he quickly became very businesslike and matter-of-fact, insisting coolly, 'It just came out during the course of some conversation with my mother that apparently I had had a twin.'

David is typically anxious to play down any hint of the family trauma and would say only, 'The bottom line of the story is that one survived and one did not. It happens all the time. Many years ago, my brother Arthur's wife was pregnant with twins and she lost both of them. They now have a son called Russell which is wonderful.' David insists publicly that he does not feel his determination to do well is any sort of compensation for the death of his brother. 'It has never, ever occurred to me,' he said. 'Two little dots came out. One dot lived and one did not. I just found out casually in the course of a conversation. "You did have a twin, you know", said my mother. I just said, "Oh did I? Oh really". At that time, my mother was great and there was no problem. It was never given any weight and it was not a problem for me. I was not made to feel any responsibility. The irony is that we are all made from a moment in time.'

But one school friend remembers it very differently. 'When he came to school the day after his mum told him about his twin dying, he looked terrible. He was shaking with emotion and he looked absolutely shattered. He swore us to secrecy about it and I think he hardly ever mentioned it again. But that day he looked awful, as though all his humour and energy had drained out of him. That day he said he felt guilty but, to be honest, I think afterwards he somehow drew strength from it, as if he had an added responsibility to achieve things on behalf of his brother as well as himself.'

David's parents were determined to do the very best for all their children. Olwen insisted that the long family tradition of looking after your own was very strongly in her mind. In any case, there was a war on and tragedy was an everyday occurrence.

England in 1940 experienced a bitterly cold winter and

it was a shivering London that welcomed baby David. The Thames froze over as temperatures tumbled to the lowest of the century. But inside the humble terraced house, with its outside toilet and its tin bath hanging on a nail in the back door, David White spent his first months and years of life in a home which was always warm and happy, air raids permitting.

Baby David did his bit for the family war effort by noisily resisting attempts to put on his tiny gas mask. Whenever the air raid sirens sounded and the family started to move to the relative safety of the shelter erected in the house, David's screams of protest began. 'It used to worry me a lot, that gas mask,' recalls Olwen. 'He just screamed like mad when I put it on him.'

David's cries often had to compete against the noise of German air raids which used to inspire his mother to retaliate by hurling curses in the direction of Berlin as she angrily crashed dishes around in her tiny kitchen. Once, the Luftwaffe almost silenced these outbursts with a near miss, which left the house structurally undamaged but somehow managed to blow out Olwen's cooker. Happily, the only casualty was the cake she was baking at the time.

The War made its grim effects felt as food rationing was brought in and, just four days after the birth of the twins, that most famous of Government campaigns was launched to combat the threat of German spies – 'Careless Talk Costs Lives'. Olwen was determined to protect her brood from the worst of the war. Her native Wales had endowed her with brisk efficiency and a warm sense of humour. A baby girl, June, completed the family four years after David was born. And while there was never much money to go around, the fiercely independent Olwen supplemented her husband's meagre wages by going out and working as a cleaner.

The wartime blackouts frequently disrupted Arthur's

trips to work. He had to get up at about 4.00am to cycle to Billingsgate and, soon after war broke out, he overslept. Arthur looked like being very late and was urgently pedalling through a dark and gloomy north London when the road simply disappeared and he went careering into a bomb crater about 50ft wide and 40ft deep.

Arthur was knocked out cold. When he came round about 20 minutes later, he found he was trapped at the bottom of a huge hole and, try as he might, he was unable to scramble up the sides and out. He started shouting for help and, after a further 15 minutes, two men arrived and shone their torches down on an anguished Arthur.

'Go on,' said Arthur, 'get me out of here will you, lads?' The faces looking down were wide-eyed in amazement. Then one of the rescuers said, 'Bloody hell. He's had a 50-ton bomb dropped on him and the bugger's still alive!'

There always was a black side to wartime humour. David's older brother, Arthur junior, was growing up fast and was quick to capitalise when a German air raid on north London blasted a part of a human arm up on to the guttering at the back of 26 Lodge Lane. Enterprising Arthur was charging the other children 2d (two old pennies) a look until his sideshow was interrupted by angry adults. The local doctor was called to remove the arm in a bag, much to the irritation and disappointment of Arthur and his ghoulish young customers.

Arthur was always a boisterous lad and came close to ending one of Britain's most promising acting careers some 20 years before it had begun, with a badly aimed house brick. Arthur recalled the incident with a wince.

'When we were schoolboys, David wanted to come to a camp I had made with my mates. I wouldn't let him, and he was hanging about trying to get in. Unfortunately, he got in the way of a brick I was throwing at our 'enemies'. It hit him on the head and nearly killed him. I was shattered, and to this day he still carries the scar.'

Olwen was the driving force of the family and, on most matters, whatever she said went. Neighbours were always treated with just enough friendliness and respect but kept firmly at a safe distance. The family was well-liked but Olwen saw to it that they always kept themselves very much to themselves.

David's early explorations of his locality were conducted in a somewhat unusual form of transport, a rickety wooden wheelbarrow. Next-door neighbour Ernie Pressland recalls David as . . . 'a little ragged-arsed sod in a barrow. His brother Arthur used to get lumbered with pushing him around. All the kids from Lodge Lane used to stick together in one great big sprawling gang. Arthur was our leader – we used to call him 'King Arthur' – and we used to go scrumping apples over near the posh houses in Totteridge.'

The Whites were one important social step up on the Presslands in that their air raid shelter was an indoor Morrison device, while their neighbours relied upon the outdoor Anderson variety to save them from the Germans. But after young Eileen Pressland caught what tragically became a fatal dose of pneumonia after a night of shivering in the cold, the family shunned either form of shelter.

Ernie recalls, 'After Eileen died, we all slept together in the same bedroom, all six kids and my mum and dad. My mother said, "We'll all go together if we go." But we all became close in the Blitz. The Whites were good friends and neighbours.'

Young David was known as 'Whitey' and, it seems, had a real dramatic talent right from his early days.

Ernie Pressland remembers, 'I had been firing potato pellets from a toy gun and David reckoned I'd copped him one in the ear. I didn't really know if I hit him but he went through such a dying spasm act that my mother went bananas and broke the gun to pieces over my back.'

It was certainly obvious to all the family that David's flair for acting was apparent from a very early age. Olwen found her children's favourite game was dressing up. Her frilly blouses and floppy hats, dresses and coats and her husband's trousers and shirts were all in constant demand from the three youngsters who loved to act out their own little plays. Arthur, the oldest, generally took the early lead in the junior White dramatic society, but David and June always seemed to be playing the biggest parts by the end.

When they got older, they pestered their mother to take them to scavenge in junk shops for even more outlandish outfits. Olwen encouraged the artistic side in her offspring. She was steeped in the Welsh family tradition of creating your own entertainment through large gatherings with every relation called upon to deliver a song or a monologue.

In fact, when the children moved on to nearby Northside School, it was June who impressed dramatically with a spirited portrayal of Queen Victoria in an early school play. At Northside School, David's cheeky sense of humour certainly began to develop. His best friend was a lad called Mike Weedon who lived just two streets away in Grange Avenue. The two youngsters made sure that life was never dull for their English teacher, an endlessly harassed lady called Miss Holmes. Mike recalls that one of David's early pranks was to spray on a little extra decoration to her dress.

'I remember once, as Miss Holmes walked up the aisle between desks with a smart blue dress on, David got a pen full of ink and flicked it on to the back of her dress. She never knew it was him as the ink blended in with the colour of the dress.'

David was always the form clown and his high-spirited partnership with Mike Weedon made sure both boys were regularly in trouble with some teachers.

'We were always getting separated because of our antics,' recalls Mike Weedon. 'Every lesson seemed to begin with

"White, get down to the front of the class. Weedon, get to the back of the class." We always tried to sit next to each other, but we played up too much.'

Certainly, Miss Holmes did not always fully appreciate David's irrepressible sense of fun. She once caned him very hard on his wrist and hand in front of the class.

Mike Weedon says, 'She was so mad at something he had done, she struck him haphazardly across the wrist and we couldn't believe it when David turned round and said, "I'm going to report you to the headmaster." And he went right along to the headmaster, Mr Maurice Hackett. Huge weals had come up on his wrist and he just stormed out of the classroom and into the head's office. She got into trouble and was told to ease off by the Head. She missed his hand and hit his wrist and it could have been quite damaging.' David was never shy about sticking up for himself. He was well below average height but, somehow, his energy and his ready wit meant that he was rarely picked on by bigger boys.

But Mr Hackett was not always so sympathetic. David and Mike packed countless scrapes into their school careers. A favourite way to start the day was to devise a new way of avoiding assembly in the morning. One day, the pair dodged down into a darkened tunnel area that ran underneath school to get out of the tedious ceremony. Unfortunately, the tunnel contained a drain which swiftly soaked them up to the ankles in water, and much worse was to come when they squelched out after assembly.

Mike remembers, 'We kept quiet until everybody had gone and crept up the stairs and round to the front door. Who should be standing there, but Mr Hackett. He caught us fair and square and we had to wait outside his room before we finally got the cane. One stroke on the hand.'

David certainly did not shine in his first years at school. He was painfully shy and in his early teens lacked any sort of confidence. But a perceptive and thoughtful teacher helped him to develop.

David said, 'When I first started at school I was not very bright and I did not do very well. I always seemed to be very backward. Then I found that there was something I could do well and that helped me a lot. I was always very physical and we had a very good young teacher, called Mr Joy, who taught us gymnastics. Because I was agile and could do things, he said, "That is very good," and he told the rest of the class to watch how I did one exercise and try to copy it.'

David had never before been used as a model for his contemporaries to match, and he thoroughly enjoyed the experience. 'It was the first time a teacher had ever said anything like that to me. That was a big turning point for me, because I thought if I can do that in gymnastics, why can't I do it in History or Geography or whatever?

'I was never very good at Maths, but at English and Science I began to creep up the scale because I realised that if I could do something well physically, it gave me a spur. Before then, I believe that deep down I had subconsciously given up. I always used to feel the lessons were so complicated and I would just give up before I started, so I was always bottom of the class. But Mr Joy proved that I could do something well. That gave me enormous confidence and it opened the door for me. I was a natural gymnast and it has been with me ever since.

'He started me reading a lot and helped me in every way. I worked at science and got an award, and I went on to become a prefect and captain of the football and swimming teams. I owe that man a lot.'

David deliberately avoided pointing out that his improvement at school exactly coincided with his discovery that he was a surviving twin. He prefers not to delve into the psychology of loss but it seems clear that his new-found purpose and sense of awareness had at least some connection with the surprising new knowledge that he was the surviving twin.

Maureen Wanders was another teacher who treated young David more gently. She spotted his flair for entertaining and recalls, 'He was a natural performer who always made the other children laugh. He seemed to stop growing when he was 13 or 14 and I think he was quite self-conscious about being short. But he was high spirited and very popular. He brought the house down in one play we put on.

'And in class he could always be relied upon to liven things up. He wasn't naughty, just great fun, with a great sense of humour. David shone at English, but drama was where his real talent lay. You could not miss his natural flair.'

David frankly recalled, 'At school, I was a well known joker and the reason why was because I was very small and very slight and, in order to survive, I started clowning. I think this is true of a lot of people who are in comedy.

'In my case, I knew that if you're little you tend to get beaten up by the bigger lads, so in order to defend myself as I was not very well built, I decided to make them laugh. It was no help being a coward. They kicked cowards. You had to use your brains. And all bullies need a court jester. I couldn't fight them with my fists so I fought them with my wits. I didn't want to get kicked to death so I made them laugh. I really worked at it so, if there was any problem, I could get them so busy laughing that they forgot about beating me up.'

David was always able to laugh off his lack of inches but just sometimes he yearned to be tall. He often looked smaller than he was because he used to be swallowed by clothes which were just a little too big for him to provide long lasting value.

'We never had much money in our family,' he said. 'Everything I owned my mother would say, "He'll grow into it," so I had jackets with sleeves that were too long and shoes that were too big. And, one Christmas, when I was 10 or 11, the thing I wanted more than anything was a bike. Come Christmas morning and there it was, but my feet wouldn't reach the pedals.

'As usual my mother had bought me a full-size model, "to grow into". My father had to put wooden blocks on the pedals and even then my toes only just touched them. My street cred really plummeted after that.'

David's mother always had great hopes for her children. She was pleased that David's schoolwork was improving, but was still anxious to help. She frequently sent David, and any other youngsters she could dragoon, up to the local library in Finchley to listen to worthy, self-improving lectures as an addition to their schoolwork.

A youngster, called Brian Barnycoat (known as Bodgy for short) became friendly with David and Mike Weedon and the trio became great pals for many years.

Even as a young boy, the most noticeable thing about David was his sharp sense of humour. He led the threesome on a trip into central London to see his radio heroes The Goons. Peter Sellers was David's childhood idol. He played his Goons records over and over again on the record player in the White front room and marvelled at the hilarious Sellers mimicry and range of voices. David was addicted to the Goons and thoroughly enjoyed watching one episode being recorded. He said, 'They broke all the rules and, of course, the older generation did not understand what on earth we were all going on about. They were so off the wall.'

David gradually realised that he had a talent to amuse, even if it did embarrass his friends sometimes. A favourite early comic stunt was to alarm the occupants of a crowded Tube train by pretending to sew his fingers together.

'He would pull a hair from his head and then go to thread it through a needle,' recalls Mike Weedon. 'He would start with his little finger and work round them all and then pass through the palm of his hand. Then he would pull it and automatically the fingers of his hands would close. He would take about ten minutes for it all to happen and people would be fascinated. We would be cringing, it was so embarrassing. We all thought he was crazy. But I suppose he was only acting.'

Not all young David's attempts at humour were quite so subtle. A hapless window cleaner, widely considered by David and his young pals in Lodge Lane to be something of a dirty old man, experienced a rather smellier and more slapstick comedy routine. In those days, when horse-drawn carts were still a familiar feature of the north London traffic, the window cleaner always carried buckets to scoop up the horse droppings to sell as manure to some of the enthusiastic rose-growers of the community. This meant his barrow was usually laden with, not just ladders, but buckets of steaming natural fertiliser.

David thoughtfully inserted two bangers deep into one bucket, lit the fuse and made a run for it. The resulting explosion left the poor window cleaner and a couple of innocent passers-by covered in horse muck.

Ernie's younger sister Julie Pressland was a good friend from childhood. She remembers the incident clearly. 'We all thought the window cleaner was a pervert so no one was very sorry for him,' she says. 'It was a real mess. There was horse shit everywhere. The window cleaner was really mad and, kids being kids, someone told him David was responsible. But, by then, David was long gone.

'That was pretty typical of David. He was full of devilment but he never did anyone any real harm. It was just for a joke. He loved to make people laugh even in those days. I remember he had an air gun and he filled another neighbour's tin bath full of holes.

'Another time we had some washing strung out on a line in the back yard and my mum kept looking out and saying, "There's a funny wind – it's only blowing the knickers." David was hanging out of his back window taking pot shots at our underwear with his toy gun! There were five women in our family so there were always plenty of drawers on the line for him to aim at.'

David did later become an accomplished cook, but one of his early efforts looked distinctly unpalatable. His mother was baking and young David came out into the yard with some pastry that he said he wanted to make into pies. He mixed it up with leaves, mud and sugar and baked it. Then, when he had cooked the alarming mixture, he sat down and ate it and, with characteristically convincing dramatic style, he pretended he was munching on a chocolate eclair!

Julie says, 'He was always very funny. And even when we were young he could walk into a room and make people laugh. It was never unkind, cruel humour but always gentle, taking the mickey out of himself instead of other people. He would make a joke about his lack of height and get everyone laughing at him. We lived on the poor side of the street. The houses on the other side were more expensive and we always used to call that the posh side.'

Julie and David spent hours just chatting in the rickety lean-to which separated their tiny back gardens. 'He was always good to be with because he was such a laugh. His imagination would always conjure up stories and jokes. But he did have a serious side.

'I remember once he planted this tree at the bottom of his garden. It was really more a yard than a garden. There were no flowers or greenery at all and he wanted to make it look nicer. He really nurtured this tree. He watered it and really tried to look after it. I think he was a sort of premature 'green'. It got to be about 6ft tall and he was really proud of it. Then the man whose garden backed on to David's chopped it down one day when we were at school. He said it cut out his light. David was absolutely gutted. Really upset.'

Julie's older sister Maureen was impressed by David's ability to mimic a wide range of different voices. 'I'll never forget David coming outside into the yard at the back on a warm summer's night and putting on a really posh voice. "Would you care to take the air on the veranda," he said and then he laughed. He had the kind of laugh which meant you just had to laugh with him.'

David was by now above average at his lessons but rarely excelled. He saved his efforts for more worthwhile causes, like arguing passionately with his pals that Elvis Presley should most certainly make that much talked about but never realised tour of Britain. David didn't know then that he had a genuine link with Presley, who had also suffered the death of his twin.

Acting entered young David's life through school plays. Mike Weedon remembers acting with him in an early play called *The Ostler*.

'He had a singing part and really shone. Even as a boy he had a real charisma about him on stage.'

David had his own room at home where he spent hours listening to the radio. His favourite show was the science fiction adventure series *Journey Into Space* and he sent off for a picture of the crew of the Discovery. He was delighted when it arrived, complete with autographs on the back.

David's house was usually the base for the youngsters and Mike Weedon recalls it was generally Olwen who took an interest in their youthful games and ambitions. 'His dad was an old sour-puss, old Arthur. David's mum was fun. But Arthur had a very bad gait and would limp and that might have been part of his bad moods. He kept out of the way and we kept out of his way. Although his dad always had an eye out that we didn't really get into trouble.'

What Mike Weedon never knew was that Arthur senior was wracked with pain from crippling arthritis. David was often deeply upset when he saw his father in agony. It left a lasting impression on him and in later life he frequently takes time out quietly to help arthritis charities.

The intrepid threesome all shared a lack of inches. They were all very short for their age all the way through school but never worried about it too much. 'We used to call ourselves "The Shorthouses",' laughed Mike Weedon. 'I got picked on a couple of times because of my size, but David was so funny and well-liked I don't think he ever got picked on.'

But perhaps the event which really shaped the future came when David was 14, just after his mother had broken the news to him about his dead twin. The school play had a problem when a young actor dropped out with measles and Headmaster Hackett was looking around for a replacement.

David remembers, 'For some reason, he decided I could do this part. I can still hear him saying, "White, I want a word with you." I thought, "Oh Gawd, what have I done now? This is it. I must be in trouble again."'

But, in fact, the Head carried the news that the boy's illness would keep him out of the production and cheeky young David White was his choice for replacement. 'I want you to take over,' he told David.

Perhaps, surprisingly, the suggestion was not then a welcome one. David might have enjoyed dressing up and larking about at home but doing it in public before the critical eyes of his pals was quite another thing.

'I wasn't very keen at all,' he says. 'I thought acting and plays were girls' things. When you're in a working-class school, being in a play seems like playing girls' games. You don't fancy doing it because it's all a bit girlish and I most definitely wanted to be seen as one of the lads.'

But the Headmaster insisted. 'I think you would be absolutely right and you are the only one I can think of to do this part,' he said firmly. The expression on David's face told its own reluctant tale so the Head added cryptically, 'Let me put it this way. Don't ask me to tell you to do it.'

With that, he left young David White to cogitate on his first casting problem. 'I was standing there for about five minutes trying to work out what he had said,' remembered David. 'Of course, I worked out that I was going to do it anyway. The difference was that he was asking me to do it. I slowly realised that if I said 'No', he was going to tell me to do it. That was it. It was a *fait accompli*, really. I had no choice – I did it under duress.'

The play was a one-act production called *Wayside War*, set during the time of the Cromwellian wars. David entered the action with a heavy heart. 'I was playing a cavalier and dressing up in all those funny clothes made it even worse. But something happened to me when I started to do it. It was somehow amazing. It was fun. It worked. After all that pressure to take part I found to my complete surprise that I was actually enjoying myself.

'It was a spy story, based on real events which had actually happened which really intrigued me. There was a spy in Bridgwater who was giving all this information to the other side. This cavalier stayed at this inn and he knew someone in the area was giving all the secrets away but he did not know who. There was a wonderful woman in this hostelry and they met and spent the evening, and later the night, together. Of course, during this he discovers that she was the spy.

'But he sort of falls in love with her and the next morning she is going off and he knows that he has got to arrest her because she is putting his side in danger. But he lets her go. Obviously he should never have done that, but he did. Because it was all based on actual happenings, for the first time it made history come alive for me. And being on stage was an amazing experience for me.

'We did it for three nights. Our parents and friends all came and it went down really well. Then they said we were going to do it in a drama festival. That was something completely new to me, I didn't know what a drama festival was. But I found out that all these amateur groups and schools put in their shows and then over about two weeks they all get performed. And you go and watch a lot of the other plays and then, on the last night, the four plays selected by the adjudicator are performed. Our play was chosen in the last four, and then after we did it we found out that we had won the trophy. It bowled me over. Suddenly there was a competitive thing in my life, and I met all these people who were enthusiastic about acting. Just being in the play was amazing. I can remember the audience laughing and it occurred to me that I was really, really enjoying it. It was a way of being clever and a success, and I'd never been much of either in school.'

David's mother was impressed. She said, 'We knew he had something special. He had this quick way with him that could lift people in the audience. I think it comes from our family. Back in Wales our family would always provide their own entertainment. Everyone stood up and did a turn, going back generations. Something of that went straight through to David. But not just to him, to all my children. Arthur and June had it, too, and it made me think of the baby that died. I told David and he gave me one of his looks.'

The stage success gave young David confidence but he still had no thought of acting becoming a career. 'I don't think I gave a second thought to taking it that seriously,' said David. 'I was much too busy having a good time.'

The teenage trio of David, Mike Weedon and Brian Barneycoat enjoyed their own company and after school would rush off on their bicycles on trips into the green countryside on the very edge of London. At weekends, they would cycle to Broxbourne to secret dens they made on the banks of the River Lea.

Next-door neighbour Ernie Pressland was called up for National Service at 18 and sold his bicycle to David who was four years younger. It was a flash model with 'Tour de France' handlebars and the price was £2.

'I was ripped off, and not for the first time,' reflected David bleakly. Even so, the trio would think nothing of round trips of 50 miles or more and all have memories of long, sun-filled idyllic days. Mike Weedon remembers, 'We were three loners really, I suppose. We didn't get into girls' company much. We really liked our bikes.'

David was unquestionably the leader of the little gang and usually the inspiration of their escapades. Mike Weedon recalls fondly, 'David organised so many pranks that it became commonplace for him to do it. If he didn't lark about, then you knew he must be in a really bad mood. He would play around all the time. He was really a fairly good student but he never stood out.'

But baiting teachers with practical jokes and at all costs avoiding taking schoolwork too seriously did not endear the trio to the school authorities. Headmaster Hackett was concerned, as the boys approached 15, that their childish pranks could turn into more serious teenage trouble-making and wisely decided that perhaps they needed a more creative outlet for their energy and mischief. Recognising David's considerable dramatic skill and potential ability to act more than the goat, he sent off the two young lads with another problem boy to Douglas Weatherhead, then the drama instructor for Middlesex who was running an evening drama group attached to the local amateur Incognito Theatre Group.

'I've got three boys here and if they don't find themselves something to do they're going to get themselves into trouble,' said the Headmaster to the amiable Mr Weatherhead, who was still a stalwart of the Incognitos some 35 years on, but sadly passed away in 1996. He welcomed the three nervous youngsters and introduced them to the Incognito Theatre, an old soda siphon factory converted by the enthusiastic amateurs with seats from a blitzed cinema, which remains their headquarters to this day.

Douglas Weatherhead recalls fondly, 'Right from the start, I could see that David was quite obviously a winner. Mike Weedon was quite reasonable but David, you could see from the start, was simply exceptional. He picked up accents and intonations beautifully. He would have been a very good serious actor, but of course his lack of height went against him. In those days, you had to be the classic, tall and good-looking Laurence Olivier type to get anywhere. I can't remember the third boy's name but we lost him quite quickly. David and Mike, who were real pals, stayed.'

David recalls that his initial euphoria for acting with the Incognitos was not totally based upon dramatic ambition. 'We went down there for the first time one Monday night because we were now inflamed with the success of *Wayside War*. And we found that there were 22 girls there and one bloke. We thought, 'Yeah, we'll have some of that.' That was our first picture of the Incognitos. I think that is what coloured our enthusiasm really.

'They had a proper senior amateur group and they also had this fabulous training group for young people as well. It was marvellous. They had their own little theatre. They trained lots of people to act. It was very good, it was a way of getting young people involved with the theatre. It was like a social group of course but there was also the chance to take parts in the senior group. They taught me so many of the skills of the theatre.

'We used to go on Mondays and Wednesdays and it quickly became much more than a hobby for me. It gradually became more and more fascinating and more and more interesting. The more I found out about acting, the more interesting it became.

'The more new doors I opened up, the more I realised there was to acting. It got steadily more difficult and because it got more difficult I always wanted more and more to get over the next hurdle, to learn the new technique or understand the next new idea. I wanted to succeed as an actor so much and I was desperate to improve my skills. But every level I reached seemed to open up new levels to aim at. The more deep and the more complex the whole business of acting became, the more involved I became. I was there for 10 years and in that time I went and acted with other amateur groups as well. As I was given more and more important roles to play, the challenge became greater.

'I never found acting an easy thing to do. It was difficult, very difficult. But because it was so difficult, it became a question of developing dedication and application to try to keep improving and developing my skills. And I learned early on that the only person who can really do all that is yourself. I tried to learn and absorb from people who knew more than me, from teachers, directors, actors or anyone, and I tried to apply that knowledge in every way I could.'

Part of David's initial audition for the Incognitos was to pretend to be much older, first 45 and then 85. Most youngsters of his age would scarcely have appreciated the difference and been inclined to bend every joint stiff to simulate either great age. But David, observers recall, was able effortlessly to suggest the difference between middle age and great age.

'David was a natural,' says Douglas Weatherhead. 'He took to acting like a duck to water. Mike was a great friend of David's and he was quite good but, of course, David was so much better that he always got the big parts while Mike was left with the small parts.

'David was also a great joker. He had a marvellous sense of humour and used to tease Mike that he was forever trying to pad out his parts. On one occasion, when Mike was supposed to have suffered a small cut on his cheek in a Drayton and Hare farce, David joked that he would no doubt finish up as a number-one accident case.

'David always kept us in fits of laughter. Whenever we took a break for coffee, he kept the whole thing going. I never did find out what sort of trouble the Headmaster thought he was heading for, but once he found an outlet in acting there was no sign of any trouble for him. That was it. He was wide-eyed with enthusiasm when he arrived.

'I remember that, like most of the young lads at the time, he never had much money. And once we were rehearsing a play with David taking a leading role when one of our rather stuffier senior members remarked rather pointedly that David had still not stumped up his annual membership subscription. I think it was half a crown at the time. I was so indignant at this and so impressed by David's talent that I said if the lad didn't pay it, I would pay it myself. And I would have done. It would have been a very worthwhile investment, don't you think?'

Despite their lack of academic dedication, both David and Mike Weedon became prefects in their final year at Northside. Their authority in handing out lines and detention to their juniors was hardly helped by their lack of inches. Both were just 5ft 4in tall when they left school.

'We did shoot up a bit afterwards,' says Mike, 'and we both finished at 5ft 6in.' The final act of leaving school was quite a traumatic experience for them. Mike remembers, 'We had always been saying that we couldn't wait to leave school, but on the last day I know we all really didn't want to go. It was a very emotional experience for all of us. We all had to go up on stage in turn and there was this great big guy called John Smith who went up and just burst out crying he was so upset.

There were tears streaming down his face and I know it affected us all. David was highly strung and a very sensitive young man. After all our big talk about the future, we were really surprised at how choked we all felt.'

The diminutive trio remained good friends long after they left school and, as soon as they were 16, they all exchanged their faithful pushbikes for much more exciting motorbikes, which instantly enlarged the scope of their adventures. David's first motorbike was an aged 350cc BSA on which he lavished hours of tender loving care.

His mother was never too keen on her precious son's new obsession, fearing the dangers of David revving around the country on the powerful machine. She was even less enthusiastic when he took the bike to pieces in her tiny hallway. Bitterly cold weather meant that this was the only place to service the bike, but Olwen gave David a fierce telling off every time a drop of oil found its way on to her carpet.

The motorbikes changed the lives of the youngsters. Their horizons were suddenly nationwide. All of a sudden, from being limited to within a few hours' pedalling distance of their homes, they could now explore the whole country. First on the list was the Lake District.

With David leading the way on his powerful 350cc machine, Bodgy riding pillion and Mike following on his smaller 250cc bike, they set out to explore the beauties of the Lakes. Unfortunately, the bargain basement accommodation turned out to be not even worth the small sum they paid for it.

'When we got there we found it was a terrible little caravan on the banks of Lake Windermere,' said Mike Weedon. 'We only got it cheap because it was falling to bits. It was parked right on the side of the lake and it was pretty miserable really, especially when I ended up getting left behind when my bike packed up.'

Despite his enthusiasm for high speed, David was usually a careful motorcyclist, yet he did come close to losing his life on his motorbike when he was racing back from Clacton with Mike Weedon riding pillion. It was a busy summer evening with the main roads so clogged with traffic that inventive David had picked a favourite personal short-cut, winding round a sequence of back roads.

As dusk fell, the two youngsters thrilled to the speedy journey and leaned energetically into every bend, until they reached a particularly sharp corner when David yelled to his passenger, 'There's too much gravel, I'm going to lose it.'

To Mike's horror, David pulled out of the bend, straightened the screaming machine and went straight on over the bank at the side of the road. With enormous good fortune, they crashed violently through the undergrowth and found the road again on the other side. Then they hit the bank and the bike just took off. When they landed they were remarkably lucky to hit the road facing straight ahead and carry on unscathed. Mike breathlessly yelled to his daring driver, 'Dave, Dave, stop. Let's have a fag.'

But the daring young man on his flying machine was seriously scared himself. He yelled back grimly, 'If I stop now, I'll lose my nerve,' and just kept on heading for home.

David's love of speed was undimmed by the experience. He later exchanged his trusty 350cc BSA for a much more powerful 500cc Shooting Star, which could comfortably exceed the magical 'ton'.

Mike Weedon recalls, 'He really cherished that 500. He did the ton more than once. He loved high speed. He used to get quite excited about having gone more than 100mph. We had no farings to make us more streamlined in those days, so David would lie down as flat as he could on the bike to get up to those sorts of speeds. He loved it.

'We used to race each other up the A1 and back down the

Watford bypass, but it was nothing really serious. We just enjoyed racing for the fun of it and hoped the police didn't manage to spot us.'

David plays down his high-speed youth and insists, 'We were never real tearaways on the bikes, we were gentleman motorcyclists. There were the rockers but me and my mates had flat caps and goggles and we weren't into all the Teddy Boy thing either. We were very shy and found it very difficult to talk to the ladies and we didn't succeed in that department at all. So we concentrated on our motorbikes. I suppose that is what young lads do –find other ways to expend their energy. We used to strip them down, heat them up, and rebuild them.

'I was so into motorbikes that in our outside toilet on the toilet roll holder was carved something like 'While You Sit Here You Will Have All Your Best Dreams', and I wrote underneath 'Or A Super Road Rocket'. At the time, that was the Mercedes Benz of motorbiking.

'Today, I drive a Jaguar XJS. In those days, a Super Road Rocket was as far away as the moon or an XJS because they cost about £750. We were earning £12 a week then. If I really pushed myself, I could save £2 a week which I did.'

The three lads also spent a few weeks with Bodgy's grandfather down in Cornwall where they were all bedded down in the same room on a huge straw mattress for the night. Mike remembers, 'It was in a little place called Mylor where there was a creek which led to Falmouth Bay. We all went out on a fishing trip in this rowing boat and tried to catch some mackerel.

'Then the tide turned and we suddenly had to start trying to row in against the tide. For a long time we didn't seem to be getting anywhere, but finally we managed to get back into the creek and back to Bodgy's grandfather's place only to be told that the mackerel were out of season. We had been wasting our time.'

Mike and Bodgy finished the day drowning their sorrows with a few beers in the local, The Pandora Inn. On the way home, they had to climb a 1 in 4 hill. A combination of disappointment and alcohol had dimmed their concentration and they lost control and completed a difficult day by finishing up in a ditch. But David missed out on this final disaster because he had chatted up a young lady down by the seaside and had taken her out for the evening. He was starting to realise that laughter was a great way of breaking the ice with girls.

'I could never impress a girl by being cool or sophisticated,' said David, 'even if I wanted to. But if I could make them laugh, they seemed to become more friendly.'

David was the first of the trio to take any interest in the opposite sex, although he was always careful to make sure that girls never came between him and his motorbike. He was always close to girl next door, Julie Pressland, who was just three years younger. 'Julie was always sweet on David,' remembers Mike Weedon, 'but I don't think there was ever any reciprocation there. We were just young guys, and girls never really came into our lives that much at the time, even David's.'

Julie insists she and David were only ever very good friends. 'I was never his girlfriend, or in love with him, or any of the other nonsense that has been suggested. I know he did have girlfriends but to me he was always so single-minded about making it as an actor that I don't think there was ever any room for a serious romance or marriage. As long ago as I can remember, he was so dedicated to making it that nothing was going to get in his way. I think he always thought, deep down, that you could either have a normal family life, a marriage and children and all that, or you could be a successful actor. He just didn't believe you could do both. He felt if you tried to carry a wife and children along as an actor, they would somehow fall by the wayside.'

Julie was perceptive enough to know that the real and enduring love of David's life was to be his acting. Certainly, he enjoyed passing flirtations with girls quick enough to follow his sharp sense of humour but he never had the obsession for the opposite sex that drove so many young men to devote their lives to the pursuit.

David reflected later, 'When I was 16, the only thing my mates were interested in was the pub, the dance hall and girls. The last thing they were interested in was acting. You had to have guts to run against the tide.'

The acting bug had bitten David for real and all his efforts were channelled into making his appearances with the Incognitos as professional as possible.

When he left school, David was wary of leaping straight in and following his brother into the precarious existence of struggling to make his way as a would-be actor. Arthur was first persuaded by their parents to take a 'sensible job' as an apprentice butcher but, like David, he knew he really wanted to act and launched boldly into the competitive world of weekly rep. David was happy and enjoying his amateur performances with the Incognitos and agreed to follow his parents' considered advice that he should get a trade behind him first. His forceful mother Olwen typically insisted, 'Actin'? That's not respectable. You need a job. You need a trade.'

David's first job was as an apprentice garage mechanic but he did not take to that, later recalling unhappily that his initial attempt at a sensible career consisted largely of, 'Lying under cars in mid-winter, this stuff dropping on you, the wind whistling up your bum.'

He left after a year and decided to train as an electrician, while still pursuing his acting interests on an unpaid basis, and joined the London Electricity Board as an apprentice but the Board made him redundant. 'I was 20 when I was made redundant by the LEB,' he recalls. 'It was an awful thing but it was not the end of the world. It was difficult for me. I had spent my life being employed by people. So my mate and I started our own business.'

David decided that if no one else would employ him, he would have to work for himself and, with a friend called Bob Bevil, he set up B and W Installations, after Bevil and White. But David sums up in one word his efforts to become a businessman.

'Pathetic. As an amateur, I was acting every night of the week in those days. I formed my own electrical business so that I could be more of a free agent. But I was doing so much acting, I was always having to take time off from work to get home, get changed, learn lines. I was packing up work at about four in the afternoon to get ready for an amateur performance at eight.

'I was getting more and more unhappy at work. I was only really happy when I was acting. We did not want to sit around and blame the Government. We were very disappointed and unhappy and we had to earn our wages as we were living at home but still needed money. We cleaned cars, did decorating, anything.

'Then, one day, I got an offer to go to drama school. I was about 21 and well into amateur dramatics. I was spending every night of the week in the theatre. I was working during the day and more or less every night I would be down at the theatre rehearsing and acting; rehearsing plays seemed to be what I did the entire time. As an amateur you did it for nothing.

'Then I won this award and the adjudicator – I think it was Anthony Von Gyseghem, a very well respected man – said, "I would never recommend anyone to take up the theatre but there is one man who has a possibility of making a career out of it," and he named me. My head was so big I couldn't get out of the room. I was absolutely over the moon.

'But at the time I was sort of engaged to this girl. My young lady lived in Lee Green, the other side of Lewisham, which is the other side of London from my home in North Finchley. It was a long way late at night in the rain. I used to take her home on my motorbike so you can tell how besotted I was, and then I had to turn round and come back home.

'I had not bought her a ring but we were unofficially engaged. We were just waiting for her eighteenth birthday to announce it. On the journey to her house that night of the award I was full of it and I said to her, "What do you think? Perhaps I could become an actor."

'There was no reply at first and then she said, "Look, if you want to be an actor, you go and be an actor, but don't think you are going to marry me. You're not. That is not what I want out of life. I want a man who is going to come home and spend a certain amount of time there. I want a husband, a two-up, two-down house, a steady income and a family. I want a reliable chap with a steady income, a car, a couple of kids."

'So much for love,' said David. 'Anyway, I was so terribly in love with this girl that I didn't want to go to drama school because I wanted to get married to her.

'At that point, I gave up the idea of becoming a professional actor. I was more interested in her at the time. But that sowed the seed and because I was totally involved as an amateur actor and no one was going to take that away from me, I went back to being a happy amateur. Within a year, we had a terrible row and we split up. I have never seen her since. I only know from a friend of mine that she did eventually get married many, many years ago. Really, the split was not over what she said, exactly, but she was a catalyst.

'By the time I was 23, I knew I was no longer going to get married. I would get close to girls and then have this fear of being tied down. It gradually became more apparent to me that I could have a go at acting and if I wasn't really any good

I could go back to being an electrician. I couldn't bear the thought of reaching 35 without having had a shot at what I really wanted. I started to think, "Right ... this is the time. I have no ties. I must have a go at being an actor." If I didn't, I knew I would never forgive myself.'

But the rejection really hurt. A former workmate said, 'David was really gutted to be knocked back like that. He wasn't really ever a great womaniser, but women liked his lively sense of humour and he always seemed to be the one in charge of the relationships. Suddenly the girl, and she was only very young, gave him the elbow and he really didn't like it. I thought he was always strange and a bit more remote with girls after that.'

Both Douglas Weatherhead and his wife Peggy were impressed by the youngster's enthusiasm and eagerness to learn. And they noted his cheeky sense of humour, too. Douglas remembers, 'I think it was mainly at his mother's insistence that he got his trade as an electrician. She wasn't having two sons who were both in this acting business. David was always a laugh. We were doing this play all about Greek and Roman senators for one of the youth festivals and David was playing a character called Didimus Hippocrates.

"At the same time, we bought a new washing machine which was being plumbed in and we asked an electrician friend to wire it in for us. We did not know that it was to be David who was working for our friend who actually did the job. That is, we didn't until we got home and found a big notice on the wall which read 'Didimus Hippocrates worked and slept here'.

Douglas and Peggy roared with laughter. Peggy remembers that, 'David was a very dedicated lad. He wasn't really interested in anything else but acting. But he was full of fun. He used to pull funny faces and lark about all over the place until it was time to go on stage when he would be as good as gold. He wasn't particularly interested in girlfriends at all.'

David has always loved to leave his mark. Colin Williams, a fellow Incognito member from those days, also worked at the same trade as David for another north London electrical firm. He recalls, 'We often met through work. I remember going to one of our friend's houses where they were having an extension done to the kitchen. David had chased all the walls and put the cables in and then he couldn't get back there so he called me in. When I went into the kitchen the first thing I saw, in David's handwriting, was 'Kildare was here' scrawled right across the wall. The room was to be redecorated so it didn't matter, I suppose.

'I know he wouldn't mind me saying that he was always a much better actor than an electrician, so I am not surprised that is why he is so successful.'

Working with the Incognitos certainly provided David with excellent training in putting on a show with the minimum of backing. The energetic Douglas Weatherhead had his young team travelling all over London by public transport, just for the chance of competing in as many drama festivals as possible.

'David never minded hard work,' says Douglas. 'Once we had to take all our props to the other side of London on the bus. I remember David and I struggling up the narrow and awkward spiral staircase on to the top deck of a double-decker with a Welsh dresser. We just laughed about it all.'

David was always desperately eager to get on stage and one evening in his enthusiasm he walked into a jagged piece of corrugated iron on one of the ramshackle buildings outside. He staggered into the tiny theatre with blood pouring from his head and said, 'I've had a bit of a bang.'

Amateur actress Vera Neck said, 'David would never walk if he could run anywhere. He came in bleeding from this nasty gash in his forehead and he dripped blood all over the stage for the rest of the evening. We all felt he should go and have stitches but he wasn't going to let a little thing like that make him miss his rehearsals. He was always supremely careless about his appearance so blood rushing down his shirt was nothing out of the ordinary.'

David would often race to rehearsals straight from work and sometimes his grubby clothes raised eyebrows among the more senior and established members of the Incognitos.

Vera Neck says, 'He sometimes turned up in dirty, grubby things. I remember being shocked at the colour of his underpants when we were rehearsing one of those 'Sailor, Beware' things and he had to drop his trousers.

'There were all these elderly ladies among the cast – I suppose he was about 20 and we were 30 something – and they all went 'Tut-tut-tut-tut'. And he couldn't blame his mum. She used to 'do' for me and she was a clean little body. But I'll never forget those grubby underpants.

'The play had a bit of rough and tumble and he disappeared over the back of a couch with his bum in the air. He had these psychedelic patterned pants with an underlying grey hue.'

Vera Neck lived in Torrington Park, Friern Barnet, and Olwen used to clean for her for three hours every week. 'She was lovely,' remembers Vera, 'very concerned for her family and very particular about her job.'

They had many conversations about David's dramatic ambitions. With his older brother Arthur, who had got into acting while doing his National Service in the Army, already struggling in the uncertain world of rep, Olwen worried greatly about her second son's ambitions.

David loved the atmosphere of earnest enthusiasm among all the members of the Incognitos and it was not long before he was snapping up some of the prime parts. He said, 'I was encouraged to act at school. I was a natural at playing the fool. I loved it with the Incognitos. I wasn't showing off, it was about entering a Walter Mitty sort of world where you could do anything, be absolutely anybody.'

He was still just 15 years old in July 1955, when noted local critic Bill Gelder from the *Barnet and Finchley Press* warmly praised his performance in *Robert's Wife* by St John Ervine. David deeply appreciated Gelder's comment: 'David White did well as a young chap wanting to do the 'right' thing by a girl.'

But it was a guest appearance for the nearby Manor Players when Bill Gelder hinted publicly that the youngster might one day earn his living from his acting. Gelder wrote: '... the extraordinarily precocious schoolboy by David White, looking like a young James Cagney and playing, though only 16, with the ease of a born actor ... possibly the highlight of the evening which was bright enough in all conscience.' The acclaim delighted David. He carefully cut out the review and made sure it didn't escape his parents' notice.

His mother, who still considered that one son risking his future in such a risky profession was more than enough, proudly noted the critic's perceptive opinion but was still insistent that David persevere with his electrical qualifications.

'It was very nice to get praise from Bill Gelder,' says David. 'He was always considered the best drama critic of the lot. If you got a good review from him, it counted. Most of the local press tend to praise the whole cast for fear of offending someone. I suppose they can't say so-and-so is a load of rubbish, but Bill Gelder could be quite hard and quite cutting and he was always respected.'

Not that David took life too seriously in those days. Julie Pressland remembers a young man who was always terrific fun to be with. 'It was great to be in David's company,' she says. 'I used to love to go around with him. He had determination. We all enrolled for some evening classes or other but most of us dropped out soon afterwards. But David was very single-minded, he carried on with his amateur dramatics. He went for it. David always believed that you should decide whatever you want to do and then go for it.

'But he was a laugh as well. It was in 1962 when David took me for my first Chinese meal. I had never had Chinese food before but he talked me into it. He said it was delicious and really raved about it. I remember I had a new suit for the evening and when we got to the restaurant and the food arrived I thought it was the most dreadful slop I had ever seen in my life. The first time you see Chinese food it can look disgusting. I kept saying, "It's very nice, it's very nice," because I didn't want to offend David.

'When I got home, I was sick all over this new suit and I never touched Chinese food again for about 15 years after that. I will never forget that night. I pretended all evening that I liked the food as much as he did. Then, at the end, he said, "Oh, we must finish off with some jasmine tea." I thought, "My God, that will certainly finish me off." I told David the next day that I had brought up his Chinese all over my new suit and he just burst out laughing. He thought it was hilarious.'

But he was also honest enough to admit later that, during those early stages of his amateur career, 'I really didn't think I had the ability to turn professional. Most people who become actors are so confident. They know for certain that they are right and everybody else is wrong. I was the opposite. I was very, very insecure – mind you, I think I'm still insecure, but I'm not as bad as I was.'

In fact, the black moods of frustration that would sometimes descend on the generally perky young man do date right back to his youth. A workmate said, 'David was a great guy to go out with because normally he was a laugh a minute. But he could suddenly turn. One night, we were in a pub in

Finchley and he had been working hard at chatting up this very pretty young girl. Then an old boyfriend of hers arrived, a very well spoken chap dressed in a smart blazer and cavalry twills. I think he was home from the Army. All of a sudden, she just turned away from David and started talking to this posh bloke. David was livid. He hardly said another word all night. When I mentioned it the next day he gave me a really menacing look and said, "I hate those stuck-up bastards. They think they own the world." I was surprised because he was still seething with anger. He wasn't that keen on the girl – it was just the way he had been dropped. He couldn't bear that.'

The ability to get laughs that he had displayed so often at school was swiftly transferred to the stage. He had enormous straight acting talent but always preferred comedy. Vera Neck says, 'He did do quite a variety of straight roles, but if there was a chance to drop a tray, sit on his bottom or drop his trousers, he was there.'

Vera is a statuesque lady of 5ft 7in, which caused some amusing moments when she and David were cast as lovers in a Spanish play. 'We had to devise ways of making me look a bit shorter than David,' recalls Vera. 'I sat at his feet rather a lot. We didn't have many love scenes because we were physically so ill-matched. On the few occasions it did happen, we just had to cheat it.

'I found him quite affectionate. We had tremendous warmth and rapport on stage. He had it with everyone. He is such a lovely actor. We chanced on a time in our group when there must have been half-a-dozen people who could, in ordinary circumstances, have earned their living as actors, had they been tempera-mentally suited to it. I wasn't – I had the talent but not the temperament. But the feeling that flowed between those few people who were there at that time was wonderful.

'David was the leading light. We loved him. He used to come to all the parties and he was always the life and soul in a muck-about way. He was a clown. He just liked mucking about.'

Another of David's regular leading ladies was Barbara Dunks. Again, she was an inch or so taller than he was, so a fair amount of knee-bending and sitting down was called for. Barbara became another firm friend and a devoted fan of the poverty stricken young hopeful. She remembers, 'He was such a callow, gangling youth when I first saw him, but I knew straight away that he had that magical something that all actors yearn for ... presence.

'He was so full of life and even at 15 you knew he was special. But he was such a monkey at making you laugh at all the wrong moments. When you were in the middle of a terribly serious interchange in rehearsals, he could just look at you and you would just break up. He just had that twinkle. The producer would be going mad but there was nothing you could do about it. He was always very serious and proper when we were doing it for real, but in rehearsals you could never be sure he wasn't going to produce a piece of mischief.

'It was so sad, though, that it seemed he could never take the hero's part because he was so short. Instead, he was automatically put into the comedy parts which he was brilliant at. But other boys, who frequently did not possess a millionth of his talent, so often became the tall hero.

'I always felt that the height thing did bother him. Knowing David, he would say it didn't, but I have seen him watch a play with the hero or leading man in a scene and I just knew that he would have loved that part.

'The trouble was that, even in amateur things, you get typecast, people start to forget you might be able to do anything but comedy. If ever there was a funny part they would think, "Oh, we'll get David to do that and 6ft Henry to do the hero." Sometimes it was simply the wrong way round. You could see it was.'

Barbara recognised that David had decided he did not want to get involved with any girls. 'He was friendly with the girls in the club but he did not seem to want to get serious about anybody. He used to come down to the theatre in his little van. We used to pull his leg about being an electrician, say he was enough to give anyone a shock.

'We were in a revue together, early on in his time with the Incognitos and we had to sing "Bye, Bye Blackbird". I remember we were in hysterics in the wings because it was so bad. Well, we thought it was bad but in fact the audience loved it because they knew us all from the serious plays and thought for us all to be in this light-hearted revue singing this silly song not very well was great fun.

'It was a real joke for all of us and, although we were all supposed to behave ourselves, we thought it was a huge joke. We were all togged up ready to sing this bloomin' song, but in all the giggling and larking about in the wings just as we were supposed to dance on, I happened to stand on poor old David's bootlace and he rolled on to the stage in a heap. Being David of course, he carried the mistake off brilliantly – he could always do that – and I'm sure the audience thought it was all supposed to be part of the show.

'There was no one better for getting you out of a mess than David. He had a mind like lightning for thinking things out whenever we went wrong. There was this scene when we were together in *The Glass Menagerie*. We had this dreadful old wind-up gramophone and at one point I had to wind it up and put the needle down to play a record.

'But something went wrong and instead of lovely music we just got this horrible scratching sound. David came to the centre of the stage and just took control. He picked up the needle and made a remark that fitted in and cut out the need for the music and we carried on as though nothing had happened.

'But it meant through David's guidance we started in the

middle of the scene and we went to the end and then back to the beginning. We were all terribly muddled but David was so brilliant that nobody even knew we had gone wrong. Apart, that is, from the prompter that night. She was so flustered at the end that she rushed on and said, "I've had four pingers in five fages. What's happening?" She was in such a state she didn't know where we were. David was never flustered. He just used to say, "Pick it up and keep carrying on."

'His brother Arthur was acting professionally by then and I always got the feeling with David that, although I knew he would love to become an actor, there was always this feeling of caution and reticence about him, especially at the beginning because, deep down, he did not really know whether he would be good enough. *We* all knew he would, but he didn't.

'He was so good and it all came so naturally to him. The technicalities of the stage never bothered him. Offstage he was just a very nice boy, always cracking jokes, always cheerful. But I think he was concerned about not having his share of serious roles. It was Brian Babb who first cast him in a leading, non-comedy role in *Next Time I'll Sing To You* and, of course, he did it beautifully. People realised from then on that he could be a serious actor. The trouble was that all of the four or five leading ladies at that time were taller than David, so it was always difficult with us.'

David's 21st birthday party was an occasion for the White family to really push the boat out. In order to cram in as many guests as possible on David's big day, they took off all the downstairs doors to make more space. David prepared much of the sumptuous spread himself and the music of Johnny Tillotson, Elvis Presley and the Everly Brothers rang out down Lodge Lane.

'It was a wonderful party,' remembers Julie Pressland. 'We all thought it was great having an open-plan house.

'I went to David's house a lot at that time. Me and David and his partner Bob Bevil and my friend Carol Haddock used to go to our local dance hall, the Atheneum in Muswell Hill, or up to Alexandra Palace for a drink and then come back to David's.

'We'd sit in his front room and talk and talk for hours on end. He had such plans and ambitions for the future, he just loved everything about acting and drama, he was so very determined to be good at every part he had. We were a foursome for a time but David and I never had a romance. I did have a crush on David but that was when I was five or six. He was literally the boy next door, a great pal.

'That was when I began to notice a more serious side. He was still great fun and often he would be larking about of course, just like before. But also he would sometimes recite long bits of poetry or quotations from Shakespeare. He was becoming very well read and getting more and more into his acting. It seemed to dominate his whole life. He loved Richard Burton and his recording of *Under Milk Wood* in that wonderful voice. David could copy that voice brilliantly and the Welsh in him really seemed to come out. We all knew then that he had an amazing, God-given talent.

'David had all the typical motorbike leather gear, but when he went out in the evening in his suit and tie he always looked impeccable. He had this gorgeous thick wavy hair and that cheeky grin. But even more, he had this remarkable personality where he could walk into a pub and just make everyone laugh.

'It seemed so effortless. He could instantly have people eating out of his hand. It was obvious to me that he was going to do much more with his life than mend fuses. He always made jokes about not being very tall. I remember once he couldn't get served in our local, The Torrington at the end of Lodge Lane, so he stood on the bar rail and just held his money out for a giggle. He didn't mind everyone laughing at him being small, he stood up there to make us all laugh.'

Not quite everyone was captivated by the David White charisma. When the Lodge Lane off licence, just one door away from the White household, was modernised, young David was in his early 20s and less than impressed by the sudden wind of change. He walked in to find that the old beer pumps had been swept away in a major refurbishment. The elegant, polished wood serving counters had been replaced by gleaming new plastic affairs. The old-fashioned off licence had been turned into a modern mini-market.

Julie and David called in for an inspection. Julie recalls, 'I asked David what he thought of the new look and he took one look round and said, "I think it's awful."He hated it and the way that all the tradition of the place had been swept away and walked straight out. The man who had done all the revamping looked crestfallen and said to me, "He's a bit of an upstart, isn't he?"'

Julie herself got a shock the night David came home rather late from another hugely successful night with the Incognitos. She recalls, 'I was 22 at the time and he gave me the fright of my life. I used to sleep in our front bedroom and I was woken up about three o'clock one morning by what I thought was the sound of someone trying to break into one of the houses. I looked out and it was David standing all forlorn with his toolbag. I opened the window as quietly as I could and he said that he was very late home from doing a play and his mum had locked him out.

'I went downstairs and brought him through our house so he could climb over the fence and get in the back way. I was frightened because I was in my nightie and my mum and dad were asleep. I kept telling him to be quiet and he kept giggling and larking about. Then, when I got him outside he got on top of the fence and of all things he started reciting the balcony scene from *Romeo and Juliet*. I was really panicking by then because I knew if my mum came downstairs and found David there with me in my nightclothes she would never believe that I was just helping him to get home. I said, "For God's sake, shut up. If my mum and dad hear you, we'll both be dead." But that was so typical of his humour, he always had a tremendous amount of fun in him.

'We got on very well together and we were always amazed that our mothers also got on really well. Because while David's mum was very broad Welsh my mum was just as broad Irish. They both had really strong accents and they used to have these incredible conversations. David used to say that the only reason they never rowed with each other was because they each did not have a clue what the other one was saying.

'In our growing up years, everybody liked David. He was always very funny with a natural gentle humour that was never directed at anyone but himself. I know they say most people who are very funny are usually manic depressives, but David never was. You never saw him depressed or down. He just had a natural sunny good nature.

'David was always very generous. He was one of the first of his contemporaries in Lodge Lane to get a car, a little Mini van that he and Bob used for their business. He was always ready to use it to help people out. When Ernie Pressland's baby daughter Sarah was suddenly taken ill with a racing heart, David rushed her and Ernie's wife Claire to hospital.

Ernie is still grateful. 'Even in those days, they were homing in on potential cot deaths. My mother knew there was something wrong with Sarah because she had had two youngsters die herself. I was at work at the time and David took the wife and the baby up to The Whittington Hospital. They wanted to get her there as fast as possible and it was just as well David was around to help.

'It turned out Sarah was born with two little pacemakers in

40

her heart instead of one. Every so often, something will trigger off the second one and her heart would go ten to the dozen and she got a loss of blood pressure. She is fine now and has a young son of her own called Daniel. We will always be grateful to David.'

David was in action again with his makeshift ambulance when Ernie's and Julie's sister Maureen needed rushing to hospital to have her baby. And to complete the job he took Maureen's husband Rob to bring her and the baby home.

Yet on arriving for the return trip, David could not resist a joke. As Maureen was coming out of the ward with the nurse who was holding the baby, David and Rob were approaching down a long corridor. Suddenly, David brushed past Rob and shouted, 'Now we'll see whose baby this is!'

It took Maureen and Rob a moment, but they did quickly realise this was a typical David White laugh. The nurse was not so experienced in this curiously quirky sense of humour and almost dropped the baby.

Only Fools and Horses hero Derek Trotter would have been deeply ashamed of David White if he had been around to see the young electrician buy his first car. He already had a share in the Mini van of course, a symbol of the struggling business partnership, but that did not quite fit the bill for the particular purpose the enthusiastic amateur actor had in mind for his motor.

'I was desperate to get into cars,' said David, 'because I knew it was the only way to pull the birds. You can't do it with your motorbike. So I went down to Colindale and bought a great, gleaming Ford Zephyr Six. It looked a lovely car but I was really, really ripped off. It was the most clapped out thing in the world. My real passion was for motorbikes and I sold my bike for £60 to buy the car and I got really ripped off on that as well.

'I think I must be the most ripped off person in the world.

The car salesman was a typical Boycie. He must have seen me coming a mile off. I fell in love with the Zephyr as soon as I saw it which must have been my first mistake. It looked fabulous and it would be worth a fortune now. It was a lovely car except that, of course, it was completely clapped out. But when you are getting your first car you know how it is. You're so keen to get behind the wheel you don't spend long enough looking underneath the bonnet.

'But I soon learned an important and very expensive lesson. The gearbox was full of sawdust and so was the back axle, and the engine was totally knackered. I seemed to spend my entire life under the bonnet tinkering with the engine trying to get the blasted thing to go. I don't think I ever had time to try to pick up any girls in the car. It never went for long enough without grinding to a halt.'

DRAMATICS

G radually, the Incognitos all came to realise that their little amateur group was witnessing some highly professional performances from young David White. In his early 20s, David was reaching remarkable heights in the world of north London amateur dramatics. David was 24 when he produced what many contemporaries agree was his finest dramatic performance, in *Winter Journey* by Clifford Odets. It was not his usual comic turn but the highly charged role of a tough New York theatrical director forcing one more decent role out of a crumpled and drunken actor.

David's director, Christopher Webb, recalls, 'The part was played in the West End by Michael Redgrave. It called for David to really put this poor actor through it. The guy is really on his beam ends when David's character blasts him once more into action. We worked very closely together on it for many nights. I pushed him very hard over and over again because I knew he had a fine performance in him. There was a real clash of wills. There is nothing like actors having a bit of hatred for their director to inspire that bit extra from them.

'We used to rehearse in empty schoolrooms and I would allow a small number of people to come and watch. I convinced David that he had to be really worked up when the scene started. I got him working on his breathing and really pumping himself up before we even started. One particular night there was a real excitement in the air and when he launched into his tirade against this other actor the atmosphere was absolutely electric.

'The scene was quite spell-binding. One or two of the girls in the tiny audience were in tears as David generated such force and will power it was almost over-whelming. It was amazing, quite brilliant. I think that was when he really decided that he had it in him to make a career of acting. But the scene was never as marvellous again. It was good on the night but never that good.'

Local critic Bill Gelder was impressed enough to announce to the readers of Finchley and Barnet, 'So far as the acting was concerned, there were three performances good enough to be judged by the highest amateur standards. Indeed, that by David White might be said without flattery to be in a professional class, it was done with such verve and explosive force. Mr White made his reputation with the Incognitos and is one of the comparatively few amateurs whom I could conscientiously recommend for the professional theatre.

'He has a brother there already (it must run in the family) but chooses instead, and perhaps wisely, to earn a steady living as an electrical engineer, devoting any surplus high-voltage energy to the interests of the local stage. Without pushing the electrical metaphor too hard, he gave a dynamic performance as the producer of the play within the play.'

By the time he was 25, David had produced many memorable performances for the Incognitos. 'I was playing all the heavies,' says David. 'Even with my height slightly against me, I played all the weighty roles: *Look Back In Anger*; *Epitaph for George Dillon*; all the Arthur Miller plays. I naturally considered myself a dramatic actor. I thought I could do anything.

'I did not realise that my height would be so very much against me when I joined rep where all the leading ladies would be 5ft 6in or 5ft 7in tall, and leading men always had to be taller than leading ladies. It was a sort of unwritten law. Nowadays it is different, and I don't think you have that if you think of all the people like Al Pacino and so on. They are all midgets running around with big roles and they are the most powerful actors. It is all right on screen, but it's not so easy on stage.'

Shortly after his success in *Winter Journey*, David had a crucial piece of good fortune.The push that he needed to turn professional came courtesy of his brother Arthur, who had landed a role in the Noel Coward play *South Sea Bubble* at Bromley. Arthur was working with director Simon Oates, an old friend, and was busy rehearsing the small but potentially amusing role of a comical coloured butler. At the last minute, Arthur was offered a much sought-after television job with the BBC's trail-blazing crime series *Z Cars* and he begged his pal to be released from the agreement.

Simon Oates recalls, 'Arthur told me, "My brother wants to be an actor," so I went to see David at the Manor Players in Finchley playing Paul of Tarsus in *A Man Born To Be King*. It wasn't much to do with comedy but I could see right away that he was stunningly talented.'

Afterwards, Simon approached David and asked, 'I hear you want to turn pro.'

'Yes, I do,' answered David immediately.

'Well, make your mind up,' said the director.

David did not need any time to consider the offer. It was the chance he had been waiting for. He made his mind up there and then.

In spite of his mother's woeful warnings, he gave his share of the ailing electrical business to his partner in exchange for the company's Mini van and joined Bromley rep.

'I said "Yes" to the offer, of course,' said David, 'But I was terrified. There are certain moments in your life – like the first time you have sex, I suppose – which you can never recreate. You can't breathe with the excitement of it. I was being paid £15 a week and I couldn't believe they were giving me money for something I would have done for nothing.'

Simon Oates recalls, 'He had to put a bit of brown make-up on for the part as he was supposed to be a South Sea Islander. It wasn't a large part but you could see his comic potential. He was just naturally funny. There was a great big talent there waiting to be honed.'

David might have been a little disgruntled to be playing yet another type of servant, 'I was always playing bloody waiters,' he grumbled. But, as David noted afterwards, 'Simon Oates has got one of those terribly evil senses of humour. He could see that I could do things and he became sort of fascinated with this during the course of rehearsals.

'*South Sea Bubble* was really quite a sophisticated Noel Coward comedy and he realised that he had in me this little rough diamond type and he could get me to do things that were slightly more bold, slightly louder, because he had this wonderful sense of humour. He just kept on getting me to do little bits of things to make himself laugh.

"The other actors did not like it at all. I didn't realise at the time they were bothered, I didn't know then that you could upset people or tread on people's toes. I just thought, "Yeah, I'll do that, great," and get a laugh. The other actors were coming up to me and saying, "That's not in the play," or "This is supposed to be Noel Coward, you know." But the director said, "Go on." That was the beginning of the end of any straight parts for me. So I never had much of a chance, really. It would be "Oh no, we can't have him. He'll dive through a hatch or something."'

Perhaps David was not quite as far from the humorous aspirations of the great Noel Coward as he feared, as The *Bromley and Kentish Times* recorded solemnly at the time, 'A small, but well acted, part is that of David White as the native butler of the governor.' Director Oates was delighted with his find: 'He made me cry with laughter.'

The date of that first paid performance was 5 April, 1965. A remarkable comedy career had begun. Oates says, 'He did go back to Bromley after the week-long run of the play. I suggested he should be taken on by the company and he was.'

David might have landed his first paid engagement but he still did not possess that essential actor's accessory, an agent. His brother Arthur was asked by old friend Malcolm Taylor, an actor who was trying to move into production, to take a part in a new run of *Under Milk Wood* which was to be staged at the Vanbrugh Theatre, the London headquarters of the famous Royal Academy of Dramatic Art. Arthur turned the job down, saying he was not available, but he suggested his younger brother. Malcolm Taylor was not too impressed by the thought. He said,'Well, it's very kind of you Arthur, but I don't really want amateurs.'

David had done only the one paid job by then but, in spite of his obvious lack of experience, Malcolm Taylor agreed to see him.

Taylor recalls, 'I relented in the end and thought it wouldn't do any harm to give Arthur's brother an audition. He came round to my flat in Maida Vale and I will always remember him sitting, shaking with fear, on my sofa. But as soon as he opened his mouth to do the part, I knew that he had real talent. He got the job.'

David and Arthur even tried working together between jobs as an imaginative ventriloquist act. Naturally, being the younger brother, David played the dummy and often complained about Arthur's cold hand going up his jumper. It led eventually to the brothers being summoned for an audition for a custard commercial. Arthur said, 'There were a whole lot of proper ventriloquists there but we got the job. We did the advertisement but I don't think the executives liked it much because David stuffed custard into his ear instead of his mouth!' The brothers clowned around relentlessly in this unlikely double act and even trawled the clubs to try to find work.

David recalls, 'I had no work at the time. I would have done anything if it was in the theatre. This bloke asked me to go down and audition, which I did, and he gave me the part. We played for four weeks in the Vanbrugh for something like £5 a week and split the box office. At the end of four weeks, I think we all earned about £30 which wasn't as bad as it sounds in those days when you haven't got a family or any responsibilities, and you haven't got a car and you're living at home. And it was a wonderful opportunity.'

It most certainly was, because in the audience one evening early in the run was an eager young agent called Ann Callender, a junior partner with the Richard Stone organisation. Ann was there with her actor-turned-writer husband David Croft, a multi-talented man destined to become the BBC's comedy stalwart with a string of successes including *Dad's Army*, *Are you Being Served?*, *It 'Ain't 'Alf 'Ot, Mum*, *Hi de Hi* and *'Allo, 'Allo*.

Perhaps as well as anyone in British television, David can spot talent when he sees it. He remembers his first experience of David White in action.

'I can claim to have really discovered David,' says David Croft. 'I went to a reading at RADA with Ann of *Under Milk Wood* and a bloke who was going to read one of the parts did not turn up. David stepped in and he was hilarious. Every time he opened his mouth he got a huge laugh.'

'My wife Ann was a very junior executive at the time and she was not really allowed to take people on. But David was simply so very exceptional.'

Ann Callender remembers, 'I had been there to see another artist, an actor called Patrick Tull, but I was completely taken by this young man who seemed unbelievably talented and really rather exceptional. My David was right of course; David White was just so funny I had to try to sign him up.

'I was very nervous about it, though, because as a very junior partner I certainly was not allowed to approach artists. We used to get hundreds of letters from would-be actors. It was a very leading agency. Ruth Llewellyn, who became Ruth Madoc, was in the class and the producer was a man called Malcolm Taylor. Afterwards, I went round backstage and said to Malcolm, "That chap is very, very talented. Has he got an agent?" I got a rather old-fashioned look and he said to me, 'Why don't you ask him?'

'By then, David was busily helping himself to food from the buffet and I went up to him and said, "I thought you were awfully good this evening. Have you got an agent?"

'He looked at me and said, "No." I took a deep breath because, technically speaking, I was not supposed to sign anyone up. I said, "Well, would you like to come and see me on Monday?"'

The response was scarcely what Ann Callender expected, 'No, not really,' said David White sharply, and walked off. Ann Callender went puce in the face with equal measures of anger and embarrassment. 'I was risking my job and my future,' said Ann. 'I just could not believe he had been so rude. I stormed back to the producer. He asked me what the matter was, as I was still shaking with a sort of frustrated fury. I said, 'I don't know who that young man is but he is very rude.' Malcolm Taylor replied that the man in question was not at all rude normally.

A few minutes later, a subdued David White approached Ann Callender and said, 'Hello, how are you? I'm sorry I was a bit rude.'

She was relieved, 'Shall we start again? You haven't got an agent, what have you done before?'

He paused for a moment to collect his thoughts and said, 'Nothing, really.'

Ann Callender insisted. 'You must have done something.'

'Well, no,' David explained. 'I'm the stage electrician.' He explained that he had stepped into the production at the last minute and that, like so many hopeful actors, he had desperately tried to get himself an agent.

David said later, 'I told her I had tried to get an agent like everybody else does. I had written about 5,000 letters to anyone and everyone in the business just by going through all the addresses I found in *Spotlight*. I wrote to every producer and every director I could find, just like poor struggling actors have always done. I used to sit down and write out 10 a day by hand and send them all hopefully off. I suppose they finished up in the waste paper bin with all the rest. It's tragic the way they don't even get looked at but I didn't know that then.

'I was abashed when Ann approached me. I don't think I could believe it. I told her I had tried to get an agent but nobody wanted me. I was still working as an electrician on and off. You don't just walk into this business, get one job and it goes on for ever. Only a very few people get that. I mean, I was even out of work for six months after *Under Milk Wood*.'

Ann Callender was not at all put off by her rebuff. She had remarked to Malcolm Taylor that very first evening that she knew David was going to be a very big star. 'That first encounter did not bother me too much when he was so rude because I realised he was just shy,' she said.

'He was, and indeed still is, an exceptionally shy person. You might have thought that was just the approach he had been yearning for, but he had just done a performance, a semi-professional performance, and I think he was a little taken aback. Afterwards, I spent a lot of time with him and found out a lot about him. I think he was introverted, he thought a great deal, always gave a great deal of study to everything and I think he was very frightened of the outside world.

'I don't say he was frightened of being manipulated because he has quite a strong character, so it would not be exactly that but he was determined to get on with what he wanted to get on with. If the money came along with the fame then that was terrific, but it really came very, very second.'

On the following Monday, David did have his appointment with Ann Callender in the impressive offices of the Richard Stone agency.

She remembers, 'There was no question about his talent. Everyone who saw him in *Under Milk Wood* must have noticed it. He was absolutely brilliant. He came and saw me and we had a long chat and I did, in fact, become his agent. Mind you, I had to put up with a lot of teasing. Richard Stone kept saying, "What on earth are you doing taking on the stage electrician? We don't handle electricians."'

David's second play at Bromley was *Diplomatic Baggage* and if his new reputation for getting laughs was not already irrevocably established at the end of his first production it most certainly was by the close of the second.

David remembers his formative moments in precise detail. '*Diplomatic Baggage* was a farce, a good old typically British farce,' he recalls. 'I was a waiter again and there was this important scene where I had to come into this hotel room where there was a bloke with two girls in a state of undress.

'The bloke orders a meal and, as the waiter, I deliver his food on this trolley with a tablecloth right down to the ground.

"Leave the meal," says the bloke, and I leave. Then he finds out that his wife is coming so he is desperate to find somewhere to hide the girls. He gets the two girls to hide in the bottom of the trolley, hidden by the tablecloth. Then he calls the waiter back to take away this trolley.

'Now my waiter had been messed about all day and by this time he was pretty fed up. So he comes in and grabs the trolley and has to pull it away thinking it was the same weight as before when he has pushed it in. The audience knows, of course, that it is much heavier with the weight of the girls. I went to walk away pulling the trolley.

'The stage directions were what you might call, 'pretty minimal'; they just said, 'The trolley is now much heavier and he falls over'. My idea for conveying that sort of grew from rehearsals but when it came to it, with all the excitement of the first night, I just really went for it much bigger than I would normally have done.

'As I pulled the trolley, I did an exaggerated version of what I thought would really happen, my feet went from under me and I flew up into the air up to being horizontal and then fell straight down on the floor. It doesn't sound that much when you describe it in words but when it happened the audience went hysterical. It brought the house down. Being physically adept, it was not that difficult for me, I thought it was quite natural. But the audience went on laughing and clapping for about five minutes afterwards.

'And I went further. I had the waiter get up, not understanding why the trolley would not move. I walked round the trolley and stared at it suspiciously. On top was a huge silver dish with a big lid. I quickly whipped it off as if suspecting there was some incredibly heavy food under there. The audience found what they thought was going through the waiter's head really amusing and they just kept laughing and laughing.

'By then, everybody in the rest of the cast was looking at me. We've been stopped now for maybe 10 minutes and the audience is still laughing fit to bust.

'I was just a little unknown and I was just doing what came naturally. I did a little bit more and then eventually I thought, "Blimey, I'll have to take this trolley off sometime," and I made my much delayed exit.

'Afterwards, the director came up to me and I thought I was going to get this almighty bollocking, but instead he just kept saying, "Wonderful, brilliant, fantastic. That's your job from now on. You are the comedy man now. And from that moment on I never got a straight role in that rep for nine months, which became a cause of great chagrin to me. In a way, that has haunted me ever since. I always feel a slight disappointment that people are pigeon-holed, that you are not considered an actor, or any good as an actor, just because you are a funny man. That has always been a thorn in my side.'

He was taken on at Bromley Rep as their last contracted artist. After he was signed, the system was changed, actors were employed simply on a four-week basis. David was delighted because it meant regular work at long last. He remembers, 'And it was hard work as well. We would start at ten o'clock in the morning and finish at ten o'clock at night. You would start rehearsing one play in the morning and finish at half-past four in the afternoon. Then at seven o'clock you were in the theatre getting your make-up on for another play. So whenever you worked on one play, you were rehearsing another.

'There again came the hard work and dedication, because I spent my entire time either learning words or rehearsing or doing a show. I was living, breathing, eating, sleeping, talking, thinking a show. The theatre completely took over my life and I loved it.

'That was what life was all about for me. It was terribly exciting and terribly rewarding for someone from my background with no training to be involved with real actors. They had all been to drama school and had much more experience than me. Some had been in the business a long time. I was absorbing everything they could give me. It was wonderful. Absolutely wonderful.

'I don't think there is anything wrong with that. I think that that is exactly the way it should be. And I would have been quite happy to have continued in that way at Bromley for ever. I thought it would be like that for ever. Of course, we all had dreams and we would sometimes sit around, people in the same situation, and we would constantly audition all the time. We would joke, of course, "Oh, you'll never be in my series" or "When I make a film, you won't be in that either." We all used to talk that nonsense but we never actually believed that any of it would come true.

'I was more concerned with doing whatever job I had got right so that I would get another job. I was always very worried about that, always very keen to impress. I never wanted to upset people in case they said I didn't do a very good job, because that could mean you were out of work. So I felt it was in your own interests to be as good and as dedicated as you could be because that meant continuity of work. If you really only wanted to be an actor, then that is all the criteria there were.

'If you wanted to be famous and all that then you could stand up to directors, but I could never do that because I did not want to get a bad reputation. I just concentrated on what I was doing because I was so interested in the theatre. I was slowly gathering knowledge.'

The doubtful pleasures of rep and summer seasons followed and David learned how to live on his enthusiasm and precious little in the way of wages.

'I spent a long time in the wilderness,' said David, 'and that is how I expected to spend the rest of my life – just fooling about on the end of some pier or other.

'I was really poor. I must have played every major town in this country, and stayed in some of the worst digs imaginable. I had to learn a lot of tricks to survive.'

David was always more worried about his acting than his wage packet and he raised his grievance about being pushed into a comedy slot with the boss of his agency, Richard Stone.

David recalls, 'Richard said to me, "You must never swim against the tide. Go with it. Go with the current. There will come a point at some time in the future when you come into still water. But don't start by trying to swim upstream when you have got something going for you. Go with it." I listened to his advice and that is what I did. I faithfully took what came along and it was always comedy.'

Following his brother into the acting business was a decision that far from delighted his parents. David said afterwards, 'The day we told Dad we wanted to become actors, he was shattered. "Why give up worthwhile trades and waste your lives?"'

David knew he would always regret it if he did not take his big chance. He was unhappy as an electrician and believed he had it in him to become a professional actor. But at the ripe old age of 25 he was still cautious. 'I gave myself a time limit. If I wasn't earning a good living by 30 I would return to my old trade. They were terrible years but, by then, I was besotted with the stage.'

Now he had a new career, David White found he needed a new name. He said, 'When I got my job in the theatre, I got three Equity members to sign my contract so that I could join Equity and sent the form off. But they phoned me up and said I couldn't have the name David White as there was already another actor registered with Equity with that name. They don't allow two actors to use the same name as it would be confusing.

'They said they could send the forms back but I was only

in the job for a month and I knew that if there was any delay I might miss my chance to get in. The woman from Equity said she could do the change over the phone, so I was on the spot. I had to decide on a new name there and then. First of all I said I'll just extend my name and become David Whitehead. She said, "No", that name was already being used as well.

'She said, "Is there any other name?" What popped into my mind was Jason. I suggested David Jason and she went away and then came back and said, "That's all right." All of a sudden I was David Jason. At the time, I had no idea where the name came from,' said David with an anxious eye on keeping a painful family secret out of the public scrutiny.

But David's mother was adamant that Jason was the name of his dead brother and that she was delighted when David chose it to keep the memory of his twin alive.

'He did what was right,' she said. 'You should never forget the death of a child. I had four children and I love them all equally and I want them all to be equally remembered. Not just the one.'

David finds this sort of personal revelation difficult to say the least. When pressed by the authors on the point he said quietly, 'My mother was a bit confused.' In fact, feisty Olwen appeared anything but confused when she spoke to the authors. Sitting in her tiny cluttered flat not far from Lodge Lane, crammed with its knick knacks and with David's picture on the cover of *TV Times* next to the television set, she was insistent. She said, 'David's father wanted him to become a fish porter like him but I encouraged him to try something different. I encouraged all of them. June was very good in a school play. I think that made Arthur and David take notice. She could have been an actress, I'm sure. But Jason should not be forgotten. Never, ever forgotten.'

David has always chosen not to confront his mother's memories. Before she died, he said in explanation, 'I discovered afterwards where the name came from when I thought about it. I had no idea when I picked it where Jason came from. But when I really began to puzzle it out I remembered my primary school days and a lovely teacher called Mrs Kent who made sure we had storytime once a week. She started to relate the story of *The Odyssey* and she told us stories of Jason and the Argonauts.

'The thing that captured my imagination, and she was a marvellous storyteller, was *Jason and the Golden Fleece*. I was really impressed by this hero from mythology battling to win the Golden Fleece. It was a brilliant story, brilliantly told.'

But a young actress who was very close to David at the time said, 'He only once ever talked about being a twin. It was very late one night when we had both had rather too much to drink. He was upset and he said something about it being a funny feeling losing a twin brother you never knew. He said he used to feel it made every birthday sad as well as happy and that sometimes he even felt guilty. He said he never talked to his mother about it. David was like that. If there was something he didn't want to think about he could block it right out. I saw him do it with people. He didn't yell or argue. If he took against someone he would simply behave as though they did not exist. It was a bit creepy, really.'

Ann Callender set about finding work for her young hopeful in earnest but she was not helped by David's shy disposition. 'He was never a very social man and he did not like turning up at agency parties or things like that. This made my job more difficult because in those days you used to invite all your mates who were producers and directors and all your actor clients who were looking for a good job to a party and hope that something would gel somewhere.

'But David was never a socialite; he did not like being paraded and he was not very keen on anything about that traditional slave market that an agency used to be. We got on terribly well and had loads of meetings about his career but there weren't many social occasions.

'He was very shy with girls. He spent a long time with Michelle Dotrice and, in fact, I thought he would probably end up marrying her, but in the end it did not come to anything.'

But David was learning about the business perhaps faster than his agent realised. The late comedian Bob Monkhouse was a friend and a fan of David Jason but he recalled a time when the young wannabe was a handful to work with.

Bob Monkhouse cheerfully recalled, 'It was back in 1971 when I met him. I had never heard of David Jason and I went to see a show called *'She's Done It Again!'* with Brian Rix playing the part of a vicar whose wife has just had sextuplets. It was a very old farce, written for Robertson Hare. I was to take over from Brian. I met David during rehearsals and loved him on sight. I didn't really see anything of David apart from his own sort of self-mockery and modesty on show. I didn't know he was an arrogant little sod!

'We opened at the Playhouse, Weston-super-Mare, with this thing. And, for me, it was like being hit between the eyes with a sledgehammer. I went out there to get laughs and there was no way anyone could get laughs apart from David. He was hysterical. He was acrobatic.

'He was wearing this white wig, with a white moustache and beard. He looked like a little old man. Everything about him was 70, except these incredible acrobatics, falls and amazing bits of business which all appeared on the night.

'We had never seen it at rehearsals but, on the night, suddenly his foot was jammed between the cushions on the couch and he couldn't get it out and there was five minutes of hysterical laughter and the other foot went in. He was just wonderful. He tumbled everywhere and the people adored him. And who was best at the end of the show? When we walked down, he walked down before me and the roof lifted off. Then I walked down as the star of the thing and everyone went quiet.

'He got a huge roar every night from the audience. Then I started doing a certain speech at the end of the show before I introduced the rest of the cast. David always got a huge ovation, much more than me or anyone else. So, after about a month of our five-month run, I said to the cast, "Look, you don't want to have to stay in make-up until after my curtain speech. Get cleaned up and I'll say, "Here's our cast as they would appear on the streets of Weston-super-Mare." They said, "Thanks Bob, that means we'll have time to get a meal after the show."

'But when David came down without his white wig, his white moustache and his white beard, nobody knew who he was, so he didn't get much of a round. Wonderful! I stepped into the middle and got the big applause. Everybody wondered where the little old guy had gone. And, do you know, David didn't twig it until the last week. Somebody pointed it out to him and he came to see me, but he took it well because we had been exchanging insults and signs all the way through.

'He used to crack me up. There was one scene where he had to come to me with the sixth and final baby in a crib. He had to come running in and give it to me. Well, the things he put in that crib that the audience couldn't see. First of all, there was the baby, then he had a horror mask on the baby, horrible lolling eyes and tongue hanging out all bloody. Then he started doing obscene things with the baby. I won't go into details but it involved the use of a frankfurter sausage and a lot of ketchup. Eventually, I used to dread this crib coming out for fear of what he had put in it. He even put all my underwear in it one time. And I still had to look in and say "What a beautiful baby."

'So I started cracking him up. There was a scene where he

was on stage with another actor and he had to look out of the window, which the audience couldn't see through. I used to stand behind it and do things of which I am now deeply ashamed. It was wonderful to see his eyes go, because nobody laughs like David. When he goes the bones turn to jelly and he just collapses with laughter. The eyes seem as if they're going to explode in his head. I think it was the funniest, happiest summer season, because of Jason, that I have ever had.

'Because we got on so well I asked him to do my radio show, *Mostly Monkhouse*, which ran for three series. He was my sidekick in 1972, 1973 and 1974 and the show did very big figures. I wrote all these insults for him to say and perform a script like I knew he could do and he was absolutely marvellous. I'm happy to say it helped him to become established.

'We don't live very far from each other and he comes over a couple of times a year for dinner. But we never did do the one dream that both of us had – a silent movie which I wrote and was going to direct. I remember when I bought my house in June 1975, we walked all round the garden and worked out the plot of the movie. But we never got it off the ground.'

David's agent could see her bashful young client needed a television chance and she turned to rising young comedy producer Humphrey Barclay as the man to provide it. She wrote to Barclay just at the time he was moving from radio to join the London ITV station Rediffusion to begin working on a completely new comedy strand.

Barclay recalls. 'I had just left radio and landed this job in television and, for the first time, I was actually a television producer. I was very new and very nervous and I was charged with putting together a children's comedy show. We had already got Eric Idle, Michael Palin and Terry Jones who were fine but they were all very cerebral and university-like. I was looking for someone who could provide some contrast.

'I approached Malcolm Taylor. He auditioned and was

very jolly and good fun but he said, "You don't want me, you want my friend David Jason."'

To this day, Malcolm Taylor finds it hard to explain this remarkable act of unselfishness. He said, 'Humphrey just explained to me that his new show was a revue-style comedy and he wanted a young actor to take part in the sketches and perhaps contribute a bit to the writing.

'I just straight away thought that David Jason would be a natural for the show and, to my astonishment, I heard myself suggesting David. I still don't know why I did it. So I suppose I was responsible for helping David to get a start in theatre and television in as much as anyone with that much comedy talent needs help. I have certainly never done anything so unselfish since then. I must have been mad.'

David is still grateful. Malcolm did become a very close friend of his but in this cut-throat business where good television chances are bitterly competed for this was a singularly selfless act.

David said, 'It was a fantastically generous thing for Malcolm to do. People think that sort of kindness doesn't occur in our business but Malcolm proved it does happen. He knew Humphrey was after a little comedy actor with a great range and was kind enough to think of me. He explained to Humphrey that I was working on the end of the pier in Bournemouth with Dick Emery and because of that recommendation, because Malcolm suggested me instead of saying "I can play that part" himself, I got the chance.

Humphrey Barclay telephoned me and said could he come down and see the show. I said, "Wonderful." I was doing very small parts in two plays back to back and one of them was doing absolutely nothing. The better one was *Chase Me, Comrade*, another typical old English farce.'

David did not make his big entrance until mid-way through the second half and Barclay, the thoughtful former classics graduate from Trinity College, Cambridge, sat surrounded by guffawing holiday-makers who were thoroughly enjoying Dick Emery cavorting about the stage in drag. As the evening wore on and David Jason still failed to emerge, Barclay was beginning to gaze yearningly at the exit.

Eventually, the moment arrived. It was a vital time in David Jason's young life and he recalls, 'For the first time in my career, I went "anti" the director. I really just followed my own instincts. My character, Bobby Hargreaves, the next-door neighbour who has just moved in, had to come on stage at a point in the play when everyone else has disappeared. The others are all chasing this guy dressed up as this Russian ballerina or whatever, and I am trying to find out if there is anybody in the house.

'At the bottom of the stairs there is a ship's bell. I have the entire stage to myself and I have to ring the bell which is the signal for everyone else to rush back on stage. Every time I cross the stage in my search I run past the bell and look at it significantly. I think about ringing it and I even make as if to ring it. This begins to wind up the audience and they start yelling, "Go on, ring the bell. Ring it. Ring it." But I make them wait and I drag it out as they are shouting and it started to drive that audience mad.'

In the audience, Humphrey Barclay, the mild-mannered former head boy of Harrow School and one-time *Cambridge Footlights* director, a master of all the most sophisticated aspects of humour, had completely forgotten all thoughts of leaving early. He was yelling and shouting with the rest of the audience, 'Ring the bell. Ring the bell.'

At last, David Jason relented and rang the bell. 'Then they really went bananas,' said the young actor. 'They knew what I was going to do. But, you see, in comedy often it is not what you do, but when you do it. This is the Laurel and Hardy message. If you watch Laurel and Hardy who have always been one of my faves, you find yourself going, "I know what you're going to do. But when are you going to do it?" I had learned that.

'Humphrey met me afterwards and he told me, "I really must say that I was thinking of leaving because it was not exactly my scene. But when you came on and did that business with the bell, I have never seen anything like it in my life. You drove that audience to distraction. Even I was yelling for you to ring it."'

David's ploy worked with the producer, but again it was not quite so popular with some of his fellow cast members. David said, 'It drove the rest of the cast crazy because no one could come back on stage until I rang the bell. A lot of people interpreted it as me hogging the limelight and I can understand how they could interpret it like that, but I was totally innocent of that. I honestly don't believe it was ever anything other than wanting to serve the audience to the best of my ability. That was my job and my joy.'

Certainly, Humphrey Barclay was convinced. 'He was just so funny,' says Barclay. 'I can still remember that first entrance very clearly. The business with the bell and his little face with those big eyes just convulsed the audience.

'I went back into his dressing room and we chatted and he was very down to earth. I swanked about being a television producer and admitted I hadn't done it for long. He said he hadn't long given up being an electrician. And I just knew for sure that he had this magical ability to make people laugh. A very funny man.

'I asked him if he would be in this TV show I was planning called *Do Not Adjust Your Set*. It sounded an awful phoney cliché but happily I was trustworthy and truthful because he was in it and he was very, very good. It was the start of a long and happy association. He was always wonderful to work with because he just communicates humour and he worked very, very hard at learning.

'I'll always remember he was so good at falling over in *Do Not Adjust Your Set*. I praised that one day and Terry Jones said, 'I can fall over and all that,' but I said, 'Yes, but not as well as David.'"

The young comedy actress Denise Coffey completed the team and *Do Not Adjust Your Set* became an innovative and successful show. But it did have a most peculiar start. David said, 'There was this wonderful moment when we all met and they told us, "This is a really major opportunity, an amazingly huge project. We want you to do six half-hour revue-type television programmes for kids. It's never been done before. We want you to be more or less adult." The attitude Humphrey Barclay and the other guys had was to treat the audience as we would ourselves. It was quite revolutionary at the time.

'Right at the start, Humphrey announced he had to prove to all the powers that be at the station that we were really worth this great investment. He took us all out to lunch and said that we had to go back that afternoon and prove ourselves to be funny.

'He said he had a studio booked and that we had to go in there and be funny. That is the hardest thing on earth with no script or direction or preparation. "How do we do it?" we asked. Humphrey said, "You've got to do it because your future relies upon it." We protested that nobody had prepared anything and Humphrey said, "Yes. That's the idea."

'I thought then that I had walked into a lunatic asylum. I thought this is crazy. We all thought it was mad, and Michael Palin freaked out completely.

Anyway, we all filed into the studio at Kingsway and we just went ... silly. We just went daft. Terry Jones kept on throwing himself backwards off his chair. Every time anybody spoke Terry Jones threw himself off his chair.

'That was all he did and I thought, "I wish I had thought of that." So I threw myself off my chair and then everybody threw themselves off their chairs. So we were all doing it. Then we thought, "We can't all do that." That piece of tape would probably be worth a fortune today because we were pathetic. We were rubbish. We had no form and no content. They just said go out there and be funny and we weren't. What we did not know at the time was that the company was so committed to the show, so far down the road with the Humphrey Barclay idea that we would have gone ahead anyway.'

Do Not Adjust Your Set, launched on Boxing Day 1967, was an instant hit with its young audience and plenty of parents tried to get home early enough to join in the zany humour. David recalled, 'It grabbed people with its anarchic humour. Adults would say, "I don't know what you're watching this bloody rubbish for," but the kids loved it. One of the highlights of each show was David Jason's appearance as special agent Captain Fantastic in a running super-hero serial that was deeply absurd. David appeared with Denise Coffey in an unlikely double act and the pair also wrote the scripts.

It was very popular and David's agent Ann Callender found herself in receipt of staggering offers to develop the item into a series of its own.

'Captain Fantastic really took off in popularity,' she said. 'There was this idea to turn it into a show of its own but David suddenly decided that under no circumstances did he want to be typecast or get involved in anything like that so early in his career.

'He felt it would prevent him from widening his scope. So, much to a lot of people's disappointment, mine included because there was a great deal of money involved, he decided not to go ahead.

'He was quite brilliant as Captain Fantastic, especially in the way he used a lot of his remarkable tumbling abilities. And to reject a lot of money and instant fame, as television could bring in those days, took guts and determination on his part. At that stage, I have to say that I thought David had it within him to become another Tony Hancock-style figure rather than the actor he became.

'I think it was sheer dedication to his craft as an actor which led him to reject the offers to develop Captain Fantastic. He felt that to have jumped towards fame so soon would mean that he would burn himself out. I remember him saying, "I would like to be a star, but I don't want to be a shooting star."

Quite why he was so adamant about Captain Fantastic still remains a trifle unclear to David. 'It is a fact that on odd occasions in my life I have been extremely dogmatic. I have made decisions that flew against everything I thought was the way to succeed and totally turned my own argument on its head. There have been two or three occasions and this was certainly one of them.

'With Captain Fantastic, we loved messing about on film, using all sorts of strange techniques and being as inventive as possible, using lots of old silent movie stunts, pinching some sketches and dreaming up other ones, with loads of visual gags and the formula worked. Colour television was just coming and they said, "What we want to do is a half-hour series of Captain Fantastic in colour."

'I said, "Great. And it will all be on film, won't it?" "No," they said. "It will not sustain half-an-hour on film. We'll do it in the studio with 10 minutes of film inserts." I was being offered this amazing deal. I'm not talking about money, but this amazing opportunity to have my own series. It was a huge chance for someone in my position. I had enjoyed being in a popular show but I was just one little individual part of the group.

'And yet although the idea of having my own series as Captain Fantastic appealed enormously, I said, "Unless we can do it all on film I don't want to do it."

'No one could believe I had said that at the time. But I did not want to carry on in those terrible cardboard cut out sets that we had got so used to working in those days. I knew it would take the essence of the character away because he was a film character.

'We were using all sorts of trick photography and clever film techniques. These days I suppose it would seem crude, but at the time I felt we were doing wonderful stuff. In the studio, it would have been just like everything else. I don't think I have ever been as begged and badgered to do anything in my life. I was coerced, I was blackmailed, I was really pushed towards doing it and I just said "No." I didn't want to do it because I just knew that if you took the filming away and put Captain Fantastic into a studio it would so weaken the character that he would no longer be worth playing. It would just be nothing, or just like everything else.

'It was a great offer and I suppose in a way Ann Callender was right, I should have done it. But with luck and hindsight you can think anything.'

David always felt a little apart from the three other male stars of *Do Not Adjust Your Set*. After three hugely successful series Messrs Jones, Palin and Idle began a campaign to move the show to a less restricting late-night slot. David said, 'We wanted to to do an adult version of *Do Not Adjust Your Set* but the powers that be said, 'No way. It's the most successful children's series we have ever had. It's obviously children's material. You guys don't know what you're talking about."

'The three of them said we want to make a late-night series with this format because our material is being so choked by the editors who keep saying, "You can't do that because it's for children." They got more and more frustrated.

'The upshot was that because they weren't allowed to turn our series into a late show they went away and came back a couple or three years later with John Cleese and Graham

Chapman and it was called *Monty Python's Flying Circus*. Need I say more?'

The last episode of *Do Not Adjust Your Set* went out on 14 May, 1969 and, having been part of such a successful team, David was understandably upset at being excluded from the future comedy plans of Jones, Idle and Palin. Though he wasn't to know it at the time, David posed for a promotional photograph for *Do Not Adjust Your Set* which was to prove painfully prophetic. David and the other three were pictured standing behind a television set which bore the caption 'Ouch!'

David's natural antipathy towards the upper-crust public school and university end of the business was already well established. David did, however, work with Graham Chapman seven years later in the film *The Odd-Job Man*. Chapman played an insurance executive deserted by his wife and on the brink of suicide. Losing the nerve to kill himself, he hires a weird little odd-job man, played by David, to do it for him. But in view of the way Chapman and the other soon-to-be Pythons left David behind, it was also somewhat ironic that in *The Odd-Job Man*, David had a scene where he held a gun to Chapman's head.

'Yes, I did feel disappointed,' says David of his parting from Idle, Jones and Palin. 'I certainly was not doing so many things at that time that I couldn't have been a part of that. But Denise and I were more actors coming from an acting background and the other guys were all from an academic world of Cambridge and The Footlights. They had done a marvellous show, where Humphrey had got to know them, called *Cambridge Circus*.

'Their way of applying their use of the language to make things funny was brilliant. They had marvellous command of language which obviously I did not have because I had come up a very different way. And they already knew each other when we started so they were always a bit of a team and a club. So they went away and they did not include Denise and I. They preferred to link up with people of similar intellectual weight like John Cleese who was quite brilliant.

'That is what happened and I think they were right, you see. Had the people in charge at the time given them their head then perhaps I would have gone along with them and that would have changed my career totally. I am not at all bitter. Because I didn't go with them I went in a totally different direction.'

That was the public reaction – privately he was devastated. A friend with whom David stayed at the time recalls, 'He liked Terry Jones and Michael Palin particularly as people, but he felt very unhappy to be excluded. He felt used, as some of the ideas they had talked about later seemed to take shape in the success of Python. He used to come back to my flat and throw himself on the floor and beat the carpet some nights when some sneering intellectual reference had gone over his head and he had caught an exchanged glance that he thought was putting him down.

'David knew he was just as good as any of them but he didn't have their background and connections. He felt vulnerable and out of his depth when they started talking about paintings or films and sometimes he was sure they did it just to wind him up. One night, after a bit of aggro in the studio, he came home raving about the 'condescending clowns' and I think ever since then David has been very suspicious of that sort of establishment background. He tends to lump it all together. If he meets someone who talks about when he was at Cambridge or drops the name of his old school or even regiment, David is quickly on his guard. He definitely didn't like being left out of the gang.

'One particular night, he came home just shuddering with anger. I've never seen anything like it. It wasn't the fame and it wasn't the money. It was just there was this great talented gang of them and he had been excluded. He knew they were brilliant and he knew they would succeed. He so wanted to be part of it all and for no reason at all it was taken away from him. It must have been very hard for him to bear. For days you could scarcely talk to him.'

While the embryonic Pythons set off on their first steps to international stardom, David headed in a distinctly different direction, to the mythical Midlands motel that was for so long the setting for the interminable ITV soap opera *Crossroads*.

To say he was underwhelmed is an understatement. After all, *Crossroads* was the show where characters could walk behind the freezer in the kitchen or across the garage for a spanner and disappear for six months. Comedians used to joke that actors who remembered their lines would be sacked on the spot. Even his best friend couldn't call it a good career move.

Ann Callender remembers, 'It was hysterical, because David did not really want to do it, but at the same time he wanted to learn the television technique for fast turnaround drama. He went into the programme, made up in Birmingham by ATV, as a rather silly gardener type and he was up there for quite a few weeks, in spite of his persistent efforts to escape.

'At first, he used to say in our frequent telephone conversations that he had been given a rather dull and tedious person to play. He said the gardener was a very boring character, but he accepted that it was very good experience although it was not a very large or interesting role.

'Then after three weeks up there I suddenly had a very angry David on the telephone. He said, "Have you seen the scripts?" I said, "No." Most play scripts were sent to me but hardly any *Crossroads* scripts were. He said, "I just can't do this any more. It is completely ridiculous." I did not understand what was going on. I said, "Calm down, David, and tell me what is wrong."

'He said, "You know that nice, boring little gardener chap

I was playing?" I said, "Yes, David."He paused and then almost spat down the telephone, "Well, he has suddenly turned into some sort of psychopathic killer." He was incandescent with rage.

'What had happened, of course, as was usual in *Crossroads*, was that the writers had switched over and the new writer was taking the story off in a new direction. I did not tell David that. Instead, I said, "I don't know what you can do about it, because you have not got much time. I think you have got to realise that perhaps the silly little gardening character was just a front and this man was in fact schizophrenic and the bad side is just starting to come out now."'

Propriety prevents Ann Callender from recalling David Jason's precise response. 'I won't tell you exactly what he said, but I can say that he just was not terribly receptive to that idea,' she recalls. 'In the end, I said, "Come on, David. You're a professional," and he accepted the situation and said, "Yeah, I'll just get on with it."

'Two or three weeks went by and I did not exactly see the programme every day. It was on while I was still at work and in those days agents did not run to television sets in the office. Then he came on the phone again and my heart sank wondering what the new problem was. He was not earning a great deal of money and he was very punctilious about everything.

'He said, "You won't believe this. I have just had the scripts for the next couple of weeks." I said, "What has happened this time? Are they going to catch you and send you to prison for some dreadful crime?" He said, "No, I'm back being a stupid gardener again." He came out of *Crossroads* not very long after that, having learned a very great deal.'

David made such an impact on life at King's Oak that Jane Rossington, the only ever-present member of the cast, completely missed it. 'I know he was in *Crossroads* but I'm ashamed to say I never noticed him.'

After *Crossroads*, David did some work in the theatre, including a memorable portrayal of Bob Acres in *The Rivals* in the West End, which led to his taking over from Michael Crawford in the long-running *No Sex Please – We're British* at the Strand Theatre and then a starring role in another comedy *Look, No Hans!* at the same theatre.

Malcolm Taylor directed *The Rivals* which opened on 1 May, 1972 and earned David a notice in *The Daily Telegraph* stating that his Acres was 'quite good fun'.

Malcolm Taylor goes much further. 'He was brilliant in it,' he said, 'and I am sure it was his performance there that gave him the chance to take over in *No Sex Please*. He was a fantastic comic actor even then. And, of course, he loved all the tumbling. He could certainly do anything that Michael Crawford did.'

Like Crawford, David also suffered his fair share of knocks while throwing himself energetically into his stage role. And, like Crawford, he decided to have regular consultations with osteopath Paul Johnson, although he was reluctant to do so at first.

'I thought it was all a bit gobbledegook,' says David, 'but I made up my mind to go and see Paul when I found I was doing myself so much body damage and I was starting to get myself all twisted up. Once I put my shoulder out, and I was constantly pulling muscles and tendons. Michael Crawford used to have Paul on contract for treatment three times a week, but I had to pay for him myself.

'Paul was absolutely brilliant and used to tweak me out. I also spent a lot of time talking to him and I became a great believer in him. I got to learn a lot about body problems and I soon learned that if I didn't do warm-up exercises, then I was going to do myself some damage. I learned, too, a lot about referred pain – that fact that your body can hurt somewhere but the damage is actually somewhere else on your body. I learned a good deal while I was doing all that falling about and it means I can now go to an osteopath and get the problem isolated and sorted out much quicker."

At one point in the run of *No Sex Please – We're British*, David spent two weeks going through the strenuous routines with a dislocated toe.

'I didn't know I'd dislocated it,' he says. 'I thought I'd just sprained it. It was all right while I rested my foot during the day, but by the time I got to the theatre I was in a lot of pain.'

Humphrey Barclay, who had television plans for David, found himself advising David on his theatre approach. He said, 'It was difficult for him when he took over from Michael Crawford because he had to do Michael Crawford's marvellous bit of comic business and then develop his own. I remember one night in my flat when we worked out a routine with a parcel that he was supposed to be wrapping and he ended up tripping over and doing his brilliant tumbling act. His face lit up with delight when he eventually got it right.'

But David Jason's style of professionalism and dedication again did not endear him to all members of the cast. He recalled, 'I remember when I was in *No Sex Please* I used to have this long piece of business which would really get the audience going and this other actor used to say, "Oh God, here comes the Milkman."

'I said, "What do you mean, the Milkman?" He said, "Let's be fair, old boy, we have all got trains to catch. You milked some scenes so much you have made us miss them some nights taking so long." I said, "That's what I'm paid for, that's what we're here for. The audience doesn't know about trains. You can't apologise afterwards and say, 'I'm sorry you didn't all have a good laugh tonight but we do have a train to catch.' When the audience buys a ticket, they buy me and they expect to get value for money. I'll walk home if that's what it takes."'

David also learned a financial lesson from *No Sex Please*.

He took over Michael Crawford's role for £100 a week. He found out later that Crawford, on the strength of his television comedy hit with *Some Mothers Do 'Ave 'Em*, had been paid much more than he was on nine per cent of the box office. 'They made a lot of money out of me,' said David darkly.

In *Darling Mr London*, he provided Ann Callender with her favourite stage moment. 'David could be a genius of a comic, especially when he was doing physical stunts. One scene involved one of the sofas that turns into a put-you-up-bed, which had been put up for obvious reasons. When the husband comes home early, David had to dive into this bed which then turned back into a sofa and folded up with him inside. It was a most dangerous and complicated piece of business, but David did it brilliantly.'

Her husband, David Croft, was producing *Hugh and I* with Hugh Lloyd and he happily included David in guest appearances. Croft recalls, 'I gave him a couple of early jobs and he was very funny. He really was such a good tumbler and faller-over. I used him for that first of all. He was supposed to be a little man with the laundry and eventually of course he had to leap into the basket just before the lid slammed shut. He was so very good, I remember that Terry Scott wasn't at all pleased.

'The most important thing about David is that he is funny. The audience laughs at him, there is never any mistaking that, he has a natural sense of fun. You can't teach people that sense of comedy and how to be funny. We developed his sense of humour but he was not particularly funny off screen – the funniest people rarely are.'

David Jason's opportunities for carving out a career with David Croft's long successful comedy television repertory company were curtailed by BBC procedures. Ann Callender said, 'David was then a BBC producer and when you have an agent and you have a husband in that position, there was a most humiliating process that you have to go through whereby your husband had to write a letter saying that under no circumstances will your artists get preferential treatment.'

In any case, David made his early television start with ITV but David Croft is still sorry that, having spotted that comic talent in its infancy in the early *Under Milk Wood* he has not been able to harness it more frequently. Croft said, 'The sad thing is that one way and another I have never been able to use him again. He used to say to me, "After all these years, you've never used me. What's the matter?" But he is a super performer, a lovely performer. The trouble is that David is too famous now to fit into my sort of show. There is no real place for a star in a team show and I have always preferred teams."

David recalls that he did, in fact, almost become a member of one of those teams. He said, 'I've been up for lots of parts in this business and some of them would surely have changed my whole life and career. There is quite a bit of luck to our game.

'When I was playing all these old men I got an interview to read for a character in *Dad's Army*. It was for the Corporal Jones that Clive Dunn was supposed to play. Clive wanted the part but he was in the Spike Milligan show at the time and David Croft and his co-writer Jimmy Perry were disappointed but looking round for someone else.

'I went in in the morning and read for them at ten o'clock and at half-past twelve my agent rang to say I had got the job. It was wonderful, a marvellous break to get in on the start of a new series. It was a lovely script and even though I did not know who else was in it, that didn't matter to me.

'But at three in the afternoon my agent phoned again to say bad news – that part in *Dad's Army*, I hadn't got it after all. Apparently, what had happened during lunchtime at the BBC was that they had gone into the bar and Bill Cotton, one of the bosses then, had said to Clive Dunn that he was sorry they were not doing any more Spike Milligan's but at least he had the new *Dad's Army* role. This was all unknown to Croft who had already cast me. Bill Cotton went to David Croft and said, "It's all right. You've got Clive Dunn for that part."'

David is philosophical about missing out. He said, 'If I had gone into *Dad's Army*, then the whole of the rest of my career would have been different. I would probably never have done *Open All Hours* or *Only Fools and Horses*.'

After Malcolm Taylor's generous act of recomendation, his friendship with David Jason grew, so much so that in 1968, when Taylor married actress Anne Rutter, who had appeared with David in *The Rivals*, he asked David to be Best Man. It was an invitation that guaranteed laughter all the way.

Taylor recalls, 'The night before the wedding, we all went out for a Chinese meal in the Edgware Road and then back to my flat after a very good night out with plenty to drink all round. In the morning, I was anxious to make sure everything was ready and I carefully cleaned my shoes. A little later, I was surprised that David insisted on cleaning them again though I thought he was just being helpful, so I did not protest.

'I did not find out what he was up to until later. It was a top hats and morning suits do in Beaconsfield. And we all got very smartly to the church and as I knelt down at the front at the beginning of the ceremony, I could hear all this barely suppressed laughter burbling behind me.

'Of course, the bastard had only written "HE" on the instep of my left shoe and "LP!" on the instep of the right shoe, so when I knelt down I was screaming for help. That was the first thing. Then when we moved into our frightfully middle-class reception in a marquee on the lawn. David stood up to make his speech. There was a sprinkling of theatricals there – Sheila Hancock was a guest and so was Frank Windsor as I was directing *Softly, Softly* at the time.

'David got to his feet. Then he stood on a chair so we could all see him clearly. He tipped his hat back and said in a loud, clear voice, "Balls..." I thought, "My God, he's flipped. He is going to lay into the whole ceremony. What on earth is he going to say next?" And one of Anne's older relations started to walk out fearing a tirade of abuse.

'But before she got very far, he went on, "Balls ... weddings and christenings are great fun." And we all breathed a huge collective sigh of relief. He went on in such hilarious style from there my real regret is that I did not think of recording his speech. It was a marvellous comedy routine.

'And as if that was not enough, David actually joined us on our honeymoon! We went for a fortnight to Corfu and after the first week David came out on his own and joined us. We were delighted to have him because he was such fun. He loved taking off the Greek waiters, doing a whole serving routine in his peculiar version of the Greek language which nobody else could quite understand. The waiters loved it and so did we.'

Corfu was always one of David's favourite holiday haunts, and often he would accompany Malcolm Taylor and Anne Rutter and their friend writer Richard Harris and his wife.

Richard Harris recalls, 'We used to have great fun. The three of us had this joke where we would refer to each other by our initials. Malcolm Taylor was known as MT, David was DJ and I was RH. We would say, "Oh hello, MT, I've just had lunch with DJ." It was just a laugh. David was obviously very talented and a great laugh. We were very young then. David had just finished working as an electrician. He usually came on his own, he never had a steady girlfriend when I knew him. He was as ambitious as any young actor and certainly he used to get frustrated. He was always a pretty solitary chap, but great fun in those days.'

MOVIES

E ven in the fairytale world of movie-making, it is very nearly asking the impossible of a film director to make a full-length comedy feature film in just three weeks, especially when those three weeks are spanning Easter, when the sets are constantly being unexpectedly dismantled and irretrievably taken away as shooting progresses, and when an unscheduled sex scene has to be shot as an afterthought to spice up the movie.

Yet amazingly, *Albert's Follies*, which was burdened with all these handicaps and more, was the film which was intended to launch David Jason to stardom. In the end, it was a disaster movie with most of the disasters happening behind the scenes. In its own way, *Albert's Follies*, or *White Cargo* as the film was eventually re-titled, was truly a miracle of movie-making, and director Ray Selfe looks back on it all with a mixture of pride, pain, pleasure, laughter and disbelief.

The miracle is that the film was ever made at all. Time was so tight that Selfe admits to being forced to use several takes in the finished movie where his star, David Jason, was not giving his performance for the camera but was simply filmed in rehearsal.

'We'd rehearse David with the camera rolling and use that take,' Selfe recalls. 'There just wasn't the time to do it properly and I was under terrible pressure to get it all done in three weeks. The production manager was continually pressurising me and I had to turn in some-where around six or seven minutes of material every day.'

As if he didn't have enough problems to worry about, Selfe's efforts to deliver a light, entertaining comedy film were further complicated when, after the cameras had been rolling for four days, a request came through to give *Albert's Follies* a different flavour. At the outset, Selfe had perceived *Albert's Follies* as an old-fashioned comedy with the well-meaning idiot getting himself into tricky situations and chasing a girl who is much stronger than he is and who isn't destined for him anyway.

So Selfe was surprised when the order to 'tart it up a bit' came from his producers as he struggled to combat the mounting difficulties he was already facing.

'They'd first of all wanted an X Certificate film, and then they'd realised it would limit their market so they asked me to go for a U certificate,' says Selfe. 'Then half-way through the fifth day of shooting, they changed their minds and asked if I would make it an X certificate. I said "No, not at this stage because it would change the whole slant of the movie."'

Instead, Selfe chose to continue with his already tight schedule at Twickenham Studios and then shoot one additional scene elsewhere. And so it came about that the film which had started out with such high hopes for David Jason, finished production in the most unlikely circumstances – in a specially hired room at the Westminster Hotel in London where Selfe, acting as both cameraman and lighting man as well as director in order to save money, shot an extra scene with 6ft 6in tall actor Dave Prowse being ordered to romp in bed with a topless blonde.

Albert's Follies, produced by Border Film Productions (nothing to do with Border TV), started out as a fairly harmless, knockabout comic tale of a boring, pen-pushing civil servant called Albert who dreams of playing out James Bond-style heroics of rescuing girls in distress. The original, ambitious plan was to have the film in 3D when Albert stepped into his James Bond guise. But lack of time and money contrived to put paid to that innovation. By the time it was ready for release, the film had ended up with the new title of *White Cargo*, a reference to part of the plot about a sexy slave trade, whereby English strippers are shipped off to harems in the East.

Selfe, who had made literally hundreds of films without ever interesting the people who hand out the Oscar nominations, was entrusted with the job of bringing the movie in within its three-week allotted schedule and within its £80,000 budget. That was a low figure by movie production standards even in 1973. But that year, the film *American Graffiti*, made for the then miniscule Hollywood budget of £350,000, was showing moviemakers that you didn't necessarily need millions to produce a winner at the box office. That film's return was 50 times the investment.

Given the huge time and financial restrictions and other pressures imposed upon him by the producers of *Albert's Follies*, Selfe nevertheless had all the credentials to deliver. His track record included making a film about Kenny Ball and his Jazzmen in a single day and that speed of work certainly impressed the backers.

Ian Lavender was originally in the frame to play hapless Albert. Lavender had made a name for himself as Private Pike in the hugely popular BBC situation comedy *Dad's Army* about

Top: A star is born. David's birth certificate.

Bottom: David with (left to right) Aunt Edie, brother Arthur, mother Olwen and father Arthur.

Top: All smiles with friend Malcolm Taylor in 1960.

Bottom: Best man David turned Malcolm's wedding to actress Anne Rutter into a laughter packed occasion.

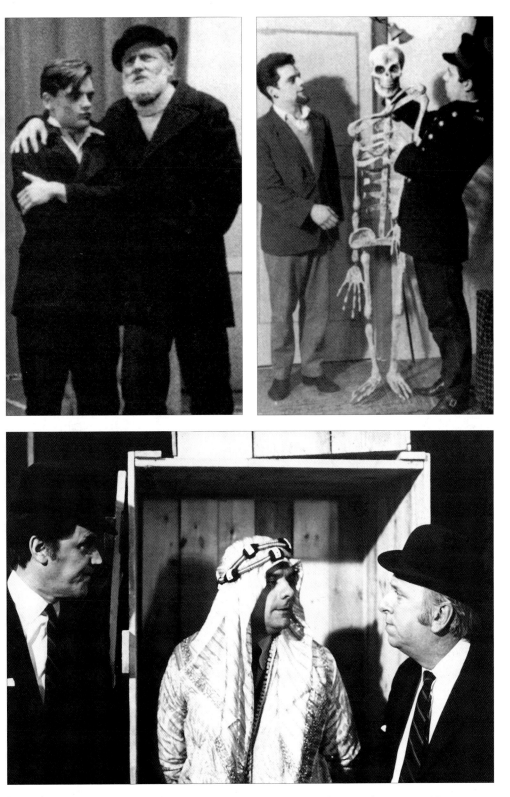

Early, but limited, acclaim came with *The Incognitos* and (bottom) David failing to sheikh the film world in the movie *White Cargo*.

Top: David in Classical garb (second left, back row).

Bottom: Making a name for himself with his amateur drama group
The Incognitos (far left).

Still an electrician – but dreaming of stardom.

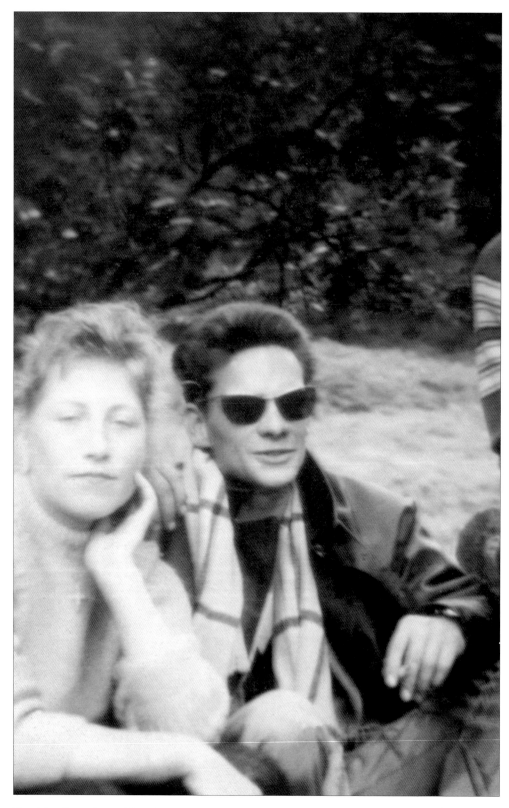

David enjoys the golden days of youth.

Halcyon days – David with school pals Mike Weedon and Brian Barnycoat.

With Heather Alexander in *Look No Hans*.

Ouch! A prophetically painful end to *Do Not Adjust Your Set*. Co-stars Michael Palin. Terry Jones and Eric Idle went on to fame and fortune with Monty Python – but without David.

Early flowering of a comic TV talent. David with Cheryl Hall in *Lucky Feller*.

David in one of his many disguises for *The Top Secret Life of Edgar Briggs*.

Star billing on a rare stage tour, all eyes in *Do Not Adjust Your Set*, and all tied up in *The Top Secret Life of Edgar Briggs*.

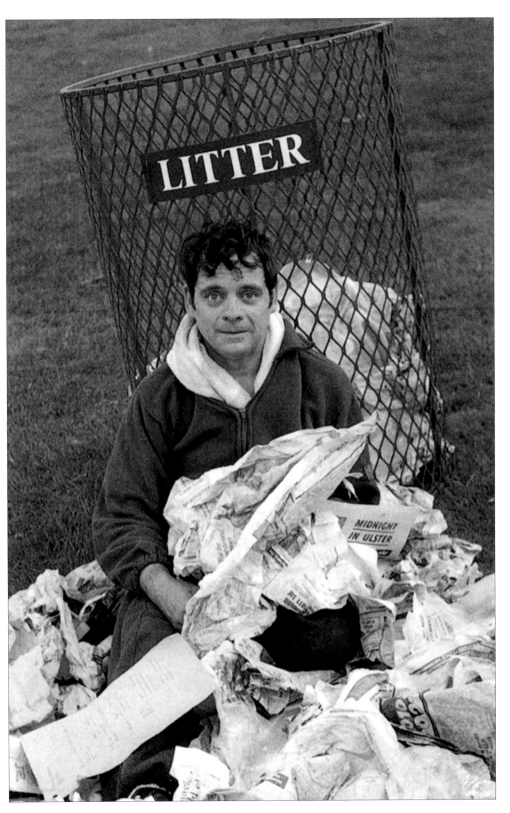

A throwaway line from David in *The Top Secret Life of Edgar Briggs.*

Falling about for the cult comedy show *Do Not Adjust Your Set*.

Stripped for action down on the farm, gunning for trouble in *The Oddjob Man*, and with Ian Richardson in *Porterhouse Blue*.

A memorable partnership. With Ronnie Barker at the comedy awards.

the antics of the Home Guard. But his impact on television audiences worked against him. Selfe considered Lavender's television image as Pike would simply be too strong and would therefore be a hindrance to the movie rather than a help.

Lavender's name might have helped attract a cinema audience but Selfe thought he was too readily identifiable from *Dad's Army* as the wet-behind-the-ears Pike. Selfe reckoned that if he was to create a brand new fool for the big screen, then he required an actor who was not instantly recognised by millions. When asked whom he favoured to take on the star role, Selfe instantly said it should be David Jason and dangled the carrot that David was unlikely to cost a fortune to sign, although he was starting to make something of a name for himself taking over from Michael Crawford in the West End stage comedy *No Sex Please – We're British*.

Selfe had worked with David some three years earlier when he was a contributor to Frank Muir's TV programme *We Have Ways of Making You Laugh*.

'I used to produce a three-minute comedy film every week for that show and David was brought in to do the commentary for one he did with Terry Gilliam on the history of the whoopee cushion,' Selfe recalls. David was duly signed as Albert.

Selfe had envisaged shooting *Albert's Follies*, which he had written as a Walter Mitty-style escapade, at various locations around London, but Border Film Productions decreed it should be shot in a studio. Selfe tried to negotiate with both Shepperton and Pinewood Studios before a deal was struck for the film to be made at Twickenham Studios over Easter in 1973. 'Nobody wanted to go into the studios over Easter because of the four-day holiday in the middle,' Selfe observes.

On the first day of filming, Selfe was anxious as always to enthuse the crew and impress upon them his ability by working at a breakneck pace. He displayed real urgency about getting the job done but the speed at which he worked caused mouths to fall open. When it came to David's very first scene, Selfe did just one take and, much to the astonishment of the crew, announced, 'Cut and print. Fine.'

'Actually,' says Selfe, 'I always believed that the first take you can cut and print. If it's not right you can go back and shoot it later.' But this audacious start astounded some of the crew, particularly a cameraman who had worked on high-budget, prestigious James Bond movies and was used to films being made with the utmost care and precision and realising perhaps a handful of seconds worth of film a day if they were lucky. He immediately came over to Selfe and asked him if he was going to go for another take just as an insurance.

'No,' Selfe told him, and quickly pressed on to the next scene. 'The cameraman smoked a pipe,' Selfe recalls with a chuckle. 'Between every take he would take his pipe out and put it into his mouth. But in the three weeks of shooting that film he always managed to get the pipe into his mouth but he never ever got the time to light it! It was all first takes.

'He kept moaning to me, "Can't you take a bit longer? Can't you do another take?" My answer was always that I'd got to finish it in the time they'd given me and there was nothing I could do about it. They were only a tiny production company. It wasn't a question of them putting any more money into it. There was no more money.'

In addition to David, Selfe had cast two other comedians, Hugh Lloyd and Tim Barrett, alongside him to play bumbling men from the Ministry. David was clearly the film's number one comedy star but he generously liked to refer to this duo as 'the comic relief'. The three of them got on extremely well and one of the very rare occasions when Selfe permitted himself more than a single take involved a scene in which Lloyd and Barrett were dressed up as gas inspectors and Barrett had to give David an address.

'We had to do four takes on that,' says Selfe, 'because they kept on rolling up with laughter as Barrett changed the address every time. Even on the take I actually used, you can see a twinkle in David's eye as he's on the brink of corpsing again.'

Not quite so funny for the cast and crew was the fact that they could not but fail to notice with increasing incredulity and much alarm that the sets of *Albert's Follies* were visibly diminishing as filming progressed. They would finish filming on a particular set one evening and head for home only to find part of that set had disappeared when they turned up to resume filming the following morning. The reason for this sudden disappearance, as they later discovered, was that several of the sets had been borrowed from another film at Twickenham Studios and had merely been reclaimed.

Selfe counted his blessings that he was fortunate enough to have in his production team a brilliant art director who managed to improvise with the utmost ingenuity.

'We had a manor built inside the studio from the remains of another movie, *The Ruling Class*, starring Peter O'Toole which had been shooting at Twickenham a few months previously,' says Selfe. 'We were also building another set on the outside of that one. But between each take, a piece of the set would get taken down and the area we were shooting in was getting smaller and smaller.

'Originally, we had a huge lounge with a corridor and several rooms off it, and a staircase. But as we finished shooting in the lounge they dismantled it, and when we finished shooting on the staircase they dismantled that, too. In the end, we were down to just a corridor with a set of double doors at the end of it.'

Inevitably, a shrinking set posed no end of problems, not least when David was due to film a scene where he had to race along the corridor, vigorously twist the handles of the double doors and throw them open.

'By this time, all that was left was half the corridor,' chortles

83

Selfe. 'And, so the set wouldn't fall down, they'd put four-by-two planks across the doors to strengthen and stabilise them and sealed the large door handles so they wouldn't open. When it came to film the scene, David being David and wanting to give his all, rushed up to the doors, grabbed the handles, gave them a vicious twist and, of course, they didn't move. He nearly broke his wrists. He swore for four minutes after that and didn't repeat himself once.'

David was not the only one feeling pain. Dave Prowse, later to become a big screen favourite with youngsters all over the world as the evil Darth Vader in *Star Wars*, had to film a scene where he stood in a coil of rope which was eventually to curl up first round his legs, then his waist, and finally up under his arms lifting him right up in the air. But as the coil travelled up his legs, Dave felt a piercing jab of pain in a kneecap.

'The rope had caught round my kneecap and pulled it right out of joint,' he says, still wincing at the memory. 'I was in agony.'

Albert's Follies was something of a reunion for Prowse and David Jason because they had known each other for many years. Prowse had appeared in an episode of the BBC's TV police series *Softly, Softly* and the Welsh director had introduced him to a little group of Welsh actors who included Jennier Hill, Ruth and Philip Madoc, and David Jason.

'I'm not Welsh myself, but I used to hang around with this group and at that time David couldn't get work to save his life,' says Prowse. 'He was paranoid about not working. He was the most insecure little guy you could come across. He was always a very funny little man. But it was strange because at that time they were trying to get his career off the ground and nothing seemed to click for him. He was a super little guy but very, very insecure.'

Prowse originally had only a small part in *Albert's Follies* but all that changed when he met director Ray Selfe. 'He said: "We can't offer you anything as small as this. You must have a major role." The next thing I know, I'm involved in script conferences. It was really strange.'

Prowse had been striving for a breakthrough for so long. He was pleased to hear that *Albert's Follies* was a film which had elevated David to the leading role. 'But it was the worst film of all time,' he says. 'It really was. At one point, David had to get over a wall to get into some big establishment and you see him climbing up the wall when it's dark and then you see him landing on the ground in daylight! It was an absolute disaster. Everything that could possibly go wrong went wrong. They were strapped for cash and everything was done in such a rush instead of things being prepared properly. Everything was done on a shoe-string, and quick.'

With two of his main cast nursing wounds, still more complications arose for Selfe from his masters. He was told that under no circumstances was he allowed to continue filming beyond 6.00pm as there would be no overtime pay.

'We never once went over six o'clock,' he remembers. 'At one minute to six, we'd get the last take in the can and then it would be cut, print and goodnight.'

That, however, suited David. He had to finish at 5.30pm every evening anyway to jump into a car to whisk him back to the West End from Twickenham through the rush-hour traffic in time to go on stage at the Strand Theatre in *No Sex Please – We're British*.

'We lost David on matinée days,' says Selfe ruefully, 'and there were days when somebody new was in the cast who had to be broken in and David couldn't make it in the afternoon because they had a rehearsal.

'David was working under terrible strain because he was doing his very action-packed version of *No Sex Please – We're British*. He must have been pretty exhausted at the end of the day.' The whole experience was a nightmare for David. He had been dazzled by the prospect of appearing in a feature film but simply appalled by the production standards.

At the Strand Theatre, David had stepped into the role created by Michael Crawford. *No Sex Please – We're British* was set in a flat above a bank, home to respectable newly-weds played by *Upstairs, Downstairs* star Simon Williams and Belinda Carroll. There to their horror, they find they are being flooded with wholesale consignments of pornographic books, pictures and films which they try to keep hidden from a nasty mother-in-law played by Evelyn Laye, a prying policeman and a couple of important bank officials. The fun comes from the attempts of David as a sheepish bank clerk to get rid of it for them by various disastrous means including flushing it down the lavatory and clogging up the rubbish disposal system.

As the bank clerk Brian Runnicles, Michael Crawford had established a supremely energetic performance, frantically rushing to and fro through the eight doors of the ingenious set, each holding a bigger surprise than the last, and David was determined to be just as acrobatic. He won huge admiration from packed houses and terrific respect from his peers for his high-octane performance.

'They took a risk with me but I stayed 18 successful months,' he was able to say later. When the curtain came down each night, David would travel the mercifully short distance home to the tiny rented flat he had moved into just off Oxford Street and fall into bed thoroughly drained. He was hardly encouraged in his efforts to get a good night's sleep by the knowledge that he had to be at Twickenham early the following morning, ready to give his all in front of the film cameras for *Albert's Follies* and yet remain fresh enough in the evening to reproduce his astonishing agility in *No Sex Please – We're British*.

Tired and exhausted as he was and aching from his

physical exertions on stage, David never let Selfe down for one moment. Selfe recalls that David gave everything to the film.

'He was absolutely excellent and contributed more than 100 per cent,' he says. 'It wasn't my first movie, although it may have looked it. But it certainly didn't look like David's first movie. I remember one scene where he had to fall out of a wagon and although he had pads on his elbows and his knees, it was a hell of a fall and it required some very agile work from him. He did it so brilliantly the crew gave him a round of applause. David always had such fantastic enthusiasm and a great sense of fun. Although it was all terribly hard work, we fell about at some of the things that happened.'

One of the more spicy scenes in the film called for David to turn up at a strip club and sit in the front row of the audience while glamorous, buxom blonde Sue Bond, a curvy Benny Hill girl, performed a striptease. From his front row seat, David's character sees the heroine of the film (played by Imogen Hassall, who later tragically committed suicide) being assaulted by Dave Prowse.

In his Walter Mitty state, David leaps up on stage and rescues her. But as the bungling loser Albert, the script called for David to leap on stage, slip up on Sue's discarded silk underwear and, in the act of reaching out a hand to stop himself falling, to pull down Sue's G-string. The scene was only made possible at all by hastily transforming a carpet showroom set from the previous's day's filming and dressing it to double as a strip club. But it was all in vain as the scene eventually ended up on the cutting room floor. Selfe was at that time working to his U Certificate brief but he says, 'I knew I would have to make some compromises afterwards when they said: "Could you put something in to tart it up a little bit?"'

Selfe needed to think and act fast and soon worked out the solution. Part of the plot involved a scenario about white slave trafficking in which strippers from London's West End clubs are abducted and sold off to harems. Dave Prowse's character is entrusted with the task of making up an assignment of strippers and decides, at the last moment, to put his own girlfriend in among them, but not before snatching one last night of love with her.

Selfe had already shot a scene in which Prowse and screen girlfriend Sue Bond were seen going out of a room to grab their last night of passion together. He had planned for their subsequent lovemaking to be left entirely to the audience's imagination. He had merely filmed them heading off together. So now, Selfe reasoned, all he had to do was to follow that scenario through to its obvious conclusion and film some bed scenes with the couple to 'tart it up'.

And so the movie, intended as a major launch-pad to stardom for David Jason, ended with Dave Prowse and Sue Bond being summoned to a hired room at the Westminster Hotel to film a sex scene together.

Dave Prowse looks back with understandable bewilderment. 'They suddenly needed Sue and me for some sexy scenes but they didn't have any money and couldn't go back to the studios so they hired a West End hotel. With Ray Selfe as director and cameraman, they had Sue and me romping around in bed trying to be sexy as part of this terrible, terrible film.'

Selfe had given Sue a start in movies by frequently using her in the short ice cream commercials he had made for the Classic cinema chains because he liked her fresh, thoroughly English wholesome look. He recalls, 'The funny thing about Sue was that she said to me when we were about to shoot this sex scene in *Albert 's Follies*, "Have I really got to go topless in this one, Ray?"

'I said, "I'm afraid so," and she said, "I've never been in a feature film yet where I've not shown my tits and I told my father this was going to be the first one. Here's another film he can't see."'

White Cargo was never going to win any Oscars, but Selfe had done his job in the most trying of circumstances. He had brought the movie in on time and on budget. 'It went out as a support movie to another film, it got a circuit release, the producers recovered their money, and it got sold to television,' he says.

But, as Prowse is quick to point out, it did nothing for David's career. 'They were trying to groom David Jason for stardom,' says Prowse, 'and *Albert's Follies* was going to get him off the ground. Unfortunately, I think it buried him even deeper than he was before.'

Ray Selfe is commendably honest when it comes to assessing the movie. 'It gets a one-star review as being terrible, but shooting a comedy is not the easiest thing to do when you have the sort of restrictions we had,' he says. 'What people don't understand is the incredible pressures we were under when making it. I don't know what David thought of it.'

David knows exactly what he thinks about it. 'It was the kiss of death,' he reflects. 'It was meant to launch me in a big way but at that time I was very green and here was an opportunity to try to do something which seemed like a good idea and everybody seemed to believe in. I believed that other people knew more than I did and I relied on them. I thought they would make it good so I worked very hard for them. I trusted more people then than I trust now. The weight of responsibility has become much more on my shoulders. It's now my decision.

'To have cameras rolling when you are rehearsing was quite horrendous. It was my first experience of filming and it certainly made me think about taking a leading part.' Unsurprisingly, there was rarely a mention of *Albert's Follies* or *White Cargo* on the David Jason list of acting credits in years to come.

'But I did another film after that called *The Odd-Job Man*. I first did it with Ronnie Barker as a half-hour television comedy and it was wonderful. But when they did it as a movie they changed the whole premise to move it up-market. But it went right away from the original story and it was total rubbish.

'Every time I got involved in a film for no money it always turned into a disaster. I couldn't do anything in a film to save my life. At one stage in my career, I was really moving backwards at a rate of knots.'

The bad memories of *Albert's Follies* stayed with David and clouded his view of British film-making. Years later, when the Carry On team got back together to make *Carry On Columbus*, top TV comedians like Rik Mayall, Julian Clary, Alexei Sayle and Richard Wilson fell over themselves to take roles in the movie. But not David. Asked whether he wanted more of a movie career, he replied acidly, 'I don't think it is possible to have one in this country. Do you think I want to be up Columbus's jacksey with Julian Clary. No thank you!'

Throughout his career, David has been prepared to take the bumps and the bruises when called upon to turn in a very physical performance. But it was while he was making *The Odd-Job Man* that he suffered a horrific accident which left his entire body seized up.

'I had to be thrown over a settee,' he recalls, 'and I ended up between the settee and a chair and landed on my head with the whole weight of my body on top of it. I was trapped.'

Fellow cast members were shocked to find David prone on the floor clearly dazed and there were great sighs of relief when he came round and appeared none the worse for the fall. But two days later David was alarmed to find his body seizing up.

'I seized up so totally that I couldn't turn my head,' he says. 'I couldn't even get my arm up to scratch the back of my head. My arm wouldn't work and my hand wouldn't work either – I couldn't close my fingers into a fist.'

David immediately sought the help of Paul Johnson, the

osteopath who had worked wonders for him during his run in *No Sex Please – We're British*. 'When Paul put me on the table he discovered I'd put my neck out at the shoulder joint. I'd pulled the tendon so badly that the joints hadn't gone back and were grating against each other. I was in agony but Paul managed to sort it all out in the end. I've taken some knocks over the years but this was by far the worst.'

Fortunately for David, Humphrey Barclay's plans for his television future were rather more professional. Barclay teamed David Jason very early on with Ronnie Barker, the man who was to become a real comedy mentor and a firm friend in later years.

Barclay remembers, 'He played an aged 100-year-old gardener called Dithers in an early Ronnie Barker series called *Hark at Barker*. David was very convincing at adding on the years. You would never have guessed how old he was. And, of course, he was very funny, as always.

'But the first major solo idea we came up with for him was *The Top Secret Life of Edgar Briggs*, a spy spoof written by Bernard McKenna and Richard Laing. I still think it was one of the funniest shows I have ever been involved with.'

The Top Secret Life of Edgar Briggs cast David as hapless no-hoper Edgar who, by a clerical error, is transferred to Counter Espionage at the Ministry of Defence. Appointed Assistant to the Commander (Noel Coleman), he manages to achieve the most remarkable results despite the fact that he is both stupid and totally unsuited to the job he has been given. David was a strange mixture of enthusiasm, apprehension and concern about the project.

Before its first screening on 15 September, 1974, he said, 'This is the culmination of eight years' work as an actor. I shall be on my own with Briggs. If the series flops, I'll get the blame. The responsibility of carrying the lead and wondering how viewers will react is a little worrying. It's like waiting to be executed.

'If it's a hit, anything is possible. Briggs is a super fellow. He's British and proud of it, and wholesome in the way that we Britons naturally are. He is devoted to his wife, although he would love to hop into bed with his beautiful and willing colleague Cathy, played by Elizabeth Counsell. There's only one thing wrong with Briggs – he's stupid. He's also so timid he'd probably collapse if Cathy openly invited him.'

Whatever the viewers thought of *The Top Secret Life Of Edgar Briggs*, David was also nervously aware that television audiences would at least be seeing the real David Jason. 'This role makes me feel rather naked,' he said. 'Until now, I've always appeared heavily disguised in wigs, heavy make-up, funny clothes and middle-European voices.'

Beating the drum for the series, Humphrey Barclay boldly predicted, 'I think Briggs, with his amazing capacity for reaching his goal by running headlong in the wrong direction, will become something of a cult. This is a new style of television comedy – fast, deadpan, laced with verbal nonsense and bundled together with a marvellously crazy logic all of its own.'

The first episode set the tone for old-fashioned knockabout comedy, with David falling over chairs, getting soaked fully clothed in a Turkish bath, taking a nose-dive over a settee and putting on a negligée without realising it.

It led *Daily Mirror* TV writer Stan Sayer to declare, 'David is a modern Buster Keaton with most of that great silent film actor's gift of timing, rhythm and skill.'

There was no doubting that David played the unfortunate espionage agent with great flair, and even *The Daily Telegraph's* TV critic Sylvia Clayton felt *The Top Secret Life of Edgar Briggs* had 'style and panache'.

Among Edgar's long-suffering colleagues who looked upon his unlikely achievements with amusement, alarm, incredulity and jealousy was Spencer, played by that fine actor

Mark Eden, later to find infamy as the Beast of Weatherfield, *Coronation Street's* Alan Bradley.

Mark remembers, 'Humphrey knew David was brimming with television potential. He had just done *No Sex Please – We're British* and everyone said he was funnier than Michael Crawford. And we all really thought Edgar Briggs would launch David as a star. It was a very well written series and David added in so many hilarious extra bits of comedy business.

'We immediately struck up a rapport because we both love comedy and we had similar a sense of humour. He used think up so many funny little stunts to improve the action and he used to ring me up and say, his voice almost quivering with enthusiasm, "Can you get in a quarter-of-an-hour earlier tomorrow, I've got an idea about that scene where you come upstairs with the milk bottle or whatever."

'And we would get in before anyone arrived and we would work it out together. He was brilliantly inventive and I just know when I watch him in series these days that a lot of that stuff is not scripted but created by him. Once, there was a scene where he had to put some things into a filing cabinet, shut it, lock it, throw the key out of the window and then find he had trapped his tie in the drawer. I had to rush over and strain to get him out, virtually by his throat. It wasn't really all that difficult because the tie slid out easily.

'But when we came to record the scene he put a little weight, a little piece of metal, into the bottom of his tie. This made it jam in the drawer and I had to yank really hard to get him out. At first I couldn't understand it, it wouldn't come free. David went into convulsions. He reckoned it made that scene more realistic but he also loved to make me laugh when I wasn't supposed to. He was one of the very few people who could actually break me up, make me laugh so much I could not go on. Not many people can do that.

'I went through rep where, when people get bored, they try

to make you laugh on stage, and I was pretty impervious to all that – or I thought I was until I worked with David Jason, because he used to get me every time. He was just so funny. He was also a very clever mimic. You would hear these amazing voices – John Wayne and James Mason were his favourites – and look round and it would be David.'

David Jason's flair for the physical side of being funny was given free rein in *Edgar Briggs* and he boldly grasped the challenge, insisting on doing all of his own stunts. Mark Eden said, 'Even when it involved big falls he insisted on doing it himself. He knew it would look better than using stunt men. Once, we were on the top floor of one of those big old-fashioned houses in London near the Regent's Park canal. The script called for David and I to pretend to be window cleaners and he had to get out on to a window sill.

'As he got out, he slipped and grabbed a rope and swung around a bit and then I had to grab him by this cardigan he was wearing but then he had to slip through the cardigan, which I was left holding, and crash several storeys to the ground. They were planning to use a stuntman for the final fall but David said, "No, no, I'll do it. It will look better," and, of course, he fell down into the pile of cardboard boxes quite brilliantly. But I wouldn't have dared to do it.

'He wanted to do everything himself. Another time, we were in one of those crazy car chases and we had to go over a hump-backed bridge so fast that the car took off. They had stunt drivers ready and waiting but David insisted he wanted to do it himself and he talked me into coming along for the most terrifying ride of my life. He kept saying it would be much better because the cameras would be able to capture out faces and our expressions of fear. The expression was genuine in my case as I smashed my head against the roof when we became airborne.

'I knew then he was going to be a star. I told everyone who

would listen at the time. We became good friends through the series but he was always something of a loner. If we went for a drink afterwards he would have half a pint and that would be it. And at lunchtimes he was always off on his own to the nearest greasy spoon café for a big fry up or meat and two veg.'

David had already developed his interest in flying. He quickly qualified as a glider pilot and would use many of his spare moments to become airborne, but when the producers found out about this potentially dangerous hobby they grounded him until filming was over. David was deeply miffed. He had moved by then into the flat that is still his London base to this day, in a pre-war mansion block just off Oxford Street.

'I used to go round for a drink sometimes,' said Mark. 'Then he bought this place in Sussex to do up. It was really remote with no phone and he would arrive for work on Monday full of enthusiasm for a piece of rewiring he had done. I think he used to enjoy hard physical work as a break from the pressures of being funny.

'But more often he came round to my house for dinner. I liked him very much and my family always enjoyed his company. But he seemed so very solitary. I don't think he ever brought a girlfriend and whenever we rang to invite him he nearly always accepted.

'I think, like a lot of comedians, he was actually quite melancholy at times. It wasn't until he got going that he would start relishing it all. When he came up with a good bit of business he would hug himself with glee, he loved it. And as *Edgar Briggs* was an action series, there was scope for him to do all his funny falls.

'David was very popular with everyone. You could not fail to respond to his enthusiasm and his determination to make the show absolutely as good as possible.'

In spite of all the high hopes, *The Top Secret Life of Edgar Briggs* never quite made it in the ratings and in the world of commercial television there is rarely any prized second series for shows which don't grab instant success in the ratings.

'The problem was that we went out just before *The Brothers*,' said Mark Eden. 'That was a glossy BBC soap opera about a transport firm that was just at its peak at the time. It was like putting something out against *Coronation Street*; we didn't have a chance. That was it, they scrapped the show. We all got letters from Humphrey Barclay saying he was sorry but that was the decision.'

As the star of the show, David's disppointment was acute. 'I was really upset about poor Edgar,' he reflected. 'I thought he was terrific but somehow he never caught on.' The irony of the failure in the ratings of *The Top Secret Life of Edgar Briggs* was that the show became a world-wide hit. It became one of ITV's most successful exports and David and the other members of the cast received fan letters from all over the world for years afterwards.

Yet when ITV moved to repeat the comedy they were blocked by David Jason of all people. 'He simply said "No",' said an angry cast member. 'It was very mean of him because, although he doesn't need the money, lots of other people do. It would have meant a few thousand quid to me that is desperately needed. Apparently, David thought he was already over-exposed. Some of the rest of us thought that was disgraceful.'

David himself declines to discuss the blocked repeats but a friend gave the following opinion: "Edgar Briggs is history. Sure, the viewers would love it but David knows just how raw he looked in those days and he is not at all anxious to share that with his public. Image is very important to an actor, and to an insecure actor like David, it is absolutely paramount. He said "No" and he meant "No".'

LUCKY

While The *Top Secret Life of Edgar Briggs* was certainly unlucky and underrated, it nevertheless fell a long way short of its objective of turning David Jason into a household name and making him ITV's answer to Michael Crawford. Crawford had given the BBC a huge comedy hit with *Some Mothers Do 'Ave 'Em* starring as a hapless failure called Frank Spencer for whom everything always went wrong. Playing Frank with consumate skill, Crawford had also taken quite staggering risks to do his own stunts, which became a spectacular feature of the sitcom. The show had caught the public's imagination and ITV chiefs had envisaged Jason, with his flair for visual knockabout comedy, as their answer to Crawford in *Edgar Briggs*.

Apart from David himself, no one was more disappointed at the failure of the series than Humphrey Barclay. But to his credit, he swallowed his disappointment, kept faith with David as a comedy actor and remained undaunted. He was convinced it was only a matter of time before David achieved a major break-through and the search was earnestly resumed to find him a suitable new comedy vehicle. The task fell to comedy writer Terence Frisby whose track record included netting around £300,000 in stage royalties for his highly successful sex comedy *There's A Girl In My Soup*, which subsequently became a hit film starring Peter Sellers and Goldie Hawn.

Frisby had first met David Jason when David's brother Arthur had played a leading role in Frisby's first play, *The Subtopians* back in 1962. In addition to being a highly promising writer, Frisby was also at that time working as an actor at Bromley Rep in Kent and he and Arthur had become friends after they had appeared in a pantomime together, Arthur playing a cannibal chief and Frisby his victim in the pot.

Frisby remembers David was often to be found hanging around the theatre. 'He'd have a few drinks with us,' Frisby recalls, 'and I got the idea that he wanted to be a theatre electrician. I didn't connect him with acting at that time.' But 13 years on, Frisby was only too delighted when Humphrey Barclay asked him to write a comedy series with David cast in the lead role.

The series Frisby came up with was *Lucky Feller*, and it was culled from a film script which Frisby had written several years before for producer Jay Lewis. When Lewis suddenly died from a heart-attack, the script went straight into the bottom drawer of Frisby's desk and remained there until it was dusted off to meet Barclay's request for a new comedy series.

In essence, *Lucky Feller* was the story of the eternal triangle – but with a difference. Frisby explained that '...it was about this innocent little man, Shorty Mepstead, trying to run his little plumbing business with his elder brother Randy who was bedding Shorty's girlfriend. In the end, Randy got her pregnant and the younger brother, Shorty, had to marry her.'

David, naturally, had the role of Shorty, the gauche innocent who still lived at home in south-east London with his mother and brother Randolph, and believed he was the luckiest person in the world because he was surrounded by such ostensibly lovely people. Cheryl Hall, a bright and pretty 26-year-old actress, won the role of Kathleen, Shorty's girlfriend who gradually coaxes him out of his shyness. Peter Armitage, later to find fame in *Coronation Street*, was signed to play brother Randy after Nicky Henson had taken the role in the pilot, and Glynn Edwards, who went on famously to play the barman at The Winchester Club in *Minder*, was Kath's father.

Once the idea of *Lucky Feller* had been accepted by London Weekend Television, Frisby was despatched to share a holiday cottage in Somerset for two days to 'observe' the latent star and fashion the series to fit him. It was not an experience which overly thrilled David

'He was just looking, listening, seeing what kind of person I was and how I behaved,' David recalled. 'Then, when he'd got enough information, he just went.'

All looked extremely promising when it came to filming the first episode. One scene, in particular set in a Chinese restaurant, had the studio audience in fits. 'I've never heard people laugh as much,' says Frisby.

The scene involved Shorty taking girlfriend Kath out for a meal. The comic scenario had Shorty, hopelessly ignorant of Chinese cuisine, so drastically over-ordering from the menu that the waiter, played by Burt Kwouk, had to pull up another table to accomodate yet more plates piled with food.

Among the offerings were two dumplings which were to provide the audience with their cue for hysterical laughter – because Shorty had ordered prawn balls. Gazing at the spread with a puzzled expression, Kath enquired, 'Which are the prawn balls?'

Frisby recalls, 'The audience laughed like you've never

heard. Then David pointed at the dumplings and said, "It must be those." Then Kath says, "Ooh, big aren't they?" and the audience laughed for another ten minutes so that David never managed to get out the pay-off line which was, "Well, they were king-size prawns." We did umpteen takes and the audience were collapsing and David broke up before every take. Everyone laughed so much those three lines took half-an-hour to shoot.'

No one ever accused *Lucky Feller* of overdoing the subtlety or good taste of comedy presentation but it all augured well for the series, especially as Frisby was agreeably surprised to discover that sitting in unobtrusively but attentively at the initial rehearsals every Monday was none other than LWT's Chairman.

'There was always this figure at the back,' says Frisby, 'and I went over to see who it was. There was LWT's Chairman, John Freeman. He told me he came every Monday simply bcause he loved watching the show.'

LWT, for their part, had plenty of faith in the project on a production level. For one key scene where Shorty floods a supermarket there was a double set – one which could be flooded and a second, dry set for other scenes.

'We took an entire set, packed it out in the studio and flooded it,' Frisby recalls. 'It was a scene where Shorty and Randy have arrived to repair the pipes at a supermarket. At the very moment Shorty is supposed to release the cock, he discovers his brother is bedding his girl and they get into a terrible fight and all the taps are open and it floods.'

Other key moments were filmed at a launderette in West London which was literally filled from floor to ceiling with foam. 'We wore wet suits with our costumes on top and we more or less floated in the foam,' Cheryl Hall recalls. 'David and I were worried how we were going to breathe, but we managed it.'

David and the rest of the cast had the luxury of five days rehearsing each episode before going into the studio to film on the Saturday. Each Sunday they had the day off, much welcomed by all because the summer of 1976 turned out to be the hottest recorded this century.

It was truly a golden summer. All parts of the UK basked in record hours of sunshine, temperatures soared, and it was so dry that the crowd at Lord's actually cheered when a few drops of rain stopped the cricket for 15 minutes. But rehearsing in stifling heat in a stuffy room at the Duke of York's army barracks in King's Road, Chelsea, was far from comfortable work for David and the rest of the cast. At 1.00pm they broke for lunch each day and David and Cheryl would escape to an equally hot, stuffy pub to queue up for a salad and a beer while cursing the fact that they were too late to find a seat in the popular beer garden at The Markham. By the time they got there, every seat was always taken.

Like so many of his co-stars, Cheryl took an instant liking to David and was immediately impressed by his flair for visual comedy and his meticulous approach to acting.

'He was so professional,' she reflects. 'His timing was so good, he was great with props and he taught me the importance of visual gags. Shorty was Mr Uncool, a man who never got anything right and we had a scene in a pub where he went to light my cigarette with his lighter. Being Shorty, of course, he activates the lighter and a huge flame shoots out and burns my entire nose. It was a tricky scene but David worked out all the angles perfectly and knew exactly where the camera should be so we could film the shooting flame then cut it so that my nose could be reddened for the next shot.

'There was one very funny moment in one of the final scenes when I was wearing a beautiful peach blouse and I had to clutch David to my bosom in a clinch. When he pulled away, my blouse was black and I couldn't understand why. I couldn't work out where this black stain had come from. The audience was laughing away about it and I noticed David looking very sheepish. Then he suddenly whispered, 'It's my bald pate!' David was beginning to go bald even then and I'd never noticed because they'd blacked it out with make-up.

'David was always 100 per cent committed. He lived, ate and breathed acting and when he wasn't acting he was always talking about the business. He had that totally focussed approach even when socialising. It wasn't just socialising, it was for an ulterior motive, a hidden agenda of who you were socialising with and whether it would do your career any good. I'd rather choose my friends by other criteria, but David was always very ambitious. He very much wanted to be a star.

'He was acutely aware that at the age of 36, as he was then, he was late coming to fame. At that time I was married to the actor Robert Lindsay who was gaining recognition in another ITV comedy series called *Get Some In*. It was a show about RAF recruits doing National Service in the 1950s and apart from Tony Selby, Bob and the other stars of *Get Some In* were all in their mid-twenties and they were all enjoying a high profile as the show became popular very quickly. David must have been looking at them and thinking, "They are my contemporaries. I'm way, way too late starting out." David was running with all his might to catch the train.'

Away from *Lucky Feller*, Cheryl found David displayed distinct traits of his TV character Shorty Mepstead, especially in his attitude to women.

'He was very vulnerable off set,' she says. 'He may have been 36 but he was very naïve as far as women were concerned. Being so committed to acting, it may just be that he hadn't had the time to discover women.

'I rather took David under my wing for a while. I gave him lifts as he didn't have a car, invited him to charity football matches where I made him sign autographs as he would never play, and tried to line him up with a girlfriend. He was unattached at the time which was of constant concern to me. I remember him telling me about some girl he had nearly married when he was in his twenties and I thought he would have had her up the aisle because he said how much he'd loved her. I'd have thought David wanted and needed marriage.

'Bob Lindsay and I were very much a married couple and so we sort of adopted David. I wanted to do some matchmaking for him, so we set up quite a few dinner parties with various girls at our house in Wimbledon. One particular evening, we lined him up with a beautiful girl called Mondy who was also unattached and feeling vulnerable because her husband, the actor Leigh Lawson, had left her to move in with the actress Hayley Mills. At the time, Mondy was a very close friend of mine. She was stunningly beautiful – her parents were Iranian and German and she had olive skin, a lovely dark mane of hair, worked in fashion design, was always impeccably dressed and was very intelligent, too.

'I thought she and David might be good together so we had a bijou soirée for 16 people at our Wimbledon home and I told David all about Mondy.

"Mondy?" he said. "That's a funny name." I told him to practise saying it and get it right for when he spoke to her.

"She's a really lovely girl," I told him, "and she's unattached."

'As the evening went on, everything seemed to be going really well. Mondy was sitting in my rocking chair and David sat at her feet. But after about half-an-hour she came up to me in the kitchen and said, "Is he having me on?" I asked what the matter was because they had seemed to be getting along like a house on fire.

"Well," said Mondy, "he's *so* attentive and he keeps telling me how beautiful I am."

'Poor David! He was trying so hard – too hard. You know women – when a man comes on to us like that you think, "Hello, this guy can't be for real!" If only David had played it a bit cooler he might have been all right. But he was so naïve about women.'

That naïveté was mirrored in the screen character of Shorty Mepstead and it certainly earned David the sympathy vote from viewers as the series progressed. *Lucky Feller* was launched on 2 September, 1976 and earned some plaudits from the TV critics. Sean Day-Lewis, writing in *The Daily Telegraph*, said, 'My response to David Jason as Shorty Mepstead is that he has a very characterful face and is more likeable than funny.'

The Stage, assessing the new sitcom in the wake of *The Top Secret Life of Edgar Briggs*, remarked prophetically, 'Somewhere there is a writer whose ideas Mr Jason can excecute to great effect but they have not met yet.'

Terence Frisby feels *Lucky Feller's* chances of big success were blighted by short-sighted scheduling. Inexplicably, a series about a man bedding his little brother's girl behind his back was given an early evening slot.

'And the girl,' Frisby points out, 'played the most abused heroine there ever was. She was knocked out, thrown about, almost drowned, electrocuted and screwed in the back of a car by the brother.

'Putting all that out at seven o'clock in the evening wasn't right at all. It was completely the wrong time and hardly anyone ever saw the programmes because everyone was still in their offices or going home and I was actually quite annoyed with LWT. The programmes, though, were top of LWT's viewing figures during a winter when LWT had a very bad time.'

There was certainly enough interest all round for LWT to invite Frisby to write a second series of *Lucky Feller*. He had wisely left the fate of Shorty and Kath in the balance at the end of the thirteenth and final programme. Followers of the series tuned in expecting to watch it neatly rounded off by Shorty finally marrying his sweetheart Kath, only to find poor Shorty being left at the altar.

'It was a really sad scene,' Cheryl Hall recalls. 'David is at the church and the scene cuts to me jumping out of a taxi and rushing on to Victoria railway station. We actually filmed at Victoria and I was wearing a complete copy of Princess Anne's wedding dress and long veil. So as not to draw attention to the fact that filming was going on, they hid a camera under one of those little arched canvas workmen's huts they'd set up outside the main entrance and the camera followed me as I ran across the concourse in my bridal gown and down the entire length of the platform.

'Kath had decided that she simply could not marry one brother and not the other so she had left them both. It was a real tear-jerker with the viewers all being prompted to pity poor David getting left at the altar. There would have been viewers all round the country sighing, "Oh, how could she leave him?"'

Followers of *Lucky Feller* never did get to see whether Shorty ever caught up with his runaway bride. LWT's request that Frisby write a sequel fell on deaf ears, largely because LWT would not repeat the original programmes.

'I was miffed with LWT for not repeating *Lucky Feller*,' Frisby explains. 'Then when John Birt became Head of Programmes at LWT he phoned me up and said some very complimentary things and told me he was going to repeat them all. But it was around the time that David was in *Porterhouse Blue*, and *Open All Hours* and *Only Fools and Horses* were on and David said, via an agent, that he was over-exposed and so he was able to stop them going out again. So, once again, I was miffed and that was the end of that. I've always called *Lucky Feller* the Unknown Comedy Series. I'd love to see those shows again. I think they'd probably stand up and I feel David was wrong to do what he did.'

David's firm reluctance to allow a second showing of *Lucky Feller* caught LWT by surprise. In 1986, they were so confident of his consent that they even sent out schedules to advertisers which clearly listed *Lucky Feller* in their programme line-up. Crucially, however, because a period of ten years had elapsed since *Lucky Feller*'s original screening, the cast had power of veto if they so wished. David most certainly did.

'I want my career to go forwards, not backwards,' he stated. 'I'm on television a lot already and I don't want viewers to start saying, "Oh God, not him again," when they switch on. Because *Lucky Feller* was ten years old they had to ask my permission and I said "No" because I didn't want to be over-exposed.'

Frisby and LWT were not the only ones who were annoyed at David's stand. 'I could have done with the money I'd have got for repeats,' says Cheryl Hall. 'But quite apart from that, *Lucky Feller* was something I was proud of. It was disappointing that one of your fellow actors had said "No." Maybe he wasn't proud of *Lucky Feller,* but I don't think there was anything he could have been ashamed of.'

Aside from his grouse over the repeats, Frisby finds no fault with David's performance. 'He was fine in *Lucky Feller,*' he declares. 'But, in those days, when he didn't get a laugh the first time, he then used to say the line again. I used to say to him, "David, if they didn't laugh the first time round, they're not going to laugh the second time." But he was so determined to get a laugh that he'd say things twice.' The generally good working relationship Frisby had with David did not, however, expand into a major friendship. Frisby comments, 'I don't know what he's like now but then, I think, he was very much locked into his own world. I think he was deeply insecure.'

At the end of the series, Cheryl Hall presented David with a lovely charcoal drawing of Laurel and Hardy, two comedy heroes whom David much revered. She'd noticed that on display in David's kitchen were little figures of Charlie Chaplin, Buster Keaton and Laurel and Hardy.

'Much later on when I went round to visit David at his flat in Newman Street,' she says, 'I saw the drawing was just collecting dust propped up on his mantelpiece. "Get it framed!" I told David. But I wasn't a bit surprised really. His flat was a typical bachelor pad and I suppose he was hardly ever there.'

The flat was up five flights of stairs with no elevator which somewhat deterred visitors and David, in any case, was reluctant to open it up for inspection.

'The trouble is, I haven't any taste,' he once openly moaned. 'I get neurotic about it. I get jealous when I go in other people's houses. My place is purely functional. Reasonably efficient. In other words, it's clean when I get it clean.'

One visitor who met up with David just before the launch of *Lucky Feller* was initally astounded by Jason at that time. He knew he was to meet the man who for five years had attracted labels like 'the new Buster Keaton' or 'the new Norman Wisdom' or even 'the new Michael Crawford'. He wasn't prepared for what he found. He said of David, 'He still lives like a bloke who might any day be re-applying for his old job as an electrician.'

Starring in a TV series had, however, done wonders for David's confidence with the opposite sex. That summer he'd walk to the nearby pub with his dark glasses on, his shirt unbuttoned and offering the greeting 'Hello, darling' to the pretty girls he encountered on the way. Almost immediately after filming finished on *Lucky Feller*, Cheryl and David went off on tour in the stage comedy *Darling Mr London*, which opened at St Anne's-on-Sea on 6 September, four days after *Lucky Feller* had hit the screen.

As the tour progressed, *Darling Mr London* was able to cash in on the TV exposure which Cheryl and David were getting from *Lucky Feller*. With a TV star cast to lure audiences into the theatres, *Darling Mr London* played to enthusiastic houses on its rounds of Southampton, Swansea, Wimbledon, Bradford and Bournemouth.

'But after working for three months together, it was a mistake for David and me to go off touring in a play,' says Cheryl. 'It was hard work. We both needed a break – but we also both needed the money. It was an uphill struggle because it wasn't a wonderful play.'

David had, in fact, toured with *Darling Mr London* the previous year on a short spring tour which took in Billingham, Wolverhampton, Bath and Peterborough. He played the central role of a hen-pecked international telephone operator called Edward Hawkins who has sought escapism in fantasy long-distance telephone affairs with a number of foreign 'call-girls'. But when the girls arrive in England for the Miss Europhone contest, they are determined to fit a face to the voice that has been charming them so consistently and they all descend at once on his home in West Drayton.

Chaos reigns. Behind the spare room door is Monique, the Parisian *femme fatale* anxious to show Edward the thrills of a French love affair, and behind another bedroom door is Sylvana who wants to make babies with Edward's help. Waiting in the wings, equally ready to get down to their underwear, are the Scandiavian sex-pots Britt and Ingrid.

The simple and undemanding plot unfolds in the unglamorous setting of the sitting room of Edward's semi where he has to explain the sudden invasion of pulchritude to his shocked wife Rose, played by Doreen Keogh, his ferocious brother-in-law Gordon (Derek Newark), and their drunken lodger Mark (Bob Grant) who, as a curate, of course views such sexual shenanigans with disapproval. A set which included six doors and French windows gave David plenty of scope to produce a fast-moving performance as he rushed from one to the other.

'All the girls were stereotyped Europeans and they somehow found it necessary to take their clothes off so they were running around the stage in bikinis or bra and pants most of the time,' says Cheryl with some disdain. 'It was one of those typical British farces with lots of scantily-clad women.' It did the box office no harm that among the nubile beauties to be found scampering across the stage in skimpy underwear each night was a voluptuous blonde Swedish actress called Lena Skoog, whose colourful personal life offstage frequently earned her acres of column inches in the tabloids, usually accompanied by a revealing photograph. Also in the cast, as French girl Monique, was the statuesque British beauty Valerie Leon, who at that time was familiar to millions of TV viewers as the predatory female in the Hai Karate aftershave advertisements.

At 5ft 10in tall in her stockinged feet, Valerie towered over David, which added to the farce. Co-starring with David was Bob Grant, the play's co-author and himself a hugely popular television actor of the moment from the sitcom *On the Buses*. All in all, *Darling Mr London* was an attractive package for anyone who liked to see television stars in person and pretty girls wearing precious little with plenty of laughs along the way. The play in general, and David in particular, garnered rave reviews.

The 'world premiere' of *Darling Mr London*, as *The Stage* grandly announced it, was at the Billingham Forum on 7 March, 1975, and the local critic Robert Brayshay of the *Evening Dispatch* wrote in his review, 'It must be one of the funniest plays to be presented there. The star of the show is David Jason, whose natural gift for comedy gets boundless scope. He draws as much humour from physical actions as as from his lines and gives an exceptionally rewarding performance.'

Another columnist noted towards the end of the play's run, 'This amusing farce had some memorable moments, especially when David Jason was on stage – which was most of the time.'

At the Theatre Royal, Bath, *Darling Mr London* was given an equally warm welcome. The *Bristol Evening Post* critic Jeremy Brien labelled it 'one of the very best farces since the early Brian Rix offerings'. He wrote in his review that David was splendid in the central role and added, 'The evening is built around the talent of David Jason whose cueing in of the laughs, elaborate contortions, and brilliant command of the throw-away line, are at the heart of the entertainment.'

Judith Boyd of *The Bath and West Evening Chronicle* found the comedy fast and furious and said, 'Most of the energy is burnt up by David Jason as Edward and his performance never loses any of its mind-boggling vigour.'

Helen Baxter of *The Peterborough Evening Telegraph* went overboard when *Darling Mr London* moved on to The Key Theatre. She said the play was brilliant and hilarious and had 'given The Key the funniest night of its life'.

As David's fame grew so did his confidence with the opposite sex. A string of attractive young women flitted quickly in and out of the life of the rising young actor. His brother Arthur took notice when they started to arrive at his home in Brighton. Arthur said, 'Every weekend David would bring a different bird to my house. And it was never the same girl twice. My wife Joy would get totally fed up with so much crumpet coming down. She would complain, 'Oh no, David, not another bird.'

As 1976 drew to a close, David could look back on a thoroughly satisfactory year. Although *Lucky Feller* had not been a resounding hit, there were plans for another series of

Open All Hours which had been well received by critics and public alike when it had quietly opened in February on BBC 2.

While the BBC looked to build on the highly promising start of *Open All Hours*, David moved to Lew Grade's ATV at Elstree for yet another sitcom. It was called *A Sharp Intake of Breath* and it turned out to be a highly significant show in the TV career of David Jason because, surprisingly, it swept him for the first time to the top of the ratings, a position he has occupied many times since.

A Sharp Intake of Breath gave David the leading role of Peter Barnes, an ordinary man battling against the perils of officialdom in assorted shapes and sizes and trying to understand and beat 'the system'. Peter's belief in freedom of choice often involved an innocent third party getting dragged into his escapades. Regular cast members included Jacqueline Clarke as Peter's wife Sheila, and Richard Wilson – now a household name as grumpy Victor Meldrew in *One Foot in the Grave* – and Alun Armstrong in a variety of roles. David's brother Arthur was asked to appear as an engineer who called to mend a broken electric heater.

Launched on 20 February 1978, two years to the day after the start of *Open All Hours*, *A Sharp Intake of Breath* swept surprisingly to number one in the ratings in its first week and stayed there. David was understandably delighted. At last the audience figures matched the aspirations of his producers.

'I've never had so many fan letters in my life,' he beamed. 'It's almost like being a pop star. I was confident about the series but I thought it would take a little time to get it right and that audiences would take a while to catch on.'

David was quick to point out that ITV's scheduling had much to do with it. He felt the relative failure of *The Top Secret Life of Edgar Briggs* and *Lucky Feller* could partly be blamed on the inability – or more probably the stubborn unwillingness – of the ITV companies to reach agreement on a single national timeslot for the shows. Both shows undoubtedly suffered from split-networking in terms of publicity and promotion. Televison editors on all the national newspapers were reluctant to write previews or stories about the cast when many of their readers would not be able to see the programme they were writing about. The alternative was for newspapers to tailor their TV previews to suit different editions in different areas of the country, but it was far simpler for TV correspondents to write about a programme which was fully networked. They were safe in the knowledge that readers in every one of their circulation areas would be sitting down to the same programme on the same day at the same time. They could all happily write about *A Sharp Intake of Breath*.

'It certainly helped the show that everyone in Britain had the chance to see it at the same time,' said David. 'It's the first programme I've ever had fully networked and it's helped a lot. But even more than that, I think a theme of an ordinary bloke struggling against officialdom appealed right across the board. Peter Barnes, the character I play, represents the little fellow against the man in authority. Ronnie Taylor, the writer, thought of the title and we all thought it was a bit odd at first. It was based on the sound people make when they are about to be unhelpful and cause you problems. But it's a worldwide language.

'You know the sort of thing – you take your Mini to the garage to get a new headlight bulb and find the foreman sucking in his breath between pursed lips then trying to palm you off with a new gearbox and a new back axle.'

Just as it looked as though *A Sharp Intake of Breath* had finally elevated David Jason to stardom, the show was hit by tragedy when its creator and writer Ronnie Taylor died very suddenly from a mystery virus at the age of 57. David was desperately upset. Not only had Ronnie become a good friend but together they had worked hard to build up the character of Peter Barnes as the little man always falling foul of bureaucracy. It had been a fruitful and harmonious partnership.

'For a comic actor to find a writer with whom he can work as well as Ronnie and I worked together was most unusual,' said David paying tribute. 'To find someone that compatible was very, very rare. We had six new ideas mapped out for the new series and Ronnie had written three when he got the virus.'

It seemed that the death of Ronnie Taylor was to be the end of the success story for *A Sharp Intake of Breath*, but David and producer-director Stuart Allen were determined to save the show.

Allen had moved over to ATV from LWT. There he had enjoyed notable success with sitcoms like *On the Buses* and *Mind Your Language*, a hilariously politically incorrect show set in a London school for foreign students, which were pulling in huge ratings. Now he had to rescue *A Sharp Intake of Breath*.

'When Ronnie died, the scripts weren't completed,' Allen recalls. 'I had to cobble together the three which Ronnie had left and I did quite a good job on them. But we obviously needed to find another writer to continue.'

By good fortune, David happened to meet comedy writer Vince Powell on an episode of the TV charades show *Give Us A Clue*. 'I suddenly realised we had the same sense of humour,' said David, 'and I persuaded him to have a go at writing *A Sharp Intake of Breath*.' Powell was indeed a logical choice.

'Ronnie Taylor had been Powell's mentor,' says Allen. 'While at the BBC and at Granada, Ronnie had encouraged Powell and Powell thought a great deal of him. There was a lot of Ronnie Taylor in his early work because he admired him so much. So he was the ideal person to step in and write *A Sharp Intake of Breath*.'

A further three series were made, including one episode where David appeared with an eye-patch because of a bad attack of conjunctivitis. Throughout, David won Allen's admiration for his comedic flair.

'I always thought David Jason was immensely clever and immensely funny,' he says. 'He was such a worker, so keen on all the detail. Everything that I admired about an artist and a performer David had, and more talent and drive than anyone I've met before or since.

'He was dedicated to his work and immensely creative with his comedy. So much so that he would get a laugh where I never would have believed there was a laugh to be had. He was superb. All he needed from me was to present him. But, unfortunately, in the end it all went wrong ...'

Allen was accustomed to success but even he was especially elated that *A Sharp Intake of Breath* had turned out so well. So the way it ended so abruptly came as a nasty surprise.

'I thought we'd done an awfully good job,' says Allen. 'I thought the shows were good and ATV wanted us to do another series. So an offer was made to David through his agent and the agent came back saying "David Jason wants a younger and hungrier director."

'That wasn't very nice', commented Allen. 'We'd never had any cross words and this was a great shock to me personally because I thought we had always got on so well together and I'd admired him so immensely because of his talent. And if you're a TV director, the way to get on is to work with wonderful talent.

'I thought I'd done so well for him. I mean, he used to come to my house at Gerard's Cross in Buckinghamshire with his lovely Welsh girlfriend Myfanwy Talog, with whom he seemed to have a very stable relationship and I thought he was just a great guy. So I was shocked and very disappointed by what had happened.

'The end came because Vince Powell was asked to write another series and then I rang him up and said, "Vince, they don't want me." Vince said, "That's ridiculous! You gave me the work and if they don't have you, then I shan't write it." So that was the end of that.'

Giving his view as to what David may have taken exception to, Allen comments 'Perhaps it was because he was jealous of my success or because he hadn't got as much then as he felt he should have had, because at that time, of course, he was only just beginning to take off. Perhaps he felt I was too admiring of him ... I don't know. What I do know is that I lost David Jason and my career waned and his went up and up.

'After that, he was out of work for a while until he fell on his feet again at the BBC – but at half the salary, of course, that he would have been getting with ATV in *A Sharp Intake of Breath*.'

An actor friend of David's recalls the incident. 'There was nothing personal about it. But then there never is with David. He just thought Stuart was coasting it, which I suppose he was in a way. Who wants to push yourself to the limit all the time? Well, David Jason for one. But Stuart just believed in doing a good job and still having a life outside. The show was up there at the top of the ratings, for goodness sake. What was the point of giving yourself ulcers? I believe David wanted someone who would be as obsessed as him. I wonder if he ever found anyone.'

When Ronnie Barker moved across from ITV to the BBC and *Hark at Barker* turned into *His Lordship Entertains*, Ronnie was keen for old Dithers to make the move as well. The aged gardener was always popular and David's ability to age up effectively led to him also taking up the role of Blanco Webb in Barker's wonderful prison comedy series *Porridge*.

Written by Dick Clement and Ian le Frenais, *Porridge* featured Barker as Norman Stanley Fletcher serving a five-year sentence in Slade prison for robbery. David played Blanco as a white-haired, doddery, short-sighted inmate for whom Fletcher always had a soft spot.

David starred in three memorable episodes *No Peace for the Wicked* and *Happy Release* in 1975, and *Pardon Me* in 1977. In *No Peace for the Wicked*, Fletch's attempts to find some some peace and quiet on a Saturday afternoon are scuppered by constant interruptions from prison officers and cons, including a visit from Blanco proudly wheeling in a wooden mule it has taken him 15 years to make. Finally, the chaplain enters and an exasperated Fletch throws him over the balcony so he can obtain solitary confinement.

Happy Release featured Fletch and Blanco in the prison infirmary together with a nasty piece of work called Norris who is in prison for just a few days. Norris cons Blanco out of all his worldly possessions – his wireless, his silver snuff box and a musical box – by cheating at Nine Card Brag. But Fletcher, using all his native cunning, hatches a plan to have Blanco retrieve all his valuables by giving his cellmate Godber a fake map of buried treasure – a hoard of £8,000 interred in Leeds. Knowing full well that Norris will obtain the map in exchange for Blanco's goods, Fletch has the added satisfaction of Norris being incarcerated for digging up the pitch at Leeds United.

In the brilliantly conceived episode *Pardon Me*, David left Slade Prison in comic style. Blanco had been inside for 17 years for the murder of his wife, a crime he had always sworn he did not commit. He felt so angry about his unjust incarceration that, when offered parole, he refused on the grounds that it amounted to an admission of guilt.

But after Fletch had successfully raised a petition for Blanco to be pardoned, Blanco was finally absolved of the blame for his wife's death and was granted the pardon and his freedom. He had protested all along that the killer was his wife's lover. During Blanco's final farewell to Fletch, the two men shook hands and Fletch urged Blanco to get even with the killer. 'Oh, he died long ago,' said Blanco. 'I know. It were me that did it!'

Playing Blanco as a man twice his real age, David was almost unrecognisable with wisps of grey hair, spectacles and a doddery gait. Producer Sydney Lotterby recalls, 'It was quite remarkable how David could add on the years so convincingly. It was often a problem because when you had a very old character in a large role you didn't always want a very old actor. David was simply so talented and so dedicated. Everyone knew then that he was something special.

'Ronnie Barker was always known as "The Guv'nor" because of his towering comedy talent. He really rated David's abilities highly so when we were looking around for a hapless nephew for the shop in Roy Clarke's *Open All Hours* we naturally did not have to look very far. David was a delight. He always used to call me "Award-winning Sydney Lotterby ..." until he started winning his own.

'We filmed *Open All Hours* up in Doncaster where a hairdressing salon called Helen's Beautique became Arkwright's corner shop. David was always known as "Little Feed" because he used to grumble jokingly that he was only there to set up the laughs for Ronnie.

'But Granville became very popular in his own right thanks to Roy Clarke's marvellous writing and David's performances. My favourite memory is the night we had Granville recreating the famous *Singing in the Rain* number. David was so keen to get it right he must have spent hours getting it just so while providing a free cabaret for the good folk of Doncaster.'

Ronnie Barker thoroughly enjoyed the recordings as well. 'David Jason, Lynda Baron and I had great times on that series. We would be in Doncaster for three weeks doing the filmed sequences for two episodes each week. So work went on until midnight sometimes, with shouting, the noise of equipment and arc lights glaring. But nobody objected, though one chap did ask how long this would be going on for as he had to get up early for work!

'The BBC generally found an empty house for sale and that would have the canteen on the ground floor, David and myself sharing one bedroom as a dressing room and Lynda using the other. We'd put up posters and silly knick-knacks making it homelier, even though it was just for those three weeks.

'Our trio's rapport showed in the spirit of *Open All Hours*. We were three mates. On location you all get together at the end of the day, have dinner, crack a bottle or two, relax and laugh. David Jason became a good friend. What a funny man. He and I have always had such rapport, ever since we first met at LWT in a half-hour comedy called *The Odd-Job Man*.

'What a wonderful sense of timing he has, with that marvellous rubber face. What a reliable and professional man to work with. I was so thrilled when he won the British Academy Award for Best Actor.'

For David Jason, Ronnie Barker was simply someone extra special. When Barker retired at the very height of his fame and popularity, David was one of the inner circle who knew all about the dramatic decision well in advance. David said, 'I first met Ronnie Barker when he asked me if I would be in *The Odd-Job Man*. It was a very funny story about a very ordinary man who lived in a council flat and loved his wife. He was the most perfect husband. In fact, he was so perfect he drove her crazy.

'His wife raved at him that she was going to leave him because he never forgot her birthday or had affairs. The guy is so depressed that he decides to top himself and the funniest part is the actual odd-job man of the title who is a really weird character called Clive who gets involved in this strange marriage.

'Ronnie Barker sent me the script and then phoned me up

and said, "Will you do it?" I thought, "Working with Ronnie Barker? Yeah! Sure I will." But I naturally thought he would want to play Clive, clearly the funniest part. But that was what he wanted me to play. I thought it was incredible. We both knew Clive was the funniest part. But he was so generous and that was the start of a long and happy association.

'Later, I was in the film version playing the same part but by then it had been rewritten and changed so much it was ruined. Graham Chapman and Diana Quick played the couple.'

One reviewer helpfully observed, 'This plodding farce hammers yet another nail into the coffin of the ailing British film industry.'

David said, 'Humphrey Barclay gave me a few small parts after that in his various series. Ronnie was always keen to work with people who could do the job very well. Ronnie was always the same, more interested in getting the job right than in being the centre of attention.

'He is basically an actor and the best comedy actor I have ever worked with. He was my hero – helpful, considerate, a wonderful teacher. I loved his generosity but I was more affected by his ability. So much so that I always used to call him "The Guv'nor" behind his back.

'That was the word I used because there was no one better at his craft in the country. This was before *The Two Ronnies* and everything he did from then on reinforced my feelings. If Ronnie suffers from anything, it's comic diarrhoea. He can't help being funny. Once, we had just finished recording an episode of one show and the audience couldn't be released until the videotape had been checked through for faults. The floor manager called out to the crowd, "We're just waiting for a clear." Ronnie cracked out, "Clear? Isn't that a Chinese homosexual?"Through the years, I have seen more of Ronnie Barker than most people and I know he was a very great comedy actor, the best.

'I enjoyed working with him so much because it is always a pleasure to work at the top level. And he was always so quick. The night we went out to celebrate his OBE, the restaurant was all decked out in decorations for Christmas. Ronnie took me up to the bar to buy me a drink and noticed a cluster of three balloons. One had gone down. "Ah," he said, "A pawnbrokers, and one of the partners has just died." He always made me laugh and he was great to work with. He brought my game up. It's like if you are playing tennis. If you have two good guys, their games will both improve.

'He told me some time before he retired that he was going to pull out of showbusiness. The BBC wanted to do more *Open All Hours* and more *Two Ronnies*, but he was finding it extremely difficult to maintain his high standards. We had lost a few comedy men like Eric Morecambe and Tommy Cooper around then and I think he was a little sensitive to that, too. When he went, he gave me something that I will always treasure. It is a poem, one of Ronnie's witty odes, and at the end of it he says, "I now relinquish the honoured title of "The Guv'nor" to my apprentice, the boy Granville, who is entitled herewith to call himself "The Guv'nor". Although the nickname started as a joke, it was always a secret mark of respect from me to Ronnie and to have him return it was just amazing. I have that poem framed in my house now and it will always be one of my most prized possessions.'

In his early days as an actor, David had moved out of the family home and into a tiny rented one-bedroom flat in Newman Street, just off Oxford Street.

'The rent was £17 a week which terrified me at the time,' he said. When his television wages started to come in, he felt it was time to invest in property and bought a cottage in Sussex with a view, as they say, to renovation.

David was a practical chap and planned to save money and occupy his free time by doing much of the work himself. But the result was a good deal more amusing to the neighbours than many of his on-screen escapades to date.

David had often visited friends who lived near East Grinstead and he had spent many a pleasant weekend helping in their garden and living the country life. He became very taken with the East Sussex area and weekends soon turned from lazy days into earnest searches for a little cottage he could call his own. He looked at literally dozens after setting himself a price limit of £15,000, which would allow an extra £5,000 for renovation.

'That was my first big mistake,' he said. 'Not wanting to get saddled with too big a mortgage, I eliminated the better possibilities. I hadn't the brains to realise that by spending a little more, I would have had a better investment.'

After much deliberation, David finally picked on a 19th century, end-of-terrace workman's cottage in Crowborough.

'It was a charming, tiny cottage and my intention was to do it up in my spare time, pottering about as a way of relaxing between work,' he said. 'Instead, it became a monster that took over my life – a major reconstruction job.

'I have never been so miserable in my life with the strain of driving to and from the property day after day in all weathers. I was very happy with my little flat but when my career started to pick up, I thought it seemed a good idea to own a place of my own. Being single and already having a London base, I didn't really want a house but I could see the sense in buying a small country cottage so that's what I set out to do. I had never owned any property before and friends told me that it was the best investment, the greatest security against inflation and all that.'

As soon as he spotted the little historic home in Crowborough, he knew his search was over. It was at the end of the row of three, the garden was neat and tidy and the price was right. It needed restoration work but David knew that doing it would give him enormous satisfaction.

Sadly, the story did not have a happy ending. When David brought in his cousin, a builder, for some expert advice he found that the cottage needed some very expensive renovation work, and quickly.

'The closer we inspected the place the worse it became,' David remembers. 'Woodworm, wet rot, dry rot. We had it all. Because I wanted to build on to an existing extension, I applied to the council for permission and had a visit from the planning officer. He told me that the original extension was illegal because it was built over a manhole. The whole lot would have to come down.'

David decided that while rebuilding the extension, he might as well build another storey on top. Then an inspection of the floorboards showed serious damp and the cottage needed new flooring throughout. In addition to that cheery news, the main beam supporting the whole of the first floor had been almost cut through to take a pipe and there was about three-quarters of an inch of wood taking a colossal strain. Then the roof needed retiling. A relaxing way to spend his weekends had swiftly turned into a nightmare for David. Each time he visited the cottage he was greeted with mounting debris and piles of bills for the work.

'They were all big ones of £300 or £400, never small ones,' he groaned. He began to dread making the two-hour drive down to Crowborough not knowing what new disaster awaited him. Frequently, he was filled with gloom when he set off on the journey back at the end of the day.

The new extension, built to replace the old one that had been taken down, posed new problems. Because it was now two storeys high, the original roof had to be extended to match. And as if he didn't have enough to worry about, David fell off the roof one day. Unable to afford scaffolding right the way round the cottage, there was nothing to break his fall, but, fortunately, his gymnastic ability helped him to land without injury. He was less fortunate a few weeks later when he slipped while mowing the lawn with a rotary mower.

The injury sounded comical when he posed for photographers in hospital but, in fact, David almost severed the toes on one foot. He was fortunate to be saved from more serious injury by virtue of the fact he was wearing thick-soled shoes when his foot slipped under the blades. He spent a complete summer in bed with his foot suspended above him. A deep cut in David's big toe caused most concern for the doctors. David was fully aware that if he lost his big toe, it would affect his balance and he would have to learn to walk all over again. Meanwhile, bills for building materials continued to pile up in the rubble that was the inside of the house.

'There was a time when I hated the place,' he said. 'It was sapping my energy and my money and I couldn't see a way out. I remembered reading that somebody had once said that you can only build a house with love, and I couldn't find anything approaching love in the way I felt about the cottage.

'But I got over that phase. A friend came to see the cottage and, standing in the middle of the rubble, looked round and said, 'Oh, this has a very good feeling about it ... a warm, happy feeling.' Seeing the cottage through somebody else's eyes, I stopped to think. And I decided perhaps it wasn't such a bad place after all.' And he simply refused to be beaten by the project.

A girlfriend, who asked not to be identified by name, said, 'I can remember him actually crying with anger that it seemed to be taking so long. He was so angry the house became a bit of an obsession. We had quite a few rows about it because it seemed to take up all his time and money and energy. In the worst row, I accused him of using the house as an excuse for not seeing me and he just looked at me stunned and said very coldly, "I don't need excuses to do anything. I'm not married and I'm never likely to be, so I do what I want when I want.

It's my life and my cottage." It was creepy really, like being slapped across the face. He just changed. Somehow in trying to organise his time, I had crossed the barrier and got too close. I thought I knew David really well until then. He was always kind and considerate and our lovelife was great. But you could go so far to get close to him and then the shutters came down.

'He was funny about that and about his family. His relationship with his brother Arthur was a bit strange. Arthur had started in the business before David and was quite successful, but even then you could see David was going places. I think Arthur was a bit jealous and sometimes would put David down in conversation a bit unnecessarily. Once, David was talking about Shakespeare and he pronounced a character's name wrong and Arthur leapt on the mistake. Things like that. David would fume but he never said anything about it, even to me.

'His old mother used to drive them both to distraction. She was very fiery and because she was a bit deaf she used to really shout quite loud. She didn't always look after herself very well and she lived in a damp, old council flat that they wanted her to move out of. But nothing they said to her had the slightest effect.

'David was a great guy to be with. No one else has ever made me laugh so much. Both in bed and out. He's not like Del-Boy at all really, but he can put on all that flashy front if he wants to. Underneath, he's sensitive and thoughtful.

'He used to go on and on about bits of business in shows. He was always working on a part, even when everyone was telling him it was perfect.

'He was very impressed by Ronnie Barker. When he was invited to Ronnie's big house in the Cotswolds he came back absolutely drooling. Ronnie had the fame and still had a happy, settled home life. I think David saw that and it was what he wanted. But Ronnie could switch off from work and talk about sport or politics. David never found it easy to switch off and, of course, he never had the happy marriage. We were great together and for a time I really loved him, but I never felt David really loved me or even really trusted me. He would never really let himself go. If he did get upset it was always because he was frustrated with something to do with work. He didn't just want to do well, he simply *had* to succeed.

'He was obsessed with the ratings and the reviews and who was getting which part and why. I've been out with a few actors and they were all on the insecure side. But David took paranoia to new lengths for me. Everything was so important to him, from the position of his name on the cast list in *Radio Times* to what fans said to him in the street. If somebody said something to him about a particular scene from *Open All Hours*, he would come back home and want to talk about whether he had really got every drop of humour out of it, even if he'd recorded it years before.

'Once, a director had talked over the top of him when he was discussing something with Ronnie Barker. He was absolutely incensed. When David talked, he thought everyone else should be quiet and listen. I never minded listening to him which was probably why we got on so well. In the end, we didn't fall out, we just sort of drifted apart. Then, one day, he asked me very formally if he could have back the key to his flat he had given me. I thought we were still going out but when he said that I realised it was over. A few years later, I saw him at the BBC. We went up in a crowded lift to the sixth floor at Television Centre together. He was talking to someone else but he saw me and his eyes flickered. I stood waiting to be introduced. He carried on his conversation and when we all got out he and this chap walked away and I was left just standing there. It was as if I did not exist. To David, I'd simply become a non-person. It took me a while to get over that.'

David declines to discuss his personal relationships. He still looks back on the difficult Do-It-Yourself enterprise somewhat ruefully, even long after he had exchanged the cottage for an expansive detached home in Wendover, near Aylesbury, Buckinghamshire, and then moved to his present home next to the Prime Minister's estate at Chequers.

These days, he is still as eager to fill his idle moments with something interesting to do but largely restricts himself to pottering about in his garden or working on his beloved motorbikes. He is still quite able to make a comedy out of an odd job however.

'Usually, I spend my spare time either digging in the garden,' he said, 'or decorating the shed or knocking a wall down, or tinkering with my bike. Some people are totally uninterested in anything practical. Their lives are more fulfilled by sitting down a lot and reading the papers or getting in the car and going somewhere interesting.

'I prefer to be doing something all the time. Whether it's painting a wall or putting some lights up, I get a lot of satisfaction out of getting a job done, then standing back and thinking, "Ah! That looks better." You should have seen me not too long ago, when I was putting up a trellis on the back wall of my house. Like a comedy it was. I was on my own and I had to work out how to get this great big heavy trellis up against the wall while actually drilling and fixing it into place.'

David's answer to the conundrum had the stamp of amazing invention. He tied one end of a rope to the trellis, then weighted another end with a brick and threw it over the wall. All he had to do then, he reasoned, was to go round to the other side of the wall, haul the trellis up into place and tie the rope to a handy tree.

'See, not only talent but also brains,' said David. 'Oh yes, very clever. And very expensive. The brick landed on the roof of my car! Undeterred by this minor set-back, I managed to pull the offending trellis skywards, and in the process dislodged two dozen ridge tiles of recently installed guttering!'

You feel that of all people, Derek Trotter, David's most brilliant comic creation, would have especially appreciated that stunt, almost as much as David appreciates Del-Boy.

By 1985, *Only Fools and Horses* and *Open All Hours* had turned David Jason into hot property and his huge TV popularity was enough to earn him the starring role in a new West End stage comedy *Look No Hans!* at the Strand Theatre where he had performed such acrobatics 15 years earlier in *No Sex Please – We're British*.

Look No Hans! by John Chapman and Michael Pertwee was a farce set in West Berlin with David cast as a British car firm sales representative called Fisher who finds himself recruited by an industrial MI5. Lynda Bellingham played his wife, whose arrival in Germany sets the cat among the dolly-birds with whom Fisher has become acquainted. They included a striking blonde Anita Graham as a put-upon stripper Mitzi, and Heather Alexander, an equally striking blonde beauty, as Heidi, who spends much of the play in black boots and a backless maid's outfit. Much play was made of the fact that both these two beautiful, very tall girls towered over David.

David made the very most of every comic opportunity as filing cabinets banged him on the head or kicked him in the shins, safe doors threw him up in the air, and every ring of the doorbell or telephone sent him into frenzied scuttling around the stage.

Somewhat predictably, the critics did not much care for *Look No Hans!* when it opened on 4 September 1985. But almost to a man they were fulsome in their praise for David who gave his usual whole-hearted, energetic performance.

In his review for *The Daily Telegraph*, John Barber labelled David 'an athletic rubber-faced comic resembling a pug dog doing a fandango.' He added, 'There is not much to it beyond a comedian in a perpetual dither and a room full of doors and a half-undressed girl behind each.'

Irving Wardle in *The Times* praised David's 'marvellous unbroken chain of manic acrobatics'. Milton Shulman in the London *Evening Standard* said, 'David Jason, who looks like a flyweight boxer but has the agility of an acrobatic dancer, is a natural comic. Without him, I shudder to think what a quick oblivion would have awaited this rather tired farce.'

David's most glowing review came from Michael Coveney writing in the *Financial Times*. He said, 'David Jason played the compulsive joker rather like Dudley Moore on speed, and with technique. Jason's television popularity is no flash in the pan. He's a genuinely funny actor, very fast and, like Groucho Marx, close to the nerve. Athletic, too. I wish him luck when he finds a vehicle worthy of his talent.'

Only Michael Billington in *The Guardian* was less than enthusiastic about David but blamed the play itself rather than its star. 'Women,' he wrote, 'are presented until the last five minutes as entirely bird-brained and female breasts and bottoms are regarded with a leering schoolboyish curiosity.

'It is impossible to credit that a dunderheaded buffoon (the energetic David Jason) would either be employed as a car firm salesman in West Berlin or that he would have been recruited by an industrial MI5. As a result, the lunatic contortions he undergoes to pass off a couple of pouting dollies as a maid and a cook when his flat is appropriated by British security are like a whirlwind in a wind.' The critic concluded, 'Mr Jason is like a man cycling uphill into the wind.'

ONLY FOOLS

In Studio 5 at the BBC's London Television Centre, they knew it was an extra special moment. Fans of the nation's favourite comedy show were assembled to watch an historic recording. David Jason had been enchanting enormous armchair audiences for 16 years with Del Trotter's ever optimistic promise to his endlessly struggling family that, 'This time next year, we'll be millionaires.' As they watched, the gales of laughter were interspersed with gasps of surprise. No one ever dreamed it would come true – but now it had.

To the fortunate few who were present, this was the ultimate *Only Fools and Horses* occasion. Laughter had threatened to overload the sound systems during the recording, but when the last episode of Christmas 1996's hilarious three-part revival was completed, and Peckham's popular but impoverished dodgy dealers had just won their lottery jackpot and walked off into the sunset, rich beyond even Del's dreams, the emotion got to everyone. Paul Barber who played Denzil who was not in the final episode rushed out of the audience to join them and so did Patrick Murray who plays Mickey Pearce and, with the rest of the cast, they were all shaking hands and congratulating each other, amazed by the standing ovation they received from the delighted studio audience. But they were also aware that this just might be the last time they got together. The crying began when the bottom lip of Ken MacDonald, better known as cheery landlord Mike, began to quiver and it spread like gossip round the Nag's Head. Almost as soon as they heard the word 'cut', just about everyone in the room was in tears.

Tears cascaded down the famous face of David Jason as he clutched co-star Nicholas Lyndhurst in an emotional embrace that was quickly joined by the rest of the clearly overwhelmed cast. And they ran down the faces of the studio audience as they stood and cheered at the privilege of being present when Jason, far and away Britain's best-loved actor, produced a fabulous and possibly final performance as Del, far and away Britain's best-loved comedy character. The eternal loser became a winner at last.

The applause and the emotion wasn't just for that evening, it was for 16 years of scintillating success and it was shared between stars who felt that this was possibly the last time the happy team would be gathered together. The audience felt that, too.

It was a bit of a risk trying to top their tremendous record with a final three-parter. But the stars seemed relaxed and assured when they got back together again. David Jason set the mood as he looked determined to enjoy every minute. An audience tends to bring out the clown in him and in between takes of his bed scene with Tessa Peake-Jones as Raquel, he was cheekily mouthing to the audience, 'She's got nothing on.'

Before recording began, David told the assembled *Only Fools* enthusiasts, 'It's great to be back on familiar ground.

There have been lots of great moments in 16 years and tonight, I promise you, will be no exception. We are all very emotional at the moment and if you could just bear with us we would all be very much obliged, and I'm sure you're in for a treat.'

David was very nervous about how the reunion would go down but he need not have worried. More than 20 million people voted with their remote controls to make the three-parter the runaway winner of the Christmas ratings battle, and almost as soon as it was in the can, the pressure began for yet more adventures of Del, Rodney and Uncle Albert to hit the screen.

'Never say never,' said a delighted David Jason with a huge beam on his face when later considering the future for Del. 'You never know ... we might be forced to bring the bugger back.'

Even with another series of his very different hit, the detective series *A Touch of Frost*, turning into 1997's top drama on ITV, his affection for the antics of Del Trotter and the sublime scripts of John Sullivan remains extra special and undimmed.

Although our favourite actor has demonstrated the breadth and versatility of his talent many times with his wide variety of roles, his special relationship with Del and the great British public is one that nobody really wants to end, because, although David Jason plays many parts to perfection, he really *is* Del Trotter.

They have an awful lot in common. They are both fast-talking, working-class lads from London whose success in life is down to their extraordinary ability to communicate with people. They are both attractive to women but wary of commitment. And they are both unbelievably popular. And after the Christmas cracker they are even financially similar now that Del has caught up in the cash stakes with David. They are both millionaires several times over. The story of *Only*

Fools and Horses is the story of the transformation of a brilliant actor into a star, a comedy craftsman into a national institution. But it could all have been so very different.

Back in the late 1970s when *Only Fools and Horses* was just an idea in writer John Sullivan's fertile mind, David was a highly-regarded comedy actor, best known for his superb slapstick abilities in ITV shows like *A Sharp Intake of Breath* and as perky shopworker Granville, the comic feed to Ronnie Barker in the BBC's *Open All Hours*.

At the time, writer Sullivan was the man with his finger firmly on the pulse of verbal London. His sensational skill as a wordsmith has always provided the essential strength of the series. Brought up in Balham, Sullivan credits his inspirational English teacher Jim Trowers as the man who opened his eyes to books and first sparked his love of writing.

'We had two books at home,' said John Sullivan. 'The Bible and a pools guide. Most blokes have to hide porno mags under their jackets, but after Mr Trowers got me interested in reading, I hid Charles Dickens novels under mine, so my dad wouldn't laugh at me.'

And Mr Trowers' council flat in Farnham, with its wildly clashing walls and carpets, certainly provided John Sullivan with food for thought when he was first describing Del's colourful home in Nelson Mandela House. Sullivan openly admits that he sat down to write *Only Fools and Horses* for one reason. Quite simply, it was out of desperation. 'I wrote the pilot out of a desperate need to get some money,' he declared.

Sullivan got the idea of writing for a living back in 1966 when he was working in a brewery in Balham where he was born. 'A friend I knew from school also worked there,' recalls Sullivan. 'It was a very boring job. It was almost like being one of those white mice waiting for a bell to ring. When it rang, these crates would come and we had to stack them. My friend Paul Saunders and I used to laugh at the same sort of things, and one day he read about the kind of money Johnny Speight was making and he suggested we had a go at writing a script.'

The two friends came up with a sitcom set in a public toilet called *Gentlemen*, but that was swiftly flushed away. 'It was a bad idea,' admits Sullivan now. But over the next 10 years, he refined his talent and eventually took a job as a scene shifter at the BBC, in a bid to get nearer the action. It worked. Sullivan said, 'I met the legendary producer Dennis Main Wilson at the BBC. I had this one thing called *Citizen Smith* which was my ace card. I always thought if this was rejected, I'd give it up. Dennis was the most perfect person to go to because he would give you a chance. He said to me, "I don't need you telling me about it, just go and do it." I took two weeks off to write it and he got it on the screen within eight weeks in a *Comedy Playhouse*.' A new writer had arrived.

Daring for its day – 1977 – *Citizen Smith* was a comedy about a six-man political movement, the Tooting Popular Front, with Robert Lindsay starring as Wolfie Smith, South London's black-bereted answer to Che Guevara.

The series ran for four years and Sullivan had high hopes of following up with another sitcom he had written for the BBC called *Over the Moon* about a failed football manager.

He had produced a very funny script and a pilot was duly made with Brian Wilde of *Last of the Summer Wine* fame starring as a somewhat sad soccer figure who had taken over a middle-ranking Third Division club and, within two seasons, had managed to take them right out of the Football League.

The comedy centred around the appointment of a new Chairman, played by George Baker, who realised his manager was an incompetent idiot but discovered on looking at his contract that he was not in a position to be able to fire him.

Sullivan was hopeful for the show's chances but the

BBC comedy bosses relegated it to the cutting room floor. They decided to kill it after Sullivan had already written three episodes.

Sullivan was sick as a parrot about the decision. Suddenly, he did not even have a ball to play with. *Citizen Smith* had finished and now *Over The Moon* had been eclipsed before it had even been given a chance to shine.

It was then that Sullivan turned to *Only Fools and Horses*. He had originally broached the idea verbally with his BBC bosses but had received only a lukewarm response. Sullivan had envisaged *Readies*, as he initially called the series, as being set in a modern, multiracial London which could be a bit violent and where the language was certainly colourful. In retrospect, he feels it was the lively language of the streets which initially frightened off his BBC superiors. 'The attitude was "We're not keen on this," he recalls. 'But with *Citizen Smith* finished and my new show killed, I had nothing. I didn't know what to do.'

Sullivan had one ace left to play. At that time, the BBC's policy was to enter into an eight-part contract with its writers in which a seven-part series was commissioned plus a pilot for something new.

'I had a contract with the Beeb to write a pilot show and so away I went,' he says. 'I thought, to hell with what they think of it. I don't really care. I've got to write something to earn some money anyway. So I wrote *Only Fools and Horses* out of a desperate need to get some money. It was the only other idea in my head.

'I suppose, maybe, they were over a bit of a barrel because of this contract. But they saw it and they must have seen something in it because they didn't even pilot it. They said they would go with it as a series. So then I had to go away and do another six episodes and that kind of solved the bank manager's problem!'

Only Fools and Horses had been born from a conversation Sullivan had one night with TV producer Ray Butt in the BBC club. The two men had worked together on *Citizen Smith* and now they were relaxing over a drink and talking about their origins and their childhoods. Butt's parents, it transpired, had a stall on Roman Road market and Butt had himself worked on street markets as a kid. Sullivan had also worked in the market when he was at school. Several of the people in his street were market folk, too, he remembered.

'We started talking about the various characters,' Sullivan remembers, 'and we both finally agreed that the most interesting people were the fly-pitchers with their suitcases and total disregard for licences. They would turn up sometimes for an hour, sometimes for ten minutes, and then they would be away on their toes. They were always funny characters, always selling absolute rubbish like mock perfume.'

Just talking about the fly-pitchers set Sullivan's fertile mind wondering. Where did they come from? What was their background? And what were their names? Invariably, they were somewhat secretive and they did not allow anyone to get to know them well.

Over the next few weeks, Sullivan and Butt would meet up at Butt's local, The Three Kings on the corner of London's North End Road and Talgarth Road, and sit talking, until gradually Sullivan began forming the idea of a family with two brothers separated by a large age gap. Sullivan had a sister 15 years older than himself and Colin, the Best Man at his wedding, also had a brother who was much older. So Sullivan envisaged a fraternal relationship where one brother was a man and the other was a little kid so that the relationship was one that was protective. The idea of an arms-round-the-shoulder fraternal love fascinated Sullivan.

From there, Sullivan began weaving in various characteristics. Crucially, he decided that Rodney, the younger brother, should be earnest and artistic and would not enjoy the life that elder brother Del lived. And yet he simply had to be tolerant of brother Del's ways. He had no choice in the matter because that was where the money was coming from.

Sullivan recalls, 'There was a guy I knew called Chicky Stocker and I used him for an awful lot of Del. He's dead now, poor chap, but he was very much the template for Del. I was using real people and real situations from my own life. And to represent the older generation, there would be this wonderful grandad, grumpy but lovable.' Finally Sullivan sent Butt a script.

'It was marvellous,' Butt remembers. 'Simple as that.'

Bursting with enthusiasm, Butt took the script to revered BBC comedy boss John Howard Davies, the man behind comedy classics like *The Good Life* and *Fawlty Towers*. This time, to Butt's joy, the response was more than encouraging. There would be no pilot, but there would be a series.

Sullivan believes that this change of heart from the BBC hierarchy had much to do with ITV's success with *Minder* starring George Cole as a London wide-boy with Dennis Waterman as his boneheaded bodyguard. *Minder* had shown that the new multiracial London with shots of breakers yards and railway arches in areas like Fulham and Camden could work on screen. But it was also because Howard Davies knew an exceptional script when he saw one.

Butt and Sullivan were elated but casting proved to be a problem. Nicholas Lyndhurst was the first to be signed up to play Rodney. He had enjoyed great success as teenager Adam going through growing pains in another BBC sitcom *Butterflies*, and both John Howard Davies and Butt agreed he was an excellent choice.

Next to be cast was Lennard Pearce as Grandad. Butt got on the phone to a woman agent he knew and said he was looking for an old man in the *Steptoe* mould. He considered

Wilfrid Brambell, who played old Albert Steptoe, who was still around and popular at that time, but Butt decided not to use him because of his strong *Steptoe* identification. The agent said she could not help but passed him on to another agent which resulted in Lennard Pearce duly being auditioned.

Sullivan, who has generally had a big say in the casting of his shows – he cast Paul Nicholas in *Just Good Friends*, Robert Lindsay in *Citizen Smith*, and Ralph Bates in *Dear John* – knew Lennard Pearce was perfect for Grandad the minute he opened his mouth. 'It was that lovely voice of his,' says Sullivan 'It was a deep, croaky voice – a great voice. As soon as Lennard went, I said, "That's him!"'

The biggest problem now remained. Who could they get to play the key role of Derek Trotter? Butt and Sullivan racked their brains, but no obvious names presented themselves.

After much deliberation, their first choice for the role of Del-Boy was Enn Reitel, who with his long face bore more than a passing resemblance to Nicholas Lyndhurst. They could certainly have passed as brothers.

An accomplished actor, Reitel concedes he would loved to have played Del-Boy. 'I was doing a series for Yorkshire TV at the time and I simply wasn't available,' he explains. 'Sure, it was disappointing, particularly when you consider what *Only Fools and Horses* has grown into. But you can't live your life with hindsight. It might have run for only one series, then bombed.'

Had he taken the role, Reitel's face might now be as famous as David Jason's. But on that score he has absolutely no regrets. 'I prefer the anonymity,' he says firmly. Since then, Reitel has starred in his own ITV series, the highly forgettable *Mog*, and has provided the voices for a whole range of *Spitting Image* characters from Lester Piggott to Dustin Hoffman.

With Reitel out of the reckoning, the then little-known Jim Broadbent was the next actor to be offered the part of Del-

Boy. But Broadbent had just opened in a play at Hampstead and it was transferring to the West End. A fine, conscientious actor, Broadbent felt he would be unable to give all his energy to the play if he was doing a TV series as well. Ray Butt could only admire him for his honesty and later used him in another role in *Only Fools and Horses* as the loathsome policeman Roy Slater, Del's former schoolmate and Raquel's ex-husband.

Continuing his search, Butt went to look at an actor appearing in a play called *Moving* with Penelope Keith. He didn't find his Del but he did find another important member of the *Only Fools and Horses* cast – Roger Lloyd-Pack who plays Trigger.

The moment Lloyd-Pack walked on stage, Butt was immediately struck by his likeness to Sullivan's description of Trigger. In the very first episode, the explanation is given for Trigger's name. Is it because he packs a gun? No, it's because he looks like a horse.

At that time, Lloyd-Pack had a strange, almost Mohican haircut and it looked to Butt like a horse's mane. The moment Butt first saw him he said to himself, 'That's the man for Trigger.'

Roger Lloyd-Pack is delighted by the role. He says, 'Trigger is great fun to do. It sort of developed as it went along. We do enjoy it and always have a lot of fun rehearsing. The characters John Sullivan writes are real characters. They are people he knows. They're not prototype sitcom characters written to a format like so many are on television. They all have a kind of real life and I think that's really what makes the series successful. Everyone identifies with those characters. You feel you know these people. They are real. I think that is why actors enjoy Sullivan's scripts so much.

'I guess there's a real Trigger somewhere. I am not sure I have ever met him though. He is a bit of a one-off really. There is a Trigger in every group. There is always someone who gets everything wrong. There is always someone who is the butt end of the joke. He is just slightly slower than everyone else and always misses the point.

'A lot of people think I am Trigger. They talk down to me, they think I'm a bit stupid. They are patronising and that is annoying. Some people do sort of jeer. But my dustman is quite sweet. He keeps coming round saying, "Can I have your autograph for my son?" And, of course, he's a dustman and Trigger is a dustman, so I feel a sort of affinity with him.'

But Sullivan still had no Del-Boy.

By now, filming dates were being firmed up for *Only Fools and Horses*, deadlines were approaching, and Butt concedes, 'I was stuck.'

The whole course of David Jason's career was changed when Butt, still racking his brains for the right Del-Boy, sat down one night to watch a repeat of the Ronnie Barker comedy *Open All Hours*.

Up came a scene where David had something of a solo performance as Granville, the ageing errand boy, clowning around in the back store of the old shop and Butt looked at him and suddenly the solution to his problem was obvious. He thought to himself, 'David's absolutely perfect for Del-Boy!'

Next day, Butt went into the office and rang Sullivan and put forward his idea of David for Del-Boy. But Sullivan was not happy at all. He could not see David in the role and when Butt then went to his bosses, they were not keen on the idea either, precisely because of David's strong connection with *Open All Hours*.

As creator of the character of Del-Boy, Sullivan felt genuine misgivings about David Jason taking on the role. 'I'd only seen him in *A Sharp Intake of Breath*,' he reasoned, 'and that was all very slapstick, falling over on the floor, opening the washing machine and all the water coming out. I thought that was his style and I was saying that Del had to be sharp, very sharp, tough, an aggressive little guy who has lived in the streets and survived.'

David later recalled, 'John couldn't believe it because I'd played this dopey, wonderful, lovable, Northern character Granville and thought there was no way I could play this brash, up-front, smart, fast-talking, fast-thinking South Londoner. John was not impressed at all. I will always be indebted to Ray. He stuck to his guns.'

Butt staunchly refused to take 'no' for an answer. He was convinced that David would fill Del's shoes admirably and he wasn't going to give up that easily. He dug his heels in then fought, quarrelled and argued his case.

David believes, too, that his cause was aided by Sydney Lotterby who had directed *Open All Hours*. Lotterby happened to mention David's name to Ray and reminded him of the time both he and Jason had worked together on a BBC pilot written by Roy Clarke which had eventually come to nothing.

Butt's very strong London accent had intrigued David and when the two men played pool after a day's filming, David always used to talk to Butt as if he was a Cockney. 'David used to take the right mick out of you,' was Lotterby's timely reminder to Butt.

Finally, Butt sent David a script after winning an agreement from everyone on the production that David should at least be allowed to come in and read with Nick Lyndhurst.

David could hardly believe his eyes when the script arrived. He found himself laughing out loud and having to pause for breath. 'I couldn't wait to turn to the next page,' he remembers. 'It was one of the best scripts I'd ever read to that point – and certainly the best characters.'

Although the script leapt off the page at David,

astonishingly he was unclear which role was being earmarked for him. 'Apart from playing Granville, I'd played old men,' he explains. 'I didn't obviously think they wanted me to play Grandad, but the thought struck me because I had always been playing silly old characters. I'd worked with Ronnie Barker as his 100-year-old gardener Dithers, and played an old man in *Porridge*. I thought Ray might want me to play Grandad. There was no reason I should naturally be the right casting for someone nearer my own age because that had never happened to me. But when he said, "What part do you think you'd be right for?" I immediately said, "Del-Boy. He's a great character."'

Sullivan remembers the read-through vividly. 'They had a little read and although they'd never met before, it was immediate – just like you see it now. They both went into their characters. It was incredible. They had this wonderful chemistry. David was perfect all along and I didn't realise just how perfect he was for the part.'

In fact, David and Nicholas did not know each other, although they had previously met briefly some three years before when Nicholas was working on a kids programme for LWT called *Our Show*. Nicholas had actually interviewed David about his series *Lucky Feller*.

After just five minutes of David and Nicholas reading together, Butt and John Sullivan grinned at each other, nodded, and agreed, 'We've got our Del and Rodney.'

And Lennard revelled from the start in Grandad's idleness. When Del described him in episode one as, 'The out-of-work lamplighter waiting for gas to make a comeback,' he had trouble containing his own laughter.

Now Sullivan had come round to his way of thinking, Butt set about winning the approval of his BBC bosses. They were worried David had been over-exposed from *Open All Hours* and was too well established in the role of Granville. Butt could understand their reservations but said he could not agree. He stressed that David would be so very different as Del-Boy. 'I knew David could do it,' he says. 'He was just absolutely right – and still is right.'

'They tried to dissuade Ray,' David recalls. 'The hierarchy said, "No, that's not a good idea." They said they don't even look like brothers. Ray said, "That's the fun of it!"'

Sullivan, his blind spot about David suddenly brushed away, was especially pleased that David Jason and Nicholas Lyndhurst looked so very different. Nicholas was just 19 years old when the first episode was filmed and he was tall, very slim, and gangling, whereas David was small by comparison and squat.

Sullivan had indicated in the scripts that he wanted the younger brother to be tall and the elder not so. Thinking ahead, Sullivan wanted them to look different to lay the doubt about whether they shared the same parentage. He also wanted to make it look as though they were the only two people in the world who believed they were brothers. Having sewn the seeds of doubt from the very start, Sullivan was able to make great capital out of and exploit the suspicion in years to come.

What was beyond question was David's own belief that he could be Del-Boy once he had read the script. 'I knew I could do it. I was convinced. And at the final reading, they said to Nick, Lennard and me, "We are going with you three!"'

Lyndhurst knew straight away that the new threesome would work. 'A lot of people upstairs at the BBC did not believe David and I could play brothers. We look so different and we have completely different styles. But as soon as we started reading the scripts together, it was obvious there was a chemistry between the two of us and with Lennard as well,' he said.

'We struck up an instant friendship that has lasted ever

since. We are never at a loss for what to say to each other. We can talk about anything. We have completely different ways of switching off, of becoming totally detached from work when we want to be. He hand-builds vintage motorcycles and is brilliant with anything mechanical. I love the outdoor stuff – like watersports and flying. But, most important, we just have tremendous respect for each other.

'When I read a script, I know how he is going to play a scene and say a line and I'm sure he knows in advance how I'm going to play my lines. So there are no big surprises when we get together. We just get on terribly well.'

Remarkably, even at that earliest stage, David was acutely aware that *Only Fools and Horses* was something very special, not just another comedy series.

'I remember going to the bar with Nick and Lennard and I remember I said, "This is not an ordinary sitcom. This is not sitcom, it's more drama. There's an unknown title for this. Everyone calls it sitcom, but what John Sullivan has done has superseded that." I sensed it.'

The very first episode, *Big Brother*, went out on 8 September 1981. And even in the opening scene, with Rodney and Grandad arguing over the pronunciation of Sidney Poitier's name, the relationship of the characters was revealed as Del came bustling in, glanced at the television, and said, 'Personally, I pronounce it Harry Belafonte, but you two please yourselves.' A young, energetic and distinctly slimline Jason was just brilliant as Del. He gazed into the mirror and said, '*S'il vous plaît, s'il vous plaît*. What an enigma. I get better looking every day. Can't wait for tomorrow.'

Jason was so alive, so energetic, so full of chat as Del he was simply irresistible. John Sullivan set out his stall straight away. Rodney's resentment at Del's dominance was right there at the very beginning. Del found Rodney doing his 'accounts' to try to keep a track of the figures behind the widely differing incomes. But, as so often afterwards, Del just blew his protests away in a blast of hilarious patter.

When he hears of the figures actually being written down, Del pauses with alarm, with his sharp Austin Reed jacket only half on. "Well, Grandad, there you are. A lot of people told me what a right dipstick I was to make my brother a partner in the business. And this only goes to prove how bloody right they were. You dozy little twonk, Rodney. This is *prima facie* evidence. The taxman gets hold of that and he'll put us away for three years.'

Del is hilariously appalled that Rodney could even consider he is a cheat, which, of course, even at this very early stage he quite obviously is. Jason is twinkling on all cylinders as he continues, jacket still only half-on, 'Cheating you? Cheating? You? What's that rumbling noise?'

'I can't hear nothing,' replies Rodney, guilelessly taking the bait.

'Oh, it's all right,' says Del. 'It's only mum turning in her grave.'

And he follows up with a full frontal attack on Rodney for having the total lack of consideration to be born a full 13 years after he was. Jacket at last shrugged into place, he says, 'You have been nothing but an embarrassment to me since the day you was born. You couldn't be like any other little brother, could you? And come along a couple of years after me. Oh no, you had to wait 13 years, so while all the other mods were having punch-ups down at Southend and going to The Who concerts, I was at home babysitting. I could never get your Ostermilk stains out of me Ben Sherman's. I used to find rusks in me Hush Puppies.'

David Jason looked to be thoroughly enjoying himself as he revelled in Del's deliciously rich dialogue, 'Mum was 39 when she fell for you. Did you know that for the first three months of her pregacy, you was treated as an ulcer? And to this day, I sometimes think the original diagnosis was correct.'

He changes the mood with a glance, suddenly warming to appeal to Rodney's better nature. 'Come on, Rodney, what kind of a man do you think I am? Everything between you an' me is split down the middle ... 60-40.'

The philosophy was all spelled out at the start. 'We don't pay VAT, we don't pay income tax or National Insurance. On the other hand, we don't claim dole money, social security, supplementary benefit. The Government don't give us nothink, so we don't give the Government nothink!'

With Grandad glowering at his strangely positioned two television sets and moaning about being given a cheeseburger instead of an emperor burger, the row between the brothers escalated so fast that Rodney left home, deciding to travel to Hong Kong to revive the only love of his life, a Chinese student whom he had fallen for at art college in Basingstoke, just before he was expelled for smoking cannabis. Of course, he didn't get far and came back with his tail between his legs six days later.

Rodney gazed out of the window at the view of architectural disasters and said, 'I missed that.' Del sounded as though he did not believe him. 'The only people who missed that were the Luftwaffe.'

David Jason knew then he was on to a winner. 'There was more weight in the characters, they were so much more full-blooded and three-dimensional than anything I had played before. Because it was so well written we could go against the normal scheme of things and try and make the characters more funny. I discovered when I read the script that it was so well written and the characters were so good that you could really concentrate on the other side of it and let the characters and dialogue work for you. I love all the sides to Del. He can be really clever and manipulative but he's got a heart of gold.

Del is a tragi-comic figure, trapped by his background, his environment and by himself. Yet he's an eternal optimist, a rubber ball who has the ability to bounce back no matter how badly life lets him down.

'Since that time, that's what we've done. You didn't have to invest very much in it. We do know that the characters can be very funny, very silly, emotional and moving. So it was a great mixture and having accepted that was the way to play it, touch wood it's worked.

'The writing is so good that *Only Fools and Horses* does not require so much effort from me. Del was once selling lace handkerchiefs and shouting, "Made in France at Chantilly. But due to a printer's error, the labels came out 'Made in Taiwan', so we can offer them to selected customers cheap."

'They are such fine scripts I do not interfere. In the early days, I used to encourage John to push the characters a bit further because I could see inside his writing that he was worth much more than making jokes. John is not just a joke writer, he is much more than that. He is a fine writer about people and relationships with real observations to make about life.

'The way he makes them work so beautifully is to have the family interact. Right at the beginning, we had this episode where Del finds some lead on a building site and it turns out to be an atomic air raid shelter. Rodney then convinces Del that we should rebuild this shelter on top of the flats and as an experiment they spend a weekend inside.

'Of course, Rodney takes it seriously and goes and gets all the batteries and so on while Del comes in his silk pyjamas with his name on the top. Then there was Grandad who was the only one of us who had really been through a war of course. The brilliance of Sullivan was that he was able to trap these three guys in a room for over half an episode. The only people who had done that before were *Steptoe and Son*, again thanks to tremendous writing.

'But what Sullivan managed to do when we were all trapped inside this shelter, busy taking the mickey out of each other but mainly Grandad, was wonderful. Rodney said, "It doesn't matter, Grandad, because in the next war we will be all right because we will be in this lead-lined shelter. We might be in here for two or three weeks."

Grandad says, "Well, what happens after we get out? There won't be anything."'

Del says, "There'll always be a little Paki shop open somewhere."

'But then, after the joke, the mood changes when Grandad becomes thoughtful and says, "Yeah, that's what they said during the last war. They said they would make homes fit for heroes. All they did was make heroes fit for homes." And suddenly this old boy, who we have been busy taking the mickey out of, has said something profound and moving that reaches out to all generations. That got to both Rodney and Del. And to me and Nick.

'I think it was at that moment that I realised that John Sullivan had got so much more inside him than an ordinary comedy writer. Not only were his scripts very funny, full of funny characters saying lots of funny lines, but he was also able to move people, to get them emotionally involved. There was real weight there.

'Once we'd done the first series and John Sullivan had seen the characters come to life as we portrayed them, it gave him the spur and he could see the way we were going and could write them from great strength. The guy is a genius.'

At first, the viewing public could hardly have agreed less. Although David, Ray Butt and John Sullivan all had high hopes for *Only Fools and Horses*, the first series did only moderately well.

'I think only about 12 people saw it and three of them were my family,' laughs Sullivan. He can afford to laugh now but, at the time, Sullivan was desperately disappointed as both he and Butt believed so strongly in the show.

What was even more galling was that they all got the impression that the BBC was somewhat embarrassed by the series and they felt it was almost being hidden away.

Sullivan remembers going up to the BBC one day where, every Monday, the foyer was filled with photographs of notable successes from either the drama, the current affairs, or the comedy and light entertain-ment departments. When it was the turn of the comedy department's output to be displayed, there was *To The Manor Born* and other sitcoms, but no sign of *Only Fools and Horses*. Sullivan also gained the impression that when it came to a second series of the show, the BBC top brass seemed to be begging for something different almost as if they wanted to get rid of a show that was a bit of a pimple to them. Neither John Sullivan nor Ray Butt was confident that a second series would be commissioned. They simply held their breath. Finally, they heard that the BBC was prepared to risk a second series, thus following the long-held BBC tradition of allowing a show to have 'the right to fail'.

Sullivan knew the first series had not done terribly well and had wondered whether the BBC would go for a second. But John Howard Davies was an astute and caring Head of Comedy and gave Sullivan a choice – something new or a follow-up *Only Fools and Horses*. Sullivan has always been grateful that the BBC is so often prepared to give a second chance to shows that are not immediate hits.

The first series did not merit a repeat and the second series also failed to make a significant impact in the ratings. But to the joy of Sullivan, David and everyone who had worked so hard on the show, repeats of the second series suddenly took *Only Fools and Horses* high into the Top Ten TV ratings. *Only Fools and Horses* was born. By the end of the third series, *Only*

Fools and Horses was pulling in 15 million viewers and it has proved to be a massive ratings winner ever since.

'The initial reaction was very disappointing,' said David. 'It was only during the third series that people really started tuning in. I was amazed by the reaction when it arrived. Wherever I went, people recognised me. I get mobbed in shops. At first I thought, "It's fantastic, like being a pop star." I had been in the business for 18 years and for about 12 of those years I was completely in the wilderness. That was how I expected the rest of my life to be –just fooling about on the end of some pier.

'I was really poor. I must have played every major town in this country and stayed in some of the worst digs imaginable and got up to some tricks to survive that would surprise even Del. One of my dodges was to be the last down to breakfast and then to Hoover up absolutely everything. Sometimes you would be lucky, sometimes it would be a minute piece of toast and a thin rasher of bacon. Then you had to try to make that last all day until just before the show when you had a sandwich. And after the show, maybe a couple of beers and a bag of chips on the way home. We had to manage on no money at all because we spent it all on Thursday nights after pay, chasing women!

'I really like playing Del because he sometimes gets the girl. When you're a character actor you rarely get to kiss the girls. It's the leading men who get the passionate bedroom scenes. But Del has love scenes, too! He just has a lot more front than I have. Del is all mouth and trousers and will go up to a girl and say "Hello, darlin". I would never do that.

'Del is wonderful to play because he is such a gentle person underneath all the brash bravado. He has that sensational sense of humour and, at the same time, he is sympathetic to those who are down. He will give a couple of extra apples to an old girl but if he sees someone who can afford it, he will rob them instead.

'The public seem to love him. I've had more free rides in taxis since Del came on the scene than I can remember. I always felt a special affinity. I know the world that Del comes from and sometimes I even try to offer an occasional line to John Sullivan. Once, in Brighton market when I was out with my brother, I heard a stallholder telling his customers to come a bit closer. He said, "At these prices, I can't afford to deliver." There is a lot of wonderful wit out there and John Sullivan's great skill is that he constantly taps into it.'

Although it was essentially a three-man show, there was no doubting that David as Del-Boy was the star. There was something incredibly infectious about his optimism and his constant promise to Rodney that 'this time next year' they would be millionaires. The public warmed to Del's wheeling and dealing, his tremendous energy, and the fact that he was always up to something somewhere, yet never really did anyone any harm.

The audience quickly cottoned on that Del would take a quid off anyone but he would never hit them over the head. And if someone was in trouble, he would be the first to try to help out. He had brought up Rodney and he respected old people, which was why he looked after Grandad initially, and then Uncle Albert. He was the type to walk round the estate at Christmas to make sure the old folk were all right, and would know where there were some Christmas puddings going a bit cheap. Del clearly cared for people. He might have a rough exterior but, if you were in trouble, Del would help you out. It was the old working-class ethic: I don't have anything but half of what I have is yours, if you need it. David has always been quick to give Sullivan great credit for his Del-Boy creation and his superb scripts. But David's own contribution to the characterisation of Derek Trotter must not be underestimated.

Presented by Sullivan with the initial outline of Del, David was able to add his own stamp to the character by drawing on his memories of a builder called Derek Hockley whom he once worked for in East London during his days as an electrician.

David recalled, 'Del was described by John Sullivan in the outline of his stage notes and I thought, "That reminds me of Derek – the rings and the gold." As I was reading it, I thought it was more and more like him. Then, when we came to the camel hair coat ... Derek always wore one.

'John, at that time, imagined Del to be pot-bellied, a beer gut, and long hair. It was at a time when hair was very thick and full. Again, I said he should have short hair. The directors did not see him like that but Derek Hockley always had hair which was dead smart, neatly parted, and had that swagger.'

For years, David did not mention Derek Hockley by name for fear of embarrassing him. But, one day, Hockley's daughter wrote a letter to David after reading David's description. She said he was in hospital and asked if David had time to drop him a line to cheer him up.

'I did, but I thought, "I'll do more than that, I'll go down and see him." But he suddenly died. He had cancer. I had seen him a number of years before when he came to see me in a show. He was very proud of the fact I had modelled the character on him. Funnily enough, they never called him Del.'

Kitting out Del was a real labour of love for the BBC costume despartment, but as you might imagine, the jewellery was not quite as genuine as it might have been. The half-sovereign rings are definitely fake and usually replaced after each series because they're so cheap the gold paint wears off. They come from stores in London's Soho and cost only a few pence. But Del's necklace with the huge D on it is quite different. Costume designer Robin Stubbs had it specially made for around £70. The camel-hair coats once came from a shop near the BBC Television Centre in Shepherd's Bush, London, but it closed down and now the buyers have to venture into the West End. Del's flashier suits come from Austin Reed in Regent Street at around £200 a time. Stubbs said, 'We have to be discreet when we go in for them. If David is recognised he is mobbed.' The ties come from Tie-Rack, his raincoat came from Dickins and Jones in Regent Street and his shirts from Austin Reed and Marks and Spencer.

Adding to David's astute portrayal of Del-Boy was John Sullivan's wonderful way with words. Into David's mouth he planted such gems as 'dipstick', 'lovely jubbly' and 'cushty', not to mention the extraordinary phrase *'Bonnet de douche'* when raising a glass as a toast – words which gave Del a language almost of his own.

Sullivan claims that 'dipstick' was the only one he actually invented. The word 'plonker', he says, was used when he was a kid and 'lovely jubbly' was an advertising slogan for a triangular-shaped frozen orange drink which he suddenly remembered and decided to resurrect. Recently, Sullivan was not a little astonished to find a hairdresser innocently using the words 'lovely jubbly' while tending his wife's hair.

The generic origins of 'cushty' purport to come from soldiers in India where there was apparently a place called Cushtabar which was supposed to be a very 'easy' posting. Its nickname was Cushty.

'Bonnet de douche' evolved during filming of an *Only Fools and Horses* Christmas Special in the Kent seaside resort of Margate. Sullivan stayed at a hotel in Ramsgate which regularly plays host to the French. In his hotel shower, Sullivan found a shower cap with *'Bonnet de douche'* printed on it. With his keen eye for words, Sullivan seized on it and ended the evening toasting everyone with the words *'Bonnet de douche'* and subsequently wrote it into Del's vocabulary.

To complete Del-Boy's background, Sullivan dreamed up the idea of giving Del a three-wheel Robin Reliant van in which to drive around. Sullivan thought about Del's image of rings, coat and briefcase and reckoned he would be practical enough to drive something that could carry all his gear. And yet he wanted it to be something that was almost opposite to Del's image. A three-wheeled van seemed to fit the bill and the BBC chose a yellow one. Sullivan gave it the final twist by dreaming up the inscription on the side, New York-Paris-Peckham.

Another vital ingredient in the show's success was David's remarkable relationship with Nicholas Lyndhurst. They developed a sixth sense about what the other was going to do and, from the outset, it has been a harmonious pairing.

So smooth was their working relationship that it came as a severe shock to producer, cast and crew when, out on location one day in the back streets of Ealing, an argument developed between the two men while they were lunching together in their camper van.

Their van was parked close to the 'butty wagon', which meant that the crew had to file past it as they queued for their lunch.

They could hear every word as first David and Nicholas raised their voices at each other then suddenly launched into a vicious argument. It became a full-blown slanging match and nervous glances were exchanged among the crew as they heard shouts coming from inside the van and sounds of a struggle. Judging by the din, the two stars were swapping blows and throwing each other against the camper's walls.

Ominously, all went quiet and then the door of the van burst open and out stormed David hurling some well-chosen insults over his shoulder at Nicholas which were duly returned with equal venom. The crew watched open-mouthed as David slammed the camper van door behind him and strode off down the street muttering to himself in fury.

The director and crew were aghast. A whole series and four

months of filming stretched ahead of them and the two stars had fallen out on the very first day.

Gradually, David was coaxed back and filming continued but, with David and Nicholas sniping away at each other and communicating with each other only through a production assistant.

The air of tension lasted through the afternoon until the tea-break when David and Nicholas happily announced that their violent row had been merely a wind-up. Everyone heaved a vast, collective sigh of relief.

David and Nicholas enjoyed their joke hugely. The camper van in which they had engineered their fake row was fitted with a smoke-glass window and they had been able to watch the glum faces of the director and crew as they listened to the argument seemingly reaching a violent crescendo. In fact, David and Nicholas were splitting their sides inside the van as they threw cutlery, boots and shoes at the van walls to make it sound as though they were engaged in a big fight.

There is a mutual respect and working friendship between the two stars that becomes cameraderie off the set as well. During filming of the second series at Studland Bay, Nicholas Lyndhurst reached the age of 21 but, in his own modest way, he had not told too many people that it was his twenty-first birthday.

When the day arrived, nobody wished him a happy birthday, there were no cards from the cast and crew and certainly no presents. Secretly, he hoped a cake might be produced at lunchtime but nothing was forthcoming. He was not too upset but merely thought that at least he could enjoy a few celebratory drinks with the film unit in the hotel bar at the end of the day.

On entering the bar, Nicholas was downcast to find it empty. The few crew members he saw wandering around the lobby declined his offer of a drink, announced they were off to Bournemouth for a meal and disappeared.

Finally, David came down from his room and a by-now desperate Nicholas blurted out that it was his birthday. David expressed surprise but immediately offered to buy Nicholas a drink in the bar.

Over a drink, David suggested playing a practical joke on Lennard Pearce. Why didn't they both go down to the gym that was being used as the wardrobe room and super-glue Lennard Pearce's shoes to the floor? So off they went to the gym and and as they walked in, Nicholas was greeted by all the cast and crew, champagne, flags, banners and presents. Nicholas was so overcome he was close to tears.

Given that David and Nicholas worked so well together and quickly established a rapport, it was vital that Lennard Pearce should dovetail in as Grandad. As it transpired, both David and Nick took an instant liking to Lennard and admired his acting ability.

If viewers had their way, *Only Fools and Horses* would run for ever. It has proved consistently popular across the widest range of viewers from Hackney to Harrods, and Her Majesty the Queen is a devoted fan. She particularly loves to watch the Christmas episodes which are inclined to include a few more laughs than her own seasonal broadcast.

Nicholas Lyndhurst also discovered that Prince Edward was a fan while working one day in the theatre at Windsor doing a Peter Shaffer play. On the last night, Nicholas generously bought a couple of large bottles of whisky as a 'thank you' to the crew and, after the curtain call, he flew back to the dressing room to collect them, tucked them under each arm and went back on stage. He was threading his way through a group of people on the stage when when he felt a tap on the shoulder. It was Prince Edward with a request to Nicholas to appear in the Royal *It's a Knockout* programme.

Nicholas Lyndhurst certainly shares one characteristic with his charismatic co-star – shyness. Neither actor enjoys the limelight. Nicholas says, 'David and I have talked about it a lot. We would both like to just do the job and go home and be left to get on with being ordinary human beings. The problem is that we seem to be ordinary human beings that everyone wants to stare at.

'This "fame" business has got to the stage where David and I both tend to wait until it's dark before we go out and do our shopping because there are fewer people about then. It shouldn't have to be like that but that is the way it has become. It's just that if you want to pop out and pick up your chicken joints and tin of cook-in sauce, it's easier to do it without seven people following you round the supermarket and ten people waiting at the check-out to ask to sign autographs and take your picture.

'People aren't particularly polite. I have got off trains before now because people make me feel like a captive. Yet there are funny moments as well. I was once walking down the road loaded down with shopping and a guy pulled alongside me in his Capri with the stereo blaring. He wound down his window and yelled, "You plonker," at the top of his voice. And then he roared off – smack into the back of the car in front of him. That was fun.'

But the sensitive Lyndhurst happily accepts the price of fame because he enjoys playing the part so much.

'We both have such a fantastic laugh sometimes. I think David and I both agree that the chandelier episode – when the Trotters were engaged to clean the elegant old chandeliers in a country mansion – was one of our favourites.'

The episode was called *A Touch of Glass* and John Sullivan rates it the hardest one he had to write. He said, 'I never write a script from page one onwards. I start somewhere in the middle or towards the end and I'll move backwards and forwards from that incident. *A Touch of Glass* was the hardest because I wrote it from the end when the chandelier falls because it was a true story that my dad told me.

'When he was an apprentice plumber they worked on this big house and it happened. He was telling me the saga to try to remind me to double-check everything was all right and don't ever just trust your luck. I was laughing and the old man's telling me, "Seven men lost their jobs through that." I told David this one day and he said, "Please, please, do it!" So I went away and wrote the end. But I had to think how did they get there? What are the Trotters doing in this big house?' Perfectionist Sullivan said, 'I have always felt with that one that the beginning didn't really work that well.'

But Nicholas Lyndhurst remembers it for a different reason. 'Even the mock-up chandeliers that were made for us were very expensive and obviously we could only do the shot where we let it crash to the floor once, so we were ordered by producer Ray Butt to be on our very best behaviour.

'David and I both have a problem with giggling from time to time and just before filming started, Ray took me to one side and gave me this really stern warning. He said, "If you laugh, you've not only blown the end of the episode, you've wasted hundreds of thousands of pounds, so not only are you off the set, you're off the series." I was terrified. I thought, "He really means it."

'When we got up the ladders and started doing the final shots, I was really determined to keep a straight face and, after the chandelier fell, Ray wanted to keep filming us looking astonished for a long time. That went on for what seemed like ages and I was struggling to hold it. Then, just out of the corner of my eye, I saw Ray watching and he quietly put his hand in his pocket, pulled out his handkerchief and put it in his mouth to stop himself laughing. Tears were running down his face. He had only been winding me up about the threat of the sack to make sure he got the shot. I did manage to see the joke later.'

Lennard Pearce's brilliance at creating Grandad's blissful ability to do the wrong thing from the best intentions was never better illustrated. What made the smashing finale even funnier was Grandad, totally oblivious to the disaster he had just caused by being in the wrong place at the right time, asking in all innocence, "Alright, Del-Boy?"

Butt was not sure of Lennard's true age when he picked him for Grandad, but in one of the early series he let slip that he had just got his bus pass. Butt also only later discovered that Lennard had been desperately ill for a long time and had thought his career was finished. In his maudlin moments, Lennard would tell Butt that he had thought he would never work again and thanked him profusely. Lennard had thought at that stage he would not even be alive and yet there he was, suddenly a nationally known figure, thanks to *Only Fools and Horses*.

The series has run for 16 years now, but it has never come closer to ending than when Lennard suddenly had a heart-attack and died.

It happened in the winter of 1984 and John Sullivan was the first to receive the grim news. Lennard's landlady telephoned him to say that he had been taken to hospital in Hampstead.

Sullivan and actress Jan Francis, who was also a good friend of Lennard's, dropped everything and went to visit him. Sullivan took with him a little pig for good luck. In the *Only Fools and Horses* production box there had been a little pig called Trotter which had been lost and Sullivan took Lennard another one, Son-of-Trotter, and left it with Lennard at the hospital.

But a day later, Lennard Pearce was dead and when John broke the news to David and Nick, they were devastated. Off-screen there was a pecking order that David and Nicholas had continued half-heartedly to play, and Lennard was like a real grandfather to them.

Lennard's death had occurred two weeks into filming an episode in which Grandad kept falling down cellars and getting compensation. Lennard had shot his last scenes on a cold snowy Sunday morning outside Kingston Crown Court and was not due to film again until the following Sunday. But when word came through that he had died, everyone was too shocked to continue and filming was immediately abandoned out of respect to Lennard.

David Jason said, 'It was a great shock. He was a wonderful actor and he had become a great friend. We were devastated. Lennard was so much a part of the show that I didn't know if we would be able to go on, or even want to. It's as if we have lost our real grandad.'

Sullivan remembered an incident at Lennard Pearce's funeral which defined Jason's affinity with the Trotters.

'David was sitting in the pew in front of me when the vicar announced hymn number 187. Suddenly, the pew began to shake and I could see David was having a fit of the giggles. I leaned forward and he held up the hymn book to show me that the page was missing. He gave me such a funny look. You could tell he was thinking that Del probably supplied the hymn books. It was as if we were both at a Trotter family funeral. David is Del.'

After the funeral, David Jason, Nicholas Lyndhurst, Ray Butt and John Sullivan had a meeting with new BBC comedy chief Gareth Gwenlan to decide what to do. Christmas was approaching and eventually it was decided to pick up filming in the New Year. None of them could bear the thought of another actor taking on the role of Grandad and the only alternative was to introduce a new character.

David said, 'He couldn't just be replaced. We just couldn't

have drafted in a lookalike so we decided that Grandad would die, just as Lennard had.

'We did what families do. We had a funeral. But the TV funeral was recorded not that long after we had been to the real funeral, so it was very hard for all concerned.'

That immediately threw the burden on to John Sullivan, who was finding Lennard's death very difficult to deal with. 'Writing a script without him was like trying to put my coat on with only one arm. It just didn't work any more.' But in spite of his feelings, he quickly re-wrote the first two episodes to convey to viewers that Grandad had been taken into hospital, although he was not seen. He also created a new character – Uncle Albert.

Butt now had the problem of casting the new, hastily-written-in character of Uncle Albert, but was astonished to find that news of Lennard's death had spread so quickly that within 48 hours he was inundated with letters from actors who wanted to replace him. Still desperately upset personally at Lennard's death, Butt slung them all on to a window sill and went away to Suffolk for Christmas, resolving to look through them on his return from the festive break.

While he was away, Butt came up with one or two possible replacements, but the established actors he contacted were reluctant to step into Lennard's shoes. They knew that Lennard was going to be a hard act to follow – not just because he was such a good character, but because he was so well liked by the public.

With filming due to pick up again on 2 January, Butt drove back to London on New Year's Eve and went into the office determined to sort the problem out. He started sifting through the letters he had thrown on the window sill and most quickly went into the bin. Then he came across a hand-written letter from a man with a beard called Buster Merryfield, who included details of his life and mentioned that he was a retired bank manager and a latecomer to acting. That was certainly different.

Butt picked up the phone and rang him at his home where Buster told him that he was currently in pantomime playing Baron Stoneybroke in *Cinderella* at Windsor. He was due on stage for a matinée at 2.30pm, but had time to go into the BBC to meet Butt and still make it to Windsor for his performance.

At that point, Butt had never heard of Uncle Albert and all he was able to do was ask Buster to read existing scripts for the character of Grandad. He was impressed and later rang David, Nicholas and Sullivan to arrange a meeting at which Buster could read with them all. They duly came in and they all sat down in a dressing room in Television Centre and read together with Buster. They all agreed Buster was in and, four days later, he was costumed up on set ready for filming.

Buster himself could hardly believe it. For 40 years he had worked in a bank, dreaming all the while of being an actor. At 57, he had taken retirement and within a week of leaving he was performing in repertory at the Connaught Theatre in Worthing. Then, suddenly, he had a key role in Britain's best-loved comedy show.

Looking back at his banking days, Buster chuckles, 'We had many Dels come in, funnily enough. Chaps used to come in and want to borrow half-a-million, and lean on the desk and light their cigars just like Del-Boy.'

While Buster was being cast, Sullivan was hard at work on the re-writes. He felt that the Trotters were like a family to the viewers as well, and therefore insisted on writing in Grandad's funeral. It had to be real, he felt, and seen to happen. He did not want suddenly to say that Grandad had gone off somewhere or that he had taken a holiday, and for him never to be seen again. But Sullivan did not know how he was going to write an inevitably sad funeral of a much-loved character into a comedy show.

There was no way either that the series could open with Del and Rodney at the graveside. So, for only the second time,

Sullivan wrote an episode without Grandad and tried to take the pain away by saying he was in hospital. Cleverly, Sullivan's re-writes also allowed newcomer Buster Merryfield to gain immediate sympathy from the viewers by having him acquire the gravestone for his departed brother.

Far and away Sullivan's hardest problem was how to write the actual funeral scene where Del and Rodney paid their great respects, where there was sorrow and grief, and yet he had to make it funny because it was a comedy show. Sullivan realised by the end of the scene that he had to break away from the gloom and make the audience laugh with relief.

Brilliantly, he came up with the idea of Grandad's old hat being buried with him, but at the very end of the scene it turned out that it was the vicar's hat which had been buried by mistake.

For David and Nicholas, filming the funeral scene was hard to bear coming so soon after Lennard's real funeral. But somehow they got through it, and *Only Fools and Horses* lived on. The actors and their writer got together in an unusual campaign to extend the length of their episodes and so lend more scope to the cult series.

David explains, 'We began with the traditional situation comedy time slot of 30 minutes for *Only Fools and Horses*. But after a few series, I kept finding myself in the situation where half-way through the week of a seven-day turnaround, we were six minutes of material over. So we had to take six minutes out of every 30-minute script and throw it away. After two or three series, it felt to me like we were cutting John Sullivan's heart out. I said, "This is just not on. We are throwing away more good material on to the cutting room floor than most comedies have in their entire 30 minutes just to squeeze into half-an-hour." So we had a discussion. I said I was fed up with it. Why didn't we make a 40-minute sitcom? So I suggested to John that we told the

BBC that we wouldn't do another series unless they were 40-minute episodes. He said he would back me up.

'The BBC said that 40-minute episodes were impossible. They insisted that it only worked in exactly half-hour slots. We asked, "Why?" The consensus of opinon was that they had never yet encountered a script that could not be cut to 30 minutes. But, eventually, they gave in and said, "OK, but on your own heads be it. It will never work."

'Then John went away and wrote a script that lasted for 57 minutes. And Gareth Gwenlan who had taken over as Head of Comedy said, "'We can't cut this. I think we can get a special out of this at 50 minutes. So we then had a seven-day turnaround to make 50 minutes. I nearly died. I got up at 6.00am and was learning my script until 8.00am. Then I went to rehearsals at 9.30am, started at 10.00am, rehearsed until 4.00pm, then came back to learn the script in the evening.

'And filming days were even worse. Nick and I were dead on our feet. I was at the end of my tether. I really had a lot of problems; I just could not turn off. I went away on holiday and after four or five days I was still getting up at six o'clock on automatic pilot. Slowly, I wound down. And the show was a brilliant success. We had created a precedent. Fifty minutes in seven days. Now we had a 50-minute format for *Only Fools and Horses*.'

Not surprisingly, the BBC came shrewdly back with a request for this new improved product which was still delivered using the old schedule. The actors revolted and were given 10 days to make each episode.

'But what we had done was to provide John with the vital elbow-room to explore the characters,' said David. 'We found that there were wonderful scenes that we had cut in the past that suddenly came back to life. I remember Uncle Albert's marvellous story about being lookout on a ship in the middle of the Atlantic during the war and hitting an aircraft carrier that he somehow failed to notice. It had been taken out so many times because it never had anything to do with any storyline. It was just a wonderfully evocative slice of life that John is always so brilliant at creating.'

While such a mutual admiration society exists between David, Nicholas and Sullivan, there is no reason why *Only Fools and Horses* should not run and run. The two stars say they are quite happy to continue as long as Sullivan keeps writing more scripts. Sullivan, for his part, says he will keep writing while David and Nicholas are happy to continue as Del and Rodney.

David now likens playing Del-Boy to wearing a comfy pair of old slippers. 'You know, when people say, "What are those terrible old slippers you've got on?" And you say, "I know, but they ain't half comfortable." They fit every contour.

'That's how Del is. I just know him back-to-front now. Providing we are all fit and healthy, there's no reason why it can't go on and on – unless, of course, Steven Spielberg offered me the lead in his next movie with Harrison Ford. Then I'd have to turn my back on *Only Fools and Horses*. But that's extremely unlikely!'

Del and Rodney did develop as the years went on. Del acquired a mobile phone, designer suits and, by the late 1980s, even red braces. David said, 'He's now modelling himself on Gordon Gekko from the film *Wall Street*. He might not look like Michael Douglas but he reckons he's got the same style. It's fairly typical of Del to want to appear flashy. Every crooked little deal he makes is the one he thinks will make him a million, like a City slicker.'

John Sullivan had been reluctant to continue writing *Only Fools and Horses*, feeling that he should be moving on to fresh projects. But public demand and an appeal from the actors persuades him to switch his mind back to Peckham's Nelson Mandela House.

David said, 'We talked him into writing one more Christmas Special and one more series and I was thrilled to bits. We always knew there was still life in *Only Fools* but without the writer's willingness, it could never live on.'

Sullivan fed in the changes in his skilfully imperceptible way as Rodney's relationship with Cassandra matured. David said, 'Rodney's affair will be a lot more successful than Del's flirtation with the yuppie world. Del could never really mix with the upper-crusters.'

Rodney and Cassandra married in February 1989 in a brilliant landmark episode that reduced David Jason to genuine tears.

'It was a sad moment for Del and me – we cried real tears together. It was emotional because Nick and I have worked so closely together and I knew that Del realises for the first time that Rodders has grown up. It was a nostalgic moment, probably the most emotional in my life. Viewers were moved, too, as honeymoon-dazed Rodney finished his first day back at work and then returned to the grotty flat that he shared with Del and Uncle Albert. That gave Del the highly-charged last words, 'You don't live here any more, you plonker!'

The episode is a personal favourite of David's. He said, 'John Sullivan approached me and said he wanted to put some music in and asked me if I had heard the record 'You Keep Me Hanging On'. I'm not a great music person so he sent me the tape. He wanted to put it in at the moment Del was left alone. We constructed that moment very carefully to make it moving, because we did not want to cheapen it.'

The series is treated with enormously tender loving care by just about everyone concerned. At the start of the 1990s, David Jason suggested that Del's behaviour be improved a notch or two. He summed up his attitude saying, 'You won't be seeing Del smoke, drink or swear as much as he used to. On the show, we all feel that we have a social responsibility, so we decided to cut things down.

'When we were filming, the producer came up and said, "We have used the word 'bloody' twice in one scene. Do we need it?" I said, "Yes," but I took the point. We are trying to have a collective responsibility. I might have the odd smoke but Del won't be swigging cocktails and puffing cigars like he used to.'

As the many millions of regular viewers will have noticed, at the end of each series there is always a question mark over whether this might really be the end of *Only Fools and Horses*.

It's partly because Sullivan cleverly writes a neat conclusion which could provide a final curtain for the series if either David or Nicholas decided they no longer wanted to carry on. There was Rodney's wedding; Del's joyous moment of fatherhood; and another episode in which Del had the opportunity to go to Australia with Jumbo Mills.

Thanks to Sullivan's keen observation of people and life, Del-Boy has been able to move with the times. Del's liking for a cocktail drink topped off with an umbrella owes its existence to a visit Sullivan made to a pub he had not been to for many years in London's Old Kent Road.

He noticed that nearby there were cocktail bars and dropped in to find that the tough guys with callouses on their knuckles who used to like a pint were now drinking umbrella-topped cocktails.

The most important shift of emphasis for David came after Sullivan had introduced Tessa Peake-Jones as Del's new girlfriend Raquel in a Christmas special. For much of the episode, it appeared that Raquel was a resting actress until she was revealed, much to Del's humiliation, as a strip-o-gram girl when she peeled off her police woman's uniform in front of Del and all his friends at his local.

Tessa's TV impact was immediate on her own life. When

she went into her local pub shortly after the episode had been screened, they started playing 'Slow Boat to China', the stripper's song, on the 60-year-old piano. And so much mail flowed in about Raquel that Sullivan seized an opportunity to bring her back in an episode where Del and the lads are on a boy's outing to Margate. Sullivan listens to the fans and he knew he had done the right thing when he found people coming up to him in the newsagent's and the baker's thanking him for reviving Raquel.

It was no surprise when Tessa was given an expanded role in the next series. First, she moved in with Del then became pregnant and provided Del with a son and heir.

David has always adhered to the theory that, in comedy shows in particular, if the cast all get on well together then it makes for a successful show. David and Tessa hit it off from the start. 'She's a super actress, super to work with,' he said, adding what a bonus that was for the series where Raquel moved into Del's home. 'If you're playing opposite someone you are supposed to be in love with, you've got to be able to do things that are believable.'

One of the most difficult scenes David has ever had to play as Del-Boy was when Tessa Peake-Jones as Raquel gave birth. 'It was a very hard thing for me to do because I've never had any experience with babies and I just didn't know whether I could make it work,' he admitted.

David was so anxious to play the part convincingly that he studied childbirth videos. He certainly got it right – a staggering 18.9 million viewers tuned in to watch Del become a dad.

The scene became a television triumph. David said, 'The videos were quite an eye-opener. I have to say that Tessa was very securely dressed in that area. I think she had 14 pairs of knickers on. When I read the script, I phoned John Sullivan up and told him he had out-Sullivaned Sullivan. It was the funniest, most moving, silliest, strangest, weirdest, oddest, warmest script ever. It was wonderful. I just fell about. I kept shutting the pages up and laughing and laughing. Then I couldn't wait to read the next page as I was already inventing what I was going to do. It was magical.

'I loved it after the baby was born and Del is a father. He has always had this thing about his mum and he takes the baby over to the window and looks out at the stars and gives a monologue about his mother to his son. 'I'll give you what I never had 'cos I've always been a bit of a wally,' Del says. 'I have been a dreamer, son. You're going to have to live my dreams for me and do all the things I wanted to do. You're going to have to tell me all about them. Tell me if they were as good as I thought they would be.' Here was this great wheeler-dealer who lays the birds really pouring his heart out in a very moving soliloquy. And it's all the more effective because Del is the sort of guy who thinks a soliloquy is a new sort of cocktail. John Sullivan knows just how to get right to an audience. He is marvellous because he is so dedicated. He worries and worries and spends hours and hours honing a script to perfection.

'You have to put credit where credit is certainly due. Without the ability of great writers, I would be nowhere. Since I have been in a position to have some control over work, I evaluate everything against John Sullivan's high standards. There are some wonderful writers in this country, but I consider John Sullivan to be the best. Not only is that my opinion but it is a view shared by many writers themselves. John is very much a writer's writer. He also happens to be a lovely, genuine man, which is a great bonus.

'One of the reasons I am able to keep going is that I try very hard to form teams of people to work together in which everyone gets on. I attempt not to have too much gossip, back-biting and unhappiness. I don't want that. It is very difficult to have a happy team. I like working with people who are fun, who are as committed to the programme as everyone else, and who take the mickey a lot. I don't go and shut myself away in the caravan. Most of the time, I am out with the crew, behind the camera, wherever there is something interesting going on. Not only do I find it interesting, but I also find it keeps people's spirits up.

'I could lock myself away in my caravan but I don't think that is very productive. I also think I can learn a lot. One day I would like to direct a television film. I would like to pass on my experience of comedy. I think *Only Fools* has lasted so long because it's not a cardboard cut-out show. It's very three-dimensional. It has the range to swing from comedy to tragedy. It goes right across society now. It used to be considered rather common but everyone watches *Only Fools* now.'

David's enthusiasm for Del always springs from the scripts. 'I never tire of reading John Sullivan's writing. Sometimes, it's only minutes after they have come through the letterbox that I've collapsed with laughing. I loved the moment when Buster Merryfield as Uncle Albert was telling one of his interminable Navy stories and he admitted he was on lookout when they crashed into another very large ship. Del says, "You mean that you were on watch and you actually ran into a 45,000-ton aircraft carrier? Blimey, they'd have been better off with Ray Charles in the crow's nest."'

Albert's abilities as a lookout are a freqent source of mirth. At the start of the fabulous *Jolly Boys' Outing to Margate*, Albert fails to warn Del, working like mad to sell some dodgy car radios, of the approach of the law. Del flips: "The entire massed band of the Metropolitan Police Force could march past singing 'I Shot the Sheriff' without him noticing them."

For Christmas 1991, the BBC really splashed out and flew Del and Rodney and the rest of the crew to Miami for a two-part adventure that was a real departure from life in drizzly Peckham. Locals were baffled by the anxiety of BBC security staff holding blankets to prevent photographers recording these two totally unknown actors at work. They headed for Florida when Rodney won a competition, but ended up on the run from the Mafia as Del turned out to be the double of a deadly mobster. Sadly, as soon as they had arrived in the sunshine state, more than 15 inches of rain delayed filming by five days. 'We might as well have been in Margate,' said David. 'The weather was absolutely awful. It should have been stable and sunny, but it rained furiously for the first week and we found ourselves in deep water. We had to have 5.00am starts to catch up. But it was a high-class production and it was enormous fun. Mind you, the Americans in the crew kept getting confused about the script. We had to keep stopping to explain to them what a 'git' was and what 'lovely jubbly' meant.'

Producer Gareth Gwenlan had to deal with the complex American labour regulations and did not enjoy the process. 'We had terrible trouble with the US unions,' he said, 'but the real Mafia were fine. I would say that it wasn't that successful, but Jason's performance was wonderful.'

Former BBC Head of Comedy Gwenlan took over after Ray Butt left the BBC. Always ultra professional, he did everything he could to maintain the high standards of the show, and was not afraid to speak up when levels dropped. He felt *A Royal Flush*, the 1986 Christmas Special about the Trotters on a country weekend, was not up to scratch.

'I wanted to cut out 20 minutes. Oh God, it went on and on. It was made under the most difficult of circumstances ever. John had great difficulty writing it. It was filmed in the middle of December in the most awful weather. We only had daylight for four hours. David and Nick were both ill with 'flu. The tent scene was filmed in the middle of the night with lights to make it look like daylight. The fact that it was ever shown was a miracle, but my favourite moment is seeing Del with the pump-action shotgun.'

One of the big disappointments of Gwenlan and the rest of the team is that *Only Fools'* humour is so essentially British that it does not sell overseas. Gwenlan said, 'It doesn't sell anywhere. We've tried to sell to Australia like *Minder* which is one of the biggest sellers. It did sell a little to Scandinavia. America would never like it as it's based on an ethos that they find odd. They don't like losers.

'But if it were up to the top brass of the BBC it would be on twice a week like a soap opera. A week does not go by when I don't get a phone call from the Controller saying, "Is there going to be one this year or any chance of a series?"'

In March 1991, David Jason finally won a British Oscar at the sixth attempt. After repeatedly losing out to more fashionable stars like Rowan Atkinson and Victoria Wood for the light entertainment gong, the *Only Fools and Horses* star was delighted and made a pledge which delighted fans of the series. He had previously taken the BAFTA Best Actor award for his dramatic role in *Porterhouse Blue*, but he was delighted to gatecrash the comedy clique. He said, 'We have been making the series for ten years and there is no reason why it can't go on for another ten years.' With typical generosity he singled out John Sullivan for special mention, saying simply, 'He gives me the ammunition and I fire the guns.'

Yet there was an edge of frustration in the background. The relationship between the BBC and David Jason and the rest of the show was often never quite as harmonious behind the scenes as it looked on the surface and the ten-year reference was a heavy public hint to the people in power at the BBC. David said frankly, 'No one has told me that we will be carrying on. I wish they would. There has been talk of another Christmas Special and I have discussed storylines but there has been a deafening silence from the BBC. It puts me in an embarrassing position. Del is my top priority but I do have lots of other offers of work and I need to know where I stand.'

The characters that Sullivan has introduced around David have all done their bit to help to keep *Only Fools and Horses* fresh and alive. One of the most popular is Boycie, the cigar-smoking spiv from the motor trade who is, definitely reluctantly, a pal of Del's.

Sullivan used to work in the car trade and met types like Boycie who have a bit of money, think they are superior, and talk about their houses and their pools. He particularly remembers a trader who got him to creosote his fence and when Sullivan arrived at the house, he was stunned to find it had acres of land, miles of fencing, and plenty of ostentatious good living.

The role of Boycie went to John Challis whom Butt remembered from many years previously while directing an episode of *Citizen Smith*. Butt had needed an actor to play a bent copper for a court room episode and remembered John. It was only a small part but Challis made such a good job of it that when Boycie was created, John got the call again.

Challis based pompous Boycie on a character he knew from his local pub. He said, 'I'm afraid he was a real figure of fun, the most sent-up person I've ever known. Yet he was always very smart, just like Boycie.

'Now I get sent up a lot, particularly thanks to one brilliant line from John Sullivan where he had Del describe would-be father Boycie as a ... "Jaffa. You know ... seedless," just because he hadn't managed to get Marlene pregnant at the time. I think that description has gone into the national consciousness.

'David and Nick and all the team are wonderful to work with and I love the show. Usually, the recognition is great but it wasn't so great when I got pulled in by the police when we were down filming in Ramsgate. I think the police were just bored with driving round and thought it would be fun to breathalyse me. In the end, after a lot of messing about they realised I was well under the limit and said, "You're free to go but can we have your autograph?"

'Boycie certainly seems to have registered with people. A video company offered me £100,000 to do an advert. I thought about it but I turned it down. I'm an actor not a video salesman and, in a funny way, Boycie is sacred. David is quite rightly very jealous of Del's character ever being used and I feel the same about Boycie.'

Sexy Marlene did eventually have her baby, little Tyler, which was a great delight to actress Sue Holderness, who plays the part so well. 'I began as a huge fan,' she said. '*Only Fools* was my favourite show and when I got the call I was actually pregnant with my first child, so I never forget how long ago it was. Marlene was talked about a lot during the first three series but never seen until I was given this wonderful episode where she and Boycie were going on holiday and needed Del and Rodney to look after their dog.

'Thank heavens John Sullivan liked Marlene and he has used me in every series since. It is just a joy to do. I get recognised and people are quite nice to me but David and Nick really suffer. They just can't move and sometimes people are really vile to Nick. They call him "plonker" and slap him on the back, but he always reacts terribly well.'

Paul Barber plays gullible Denzil, who is often on the receiving end of one of Del's scams. Paul is deeply impressed by the dedication of the whole team. He was involved in the memorable scene involving a rare butterfly that he and Del inadvertantly crushed by slapping their hands together. Just before they filmed the vital moment, they were interrupted by rain. In a quiet moment, Paul suggested to producer Ray Butt that it would be even funnier if Denzil was roller-skating while they did it.

Paul recalls, 'Ray just said, "That is a brilliant idea." But the only trouble was that we had to wait for two weeks for me to learn to roller-skate. But they took the care to do that. I think that extra loving care and attention is one of the reasons that *Only Fools* is so special.

'It's great working with David. I am always very nervous and I sometimes fluff my lines and he is always wonderful at quickly helping me out.'

The late Ken MacDonald played cheery Mike, long-suffering landlord of the Nag's Head, and said he loved the job so much he would almost do it for nothing.

'The guy I miss the most is dear old Lennard Pearce. He gave us one of the 'in'-words of show. When we read through the script and pick out the lines that will produce a real belter of a laugh, we always call them "a Wendy House".

'That's out of respect for Lennard and it dates back to one of his own lines. Rodney announced he was going to move out to a place of his own, and Grandad said, 'What ya gonna get, a Wendy 'ouse, then?" It brought the house down. The studio audience didn't stop laughing for 20 minutes. Lennard was a very great actor. Whenever David Jason and the rest of us meet, we always talk about him.'

Pat Murray plays wide-boy Mickey Pearce and he is a devoted fan of David Jason's talent. 'David is just exceptional,' says Pat. 'I love to watch him turn into Del. Sometimes, when we're on a break or waiting for something technical, someone will say, "Come on, David. Be Del for a minute or two," and he just changes. It's fantastic. It's a very happy show, there is a real team feeling.

'My most frightening time was when I cut my arm falling through a window a day or so before we started filming. I had my arm in a plaster cast and I thought I might lose the part. But John Sullivan wrote it into the script that I had been beaten up by the Driscoll brothers. Fantastic.'

But it only comes over as effortlessly funny because everyone involved with the show works incredibly hard. One of the most memorable moments over the 16 years of *Only Fools and Horses* was the time Del, by now a would-be yuppie, was on the chat-up in a wine bar and ended up falling flat when he leaned on a bar flap not noticing it had been lifted. Instead, he found himself leaning on air.

John Sullivan wrote the classic prat-fall into the script of the *Yuppy Love* episode after seeing a flash Harry missing his footing one night when he went to lean on a bar.

Sullivan recalls, 'The scene was not in the original script because we couldn't get Roger Lloyd-Pack for Trigger. I got a last minute phonecall saying they could get Roger for one day, did I want to do anything? We had them in the wine bar and we had a bit of time because the script was a bit short and I thought I'd bring in the scene I'd seen in a wine bar in Balham. It's become a sort of classic scene but it was written in ten minutes.'

It looked an easy scene for David to do. But the natural instinct of anyone falling is to try to break the fall. David turned it into one of TV's unforgettably funny moments by falling down like a log. It is one of the most memorable *Only Fools'* moments but for David Jason it was another exercise in faultless comedy technique.

He recalls, 'When John told me about the flash Harry missing his footing he said that the guy had recovered himself just in time and then looked round the room to make sure nobody had seen his mistake. He did not see John looking and was delighted no one had seen him.

'I said, "It's brilliant, John. But I would have to do the whole fall." He said, "No, that's not the way I saw it." I said, "I know that's not the way you saw it, but if I do it I want to do the whole fall." He said, "OK, I'll put it in."'

What became a magical moment for millions of viewers was really the result of meticulous planning. David Jason took John Sullivan's amusing idea and went to work.

'First of all, we had to have a shot of Del-Boy and Trigger with the flap going up and going down while they have their conversation. Then you had to drag the viewers' attention away over to the two girls and then have a shot of Del leaning against the bar. Then Del says, "Just act casual, Trig," as the barman comes out and leaves the flap up and we cut across to the two girls again to distract the viewers. Then we come back to Del falling.'

The result was one of the funniest moments in the show's long and happy history. But for David it was, 'A good idea, a lot of work, and a lot of construction. It's a bit of science, it's a bit of experience and it's a bit of knowledge, but you have to work at it. I had a very small mattress to fall on to. And that is the bit that is extremely difficult. It is the difference between being real and comic. The problem is when you fall you go so far and then your instincts take over and your head and eyes will turn to see. Then your arm goes out, then your leg. The difficult part is not obeying your instincts and going against what is natural. It's funnier that way. Also, while I was down I got somebody to give me a wine glass so that when I got up I still looked as though I had the same full wine glass. How many people noticed that I don't know. It was just another funny little joke that we put in.

'Just the other day, a chap came up to me and said, "You know when you fell through the bar?" I said, "Yeeees." He said, "Tell me something, because I've got money on this. Did you rehearse it or was it an accident?" How's that for professionalism! That's how high my abilities are regarded! In some ways, I suppose that was a backhanded compliment. The guy meant it. People think that if it's comedy, it's only daft, whereas a great heavy piece of drama is seen as desperately artistic.'

But as David points out, it's not just remembering everything, there's the pressure of getting everything right. David has to face calls at six o'clock in the morning and may not finish until eight o'clock at night. But it is the day in the studio, he ventures, that is the heaviest.

In past series, Sunday has been the studio recording day and David has to arrive at 10.00am in the morning and be on camera from 10.30am, not finishing till 9.30pm. He rehearses all day and then at 6.00pm he has an hour off.

'Then, just when you're really at the bottom, when you're really very tired, they say, "Twinkle, twinkle, you're going to be a star,"' David explains.

On recording days, the audience arrives around 7.30pm and David and the others have to perform in front of them and make them laugh with cameras and sound to worry about, people rushing backwards and forwards, lines to remember, pauses to anticipate the hoped-for laughs. That, he concedes, can be very stressful.

The idea that *Only Fools* is guilty of glamorising petty crime is firmly rejected by David Jason. 'We do have a responsibility. We know we do. There is always a danger of being imitated by stupid people. If we were shown jumping off the Clifton Suspension Bridge I dare say some wally would try to emulate it. We always show that Del is essentially a failure. And when it comes to the crunch, he is actually very honest. He is also very vulnerable. If he was harder and more successful, there would be more danger of him glamorising cheap thiefdom.'

Over the years, the *Only Fools and Horses* cast and production teams have watched the show grow in popularity to the point now where Christmas is not Christmas unless TV viewers can sit back and watch the Trotter family in a TV special. Every year, it is the jewel in the BBC's festive crown. But at Christmas 1996, the three-show series amazingly capped everything that had gone before.

With David Jason and Nicholas Lyndhurst both in great demand for other projects, it took 14 months' planning just to get them together to film the ground-breaking three-parter. The story had Del and Rodney discovering they had an incredibly rare Harrison watch in an old lock-up. And with typical Sullivan brilliance, Rodney recalled from a scene in the very first 16-year-old episode exactly where the receipt was. It was as though *Only Fools* had gone full circle.

The shows were simply packed with magical moments but the sight of Del and Rodney dressed as Batman and Robin still lives in most people's memories as one of the funniest sights of all time.

The audiences were sensational: 21.31 million, 21.33 million and 24.35 million for the fabulous finale which had Del, Rodney and Uncle Albert wandering up the Yellow Brick Road with their £6m fortune. There wasn't a dry eye in millions of houses when that went out on 29 December.

And although it was officially intended to be the end, the success and the joy of the reunion shows had everyone thinking about another *Only Fools and Horses* possibly around the time of the millenium.

But, sometimes, you can't please all of the people all of the time. Chris Woodhead, chief schools inspector publicly criticised the idea of the Trotters as role models for the young.

John Sullivan sprang to the defence of his characters. 'What is so wrong with Del and Rodney? Derek Trotter is a man who, through his own endeavours, brought up his kid brother Rodney after they lost both parents, cared for and fed his ageing grandfather and later his Uncle Albert. He makes no excuses for loving Raquel and their son Damien. He has worked every hour God sends to put groceries on the table. He is optimistic and resolute despite all the slings and arrows of outrageous fortune – and Del wrote the book on outrageous fortune – he picks himself up, smiles at the world and continues with his everlasting dream. Admittedly some of his 'business arrangements' may not fare too well in a court of law, but compared with the activities of some of our politicians and captains of industry, Del is squeaky clean.

'Does Mr Woodhead honestly believe that the British public, particularly our young, are so thick that they actually ape everything they see on the screen or the stage? Does Shakespeare's *Romeo and Juliet* induce young people to commit suicide? Did Charles Dickens endorse pickpocketing as a fun career in *Oliver Twist*? Throughout the series, I have tried to emphasise the basic decency of the Trotters. They are not violent, they don't take drugs and they don't drink and drive. They respect the old and the very young. More importantly, they have strong family values, loyalty and love and the ability to laugh at themselves. If more people followed their example, Britain might be a happier place.'

Only Fools and Horses has millions of faithful followers but none more devoted than the band who have formed themselves into the official *Only Fools and Horses* Appreciation Society. Perry Aghajanoff and Andy Banks run the club from their homes in Essex. They put out a lively quarterly magazine called *Hookie Street* and enjoy good relationships with the cast and the BBC. Membership is growing fast and *Only Fools* followers from as far afield as Croatia and Bangkok have joined up.

PORTERHOUSE

David Jason's heart was in his mouth at the Grosvenor House Hotel in 1988 when he waited to hear the announcement of the award for Best Actor at the British Academy of Film and Television Arts awards dinner.

For several years, David had regularly been nominated for an award in TV's Light Entertainment section for his role as Del-Boy in *Only Fools and Horses*. Somewhat mystifyingly, he had always been passed over.

But this year it was different. Now, here he was, up for a straight acting honour for his role as the wily old porter Skullion in Channel 4's marvellous production of Tom Sharpe's comic novel *Porterhouse Blue*.

Robert Knights, who directed David in *Porterhouse Blue*, remembers arriving for the dinner to find there appeared to be no clear route to the stage from the table where he and David had been placed for the evening.

His heart sank. It seemed to indicate that David was yet

again destined to be passed over and would come away empty-handed. Knights inwardly resigned himself to hearing the name of Robbie Coltrane read out as Best Actor for *Tutti Frutti*, a drily funny series about a 1950s Glasgow pop group called The Majestics. But to a great roar of appreciation from a packed dinner-jacketed audience, the winner was, 'David Jason for *Porterhouse Blue'*.

There was no disguising David's utter delight. Knights's recollection is of David leaping four feet in the air and almost running across shoulders to get the stage. He made it, all right, and his gratitude and respect for the others he had beaten to the most coveted of the BAFTA awards was evident for all to see.

It was an important award for David in every sense and it came with marvellous timing in his career. David had enjoyed tremendous success in *Only Fools and Horses* but *Porterhouse Blue* had allowed him to show he had a much wider range as an actor. The part of Skullion was exactly what David needed at that time. Anything less like *Only Fools and Horses* or *Open All Hours* was hard to imagine.

When David's name was originally put forward for Skullion there were, however, some reservations. Initially, Knights felt David might be too young to play an irascible 64-year-old porter. Knights also wanted to be sure in his own mind that David was not simply a sitcom actor who could succeed only on a certain level. Knights decided to check up on him and was pleased to hear from various people in the business that David was a real actor with a varied range.

Also in David's favour was the fact that he had played much older men in the past – Blanco in *Porridge* and Dithers in *Hark At Barker* – with great success. David, despite his star status, was humble enough and committed enough to the idea of playing Skullion, to audition for the part. Knights needed just two meetings with David to satisfy himself in his own mind that David was indeed the right choice.

Looking back, David later recalled, 'I had to audition for *Porterhouse Blue* because I had to convince them that I could do it. They were worried that they would get a sitcom performance – over-the-top. Everyone was very concerned. They began to get nervous about me. I said I'd grow a moustache. "Oh no," they said. "You said a moustache? Don't do that." And I had these eyebrows made. Everyone was shaking their heads and I had to stick to my guns.'

Set in Cambridge University, the story of *Porterhouse Blue* centred around fictional Porterhouse college where oar-pulling and feasting take priority over academic achievement until a new college head, played by Ian Richardson, makes drastic changes. Women are to be allowed in, contraceptive machines installed, and finally head porter Skullion, after finding it hard to adapt to change, is sacked after 45 years of service.

'Skullion attracted me because I loved the stiffness of the character,' David explained. 'An ex-Army man who has built-in discipline and a wonderful attitude of subservience. He likes being like a soldier again – do a job, do it well. I loved that character and I tried to bring all that out in him.'

When the cameras started rolling, David could not have looked more different from Del-Boy Trotter. Pushing an old bicycle up the street, David was wearing a starched collar, his tie was straight, and there was a carnation in the buttonhole of the staid three-piece suit topped off by a gold watch and chain.

In addition, David had bushy eyebrows and wore a bowler hat on top of his slicked-back hair. The part called for David to age about 20 years and it took eight hours to dye his locks a whitish-grey.

David had a complex scene on the first day's shoot where Skullion goes on television.

'We had meetings and discussions,' David recalled, 'then started shooting. Those first two or three days I was struggling a bit. I was very uncomfortable the first few days.' Any worries

Knights may have had about David, however, completely disappeared two days into filming.

It was a night shoot in a park round the back of Waterloo which was supposed to be the back of a garden at Porterhouse College and conditions were anything but easy for actors and crew alike. Knights recalls that not only was the park flea-infested because of the Waterloo dossers, but there was a woman noisily servicing a man at regular intervals behind the bushes.

The scene to be shot was one where John Sessions as student Zipser falls into the college having climbed a wall. David, as Skullion, hears him and turns round like a stag at bay, unmistakably elated that there is a student misbehaving and he has spotted him.

On the first take, Knights wondered whether David might have gone slightly over the top, so they went for a second take. When Knights saw the rushes, he went for the first take. From that moment, David showed Knights what he was going to do and the part became his.

Some of the dialogue in the script reminded David of his own father.

'Like Skullion, my father was a strict, self-reliant man,' he said, 'who didn't like change and couldn't understand the modern generation. It's quite uncanny and sad for me in a way, because he even looks like my father.

'My father was a traditionalist. He came from a generation who believed in hard work. We were brought up to respect the law – an honest day's work for an honest day's pay.

'In a way, the part was a tribute to him. I needed a model, someone I could believe in to help the characterisation, and memories of my father gave me what I needed.'

He added, 'We weren't very close and he used to be crotchety with me. But I think his distant attitude was due to the terrible pain he suffered from arthritis.'

Undoubtedly the funniest and most memorable scene of the

entire *Porterhouse Blue* series was when an outraged Skullion finds Zipser disposing of hundreds of condoms by filling them with gas and pushing them up through his chimney as balloons, from where they float and bob through the air coming to rest on the scrupulously manicured college lawns. Here, Skullion has the job of bursting every one of them.

Two Cambridge colleges gave permission for their stately quadrangles to be used for filming but then withdrew when they learned the precise details of the script. Finally, the scene was shot at a Jacobean mansion called Apethorpe Hall near Peterborough as only some two-and-a-half days of filming out of the ten weeks was actually able to go ahead in Cambridge.

Ideally, the scene called for a still, moonlit night where the condoms, if filled with a drop of water, would hang in the air. But instead, Knights encountered high winds which nearly destroyed the scene. Annoyingly, the condoms kept taking off and popping in the gusts.

David had to wait patiently to perform his extraordinary condom-popping scene while the problem was sorted out. Eventually, a team of middle-aged ladies inflated the condoms from cylinders of helium and then they were attached to the grass by invisible thread.

At long last, some 500 inflated condoms were in place close to the ground while others were poised for release into the wind to fly past the camera.

When all was ready, David asked Knights how he wanted the scene to be played. It was then that Knights told David to remember those Japanese soldiers who occasionally emerge from the Phillipines swearing allegiance to the Emperor. 'Play it like a Japanese soldier for whom this is the last bayonet charge,' said Knights.

As the cameras rolled, David charged forward holding a broom like a bayonet. He began popping the condoms, stabbing at them while uttering demented Japanese-style cries.

A pin had carefully been inserted into the broom so that the condoms would burst more easily.

Knights still laughs at the comic touch David added himself. After one or two stabs with his broom, David stopped to rub his eyes as if some horrible gob of spermicide had hit him smack in the eye. Wiping it from his face, he charged back into battle again then turned it into a sort of Fred Astaire dance where every step crushes the head of a condom. It fitted the classic description in Tom Sharpe's book and David had made it a classic TV comedy scene.

'It was quite amazing,' said David. 'There were hundreds of these inflated condoms staked out on the lawn. I had to go round bursting them with anything handy. We started filming at 7.00pm and it went on until daybreak. We had quite a lot of complaints from farmers who found stray "balloons" on their land!'

Porterhouse Blue had a distinguished cast which included Ian Richardson, Griff Rhys Jones and Charles Gray, but it was David who always caught the eye. Winning the BAFTA award was the icing on the cake.

'That was the first time I think I was considered as an actor,' says David. 'I was reviewed in the more up-market papers. You had Ian Richardson and my character reflected his, so that we were on a par andI was considered an actor of weight. I would not have been considered as such had I not been in *Porterhouse Blue* and had I not been opposite an actor like Ian Richardson.'

David has won shoals of other awards both before and since but the acting award was very special to him. Yet if he harboured dreams of the BAFTA prize leading immediately on to greater things, then he was in for a disappointment. For a couple of weeks afterwards nothing happened, and then there was an inquiry from Menichem Golan of Cannon Films as to whether David might be interested in making a film.

Not long afterwards, a large Mercedes with a uniformed driver bearing a script pulled up outside David's house in Buckinghamshire.

'I played it casual,' David later recalled, 'and opened the door after a suitable delay. Man in hat, gives me a package. I go in, tear it open and find I'm reading the part of Tom Shepherd. I look through the cast list – it's always dangerous – and I'm half-way through and the character has not appeared yet.

'Finally, about three-quarters of the way through, I see him: Gatekeeper. "Car drives into chocolate factory. Tom Shepherd comes out. 'Yes sir, good morning sir.' 'I'm here to see the managing director.' 'Up there on the left, sir.'"

'I had three of those. They got smaller and smaller and in the last one Tom Shepherd got run over! My agent got on to casting and began to bawl them out. She did say there was not a hope of me doing it.'

The other offer to come David's way after his BAFTA triumph was a part in *Doctor Who*.

'Now I think *Doctor Who* is quite good,' David reflected later, 'but I was getting lower and lower. I had been nominated as Best Comedy Actor for about three years running, then to win Best Actor I was pipping them all at the post. I thought it might have meant something.'

It certainly meant a lot to David. 'I think that was the greatest accolade I've managed to receive,' he said of his BAFTA award for *Porterhouse Blue*. 'It put me into a different category from "That's the bloke who can only do funny cockney voices."'

While making *Porterhouse Blue*, David met the author Tom Sharpe and talked about filming another of Sharpe's books *Wilt*. It eventually became a film starring Griff Rhys Jones.

'At the time, the rights had been bought by one of the famous film directors and it wasn't available,' David remembers. 'So I just went, "Oh dear!" But, of course, Griff and his company were probably a bit better informed and made more enquiries and found it had come up on offer. The one thing I wanted to do was *Wilt*, but Griff has done it, the swine!'

At one time, *Porterhouse Black*, a sequel to *Porterhouse Blue*, was planned by Channel 4. But, to David's disappointment, the idea was abandoned when Channel 4 boss Jeremy Isaacs left his post.

Until *A Touch of Frost*, the variety of David's abilities was not always widely appreciated, especially when you consider that some of his acting is done without ever being seen. He does not underestimate his ability to do funny voices.

For David's is the versatile voice behind the remarkably successful children's cartoon character *Dangermouse*, a serious hit on both sides of the Atlantic, and a string of other animated entertainments.

He was delighted with the success of *Dangermouse* and the characters which followed. 'One of the reasons I wanted to get involved with cartoon characters was that I was fascinated by them when I was a boy,' said David.

'I loved the way they broke the bounds of reality. They could blow someone up and leave the Earth to go round the Moon, come back, and everyone would still all be in one piece. I found that breaking the rules and being anarchic was very funny with animation. You can't do it nearly as well with live action. I just love cartoons if they're well made.

'In the days when I was growing up, there was no real television. I used to go to the pictures on Saturday mornings and it was all Disney then. My favourites were Pluto and Donald Duck. I'm a dog man so that is probably why I like Pluto.

'I really enjoy doing voices. When I was a kid at school I used to imitate the masters and terrify the other kids when they were swinging on ladders or messing about. They would freeze in their tracks; it was hysterical.

'Ever since I saw that Goon show being recorded as a kid,

Peter Sellers was my idol. I always followed his career very closely and tried to emulate him. But I know I would never be able to reach his dizzy heights. He was an extraordinarily talented man. I did meet him once when I was putting a couple of silly voices on one of his records. He was lovely, absolutely charming. I can't for the life of me remember which LP it was, and I'm sorry about that because I would very much like to get a copy.

'We recorded it in the famous Abbey Road studios in London. We all sat round a table in the studio and I sat there in awe of the man. Then we all sent out for a Chinese takeaway. I was so impressed by Sellers I couldn't speak to him. He was just so amazingly wonderful and famous and there I was in his company. I have got practically all The Goons recordings. Sometimes, when I'm in the car and I'm feeling a bit fed up, I listen. It's beautiful, escapist stuff, completely mad. As long as it entertains, that's what it's all about.

'I've developed that sort of mimicry because it was all part of being an actor. I have a good ear and I listen. I did a lot of the radio series *Weekending*. I did James Callaghan, Tony Benn, James Mason, Enoch Powell and lots of others with varying degrees of success. I do some much more accurately than others and it's a vocal range that I employ in the cartoon work. People say, "You've got a brilliant ear, you must be able to sing." But I can't. I'm tone deaf.'

The cartoon career all began in the most unlikely circumstances back in 1977. Brian Cosgrove, the boss of Cosgrove Hall Productions, which is now the Manchester-based animation subsidiary of Thames Television, was looking for a man to be the voice and personality of *Dangermouse*.

But David Jason did not exactly get off on the right foot for the audition. Brian Cosgrove recalls, 'David arrived for the voice testing session in Wardour Street with his leg all bandaged up. I thought it looked a bit funny and wondered if it was some sort of joke, but he said he had damaged his foot in an accident with a hover mower.

'So he was really not very comfortable and he came along with another actor who really was not very good and was drunk into the bargain. David did his best but he was a little put off by this chap who was tanked up, and by his injury. In spite of the problem, I could see the quality straight away. He searched so hard to get what he saw of the character into his performance. But David was annoyed because he felt he hadn't got the voice right and he really wanted the job. He told me he liked cartoons and this was more than just another job to him.'

David said later that they were trying to make *Dangermouse* really laid back, '... a Roger Moore-ish type special agent.'

Brian said, 'He was a bit down about it but when I listened to the material his unique ability in this field was very evident to me. He was marvellous. Of course, it is well known that he is a good actor but also he can do things with his voice that help to create a whole personality in the peculiar way our medium requires. He was relieved when I told him later that the job was his. Our friendship began that day and has grown ever since.

'David is a perfectionist but not one who is painful to work with. If he has got an idea he discusses it and says, "What about this?" or "What if we did that?" He adds things to shows and inspires excitement with other people. He is very good to work with.'

Having landed the role of the suave and debonair mouse who faces all those dastardly villains, David Jason became remarkably protective of his character. Brian Cosgrove said, 'When you are using lots of writers, mistakes can sometimes creep in. But David takes great care to monitor the script. If anyone had him living in Oxford Street instead of Baker Street, David would be straight on to it, pointing out the mistake and rightly insisting on accuracy.

'He does love a challenge and he is so good at creating different voices that sometimes after an audition he would be playing three or four extra characters as well as the standard one.

'Sometimes they would be quite difficult roles and he would grumble about them and say, "Look, I've got this to do or that to do." But then he would do it superbly and we would all talk about it afterwards and we would know he had thoroughly enjoyed it. Although he had complained and it had been difficult, you would know he had really enjoyed himself so it did not stop us giving him a challenge.

'David never rests upon his laurels. That is the other major thing I have noticed about him. It would have been very easy for him to have settled on the role of Del and that style of character and he could have done a variety of roles out of the same box. He has deliberately not done that. He has gone for different roles, for chancing his arm if you like. And also for searching for something that will move him on. He does not want to stay in one place. He wants to stretch himself. And David also seems to have a good feeling for the right material. He is offered a lot of scripts and he weeds them out very carefully.'

David has enormous respect for the people who create cartoons and is one of Cosgrove Hall's most faithful fans. 'Even if I am in a hurry and there is a good cartoon on, then everything has to wait until the cartoon has finished because I know they only last three, four or five minutes,' said David.

'People forget that the artists who make cartoons are very talented. They get denigrated because they are not Renoir. But they are in their own way. And they are probably seen by more people than any of the great artists and appreciated more, and yet those artists are revered – I'm not belittling those artists – I'm saying we don't look at cartoons with the same critical eye.

'Early Disney and other old American cartoons are now beginning to be taken more seriously, even the actual artists behind them. And collectors are always on the lookout for them.

'The relationship with Brian worked very well. He draws a character and then asks me what I think. I try to find a voice that comes out of the drawing that looks as though it belongs and does not sound like an actor reading lines behind a moving picture.'

The partnership between Brian Cosgrove's artistic talents and David Jason's acting ability has helped to turn *Dangermouse* into an international success story. The super-cool sleuth has been sold to more than 50 countries around the world. In America, where the programme was the first British cartoon to be syndicated from coast to coast, he is particularly popular.

Marvin Kitman of the New York *Newsday* eulogised, '*Dangermouse* is not just a cartoon show. It's a way of life, a religion. Dangermouse has been elevated to the status of cult figure.'

After Brian Cosgrove became so close to David, he sometimes felt guilty about employing his pal so frequently. 'Each new project we found ourselves saying, "Oh, we can't use David again," but the most important thing is that we find the right actor. And more often than not, that means turning to David yet again.

'He has been our Count Duckula. He has been our Toad in *Wind in the Willows*. He has been the giant in *BFG*, the Roald Dahl story. And he's been Hugo in our production *Victor and Hugo*.

'But honestly, we do not always go for him first when casting. When we were looking for someone to play the giant in *BFG*, we tried a lot of fine actors, including Trevor Howard as an indication of the calibre of cast we went for. Now Trevor Howard was a lovely man and he did a nice voice, but it was Trevor Howard, not the giant.

'We had tried lots of other people and then, one day, I was having lunch with David, who had been too busy to test at first. He said, "Would you mind if I put a voice down?" He's like that – not grand or at all pompous. And he put this voice down and that was it.

'It was very similar when we were casting *Wind in the Willows*. We tried him out for Ratty and he did a marvellous Ratty. Then I tried out another actor for Toad who was not totally satisfactory. Again, I thought David was unavailable and we still had not found our Toad when he came up to me and asked if he could put down a Toad voice. He said, "I'm not after it or anything, I just feel that if I put something down it might help you find a bit of direction that I feel would be worthwhile."

'There was a particular aspect of Toad's personality that we were finding impossible to capture. Toad is rather a nasty little character in some ways in Kenneth Grahame's original book, yet there is a madness and an undisciplined quality to him as well.

'And yet he has to be likeable as well for the story to work because the other characters do have affection for him. David is a very fine actor and he managed to encapsulate exactly what we were thinking.

'We have always laid great importance upon getting the soundtrack right. We use the very best actors we can find. I like to think that we have become good friends with David over the years and that he now feels comfortable with us. There is no searching for supremacy with David, the job comes first. Mind you, he does not suffer fools gladly and he is very careful about whom he works with.

'This industry can be very competitive and cut-throat but I doubt if anyone will have a bad word to say about David. He is good company and a funny fellow but he would be the first one to say that he is a comedy actor, not a stand-up comic. He couldn't just stand up and tell a string of jokes, but when he is telling you an anecdote he makes you fall about.

'But he is not the type who hogs a conversation. You can

come back and tell him a joke and tell him some of the things that have happened to you and he will laugh out loud at them. He is not a selfish actor.'

David's voice has earned him a fortune over the years and not just from Brian Cosgrove's carefully crafted cartoons. David is one of the kings of the commercial voice-overs.

He is always in demand to find just the right voice to promote dozens of firms from Esso and the Woolwich Building Society to Alpen and the TSB. It is a lucrative sideline which is much, much better paid than even the best paid television drama work. As one of the voice-over kings, he was paid a staggering £100,000 by the Abbey National Building Society for just one day's work.

If the BBC had had the foresight to sign up their most popular star on an exclusive contract, David Jason would not have been available to take the lead in an enterprising new ITV comedy back in 1988. As he was summoned only from series to series and therefore open to offers, he was interested to hear from Yorkshire TV and their plans for a series called *A Bit of a Do*.

David Nobbs, the writer of the classic Reginald Perrin books and television series, had a new idea about a series of odd Yorkshire functions during which a series of odd Yorkshire people hurtled in and out of each others lives with hilarious abandon.

The main character was tough-talking Ted Simcock, a garrulous businessman modelled in the author's mind upon fiery Freddie Trueman. Ted owned a foundry which made toasting forks and boot scrapers which bore the faces of Prime Ministers. When Nobbs was asked to lunch to meet David Jason with a view to discussing him playing Ted, he wondered how television's Del-Boy would measure up.

'I was obviously pleased they chose David in that he is a big name and I knew he would attract a big audience,' said

Nobbs. 'But sometimes you get the feeling that someone is not how you saw the character and I felt a bit of that. I tried to dismiss that because David is a very fine actor and, in the end, I thought he played Ted wonderfully. I thought he became Ted Simcock.

'Ironically, I was late for lunch because I had been to a bit of a do, a funeral actually. But we still got on very well and his agent rang back in the afternoon to say he had decided to take the part. I was delighted because Ted is one of the hardest characters for an actor to play. He had a very characteristic speech rhythm and David caught this perfectly. Then it all fell into shape.

'I thought he brought so much to Ted and it was so much easier to write the second series with him in my mind. I loved him when Ted was hosting his party dressed as Napoleon and his world is collapsing around him because he has been conned by a woman. He made it funny and moving at the same time. He is a fine actor to work with. A real professional.'

David enjoyed his two series of *A Bit of a Do* and said, 'I liked playing Ted but I did not like him as a man. He is so chauvinistic, so self-centred and so unbelievably arrogant. Having gone through so many areas of the character, there are some times that you think, "God, he really is a pain." But that is what made him interesting to play. He thinks he is irresistible to women and that attracted me as an actor. I liked him because he was so different from Del. David Nobbs is a good writer, I liked the scripts very much. I thought it was a sort of working-class Dallas with a sense of humour.'

David's search for more challenging roles did produce two notable one-off performances in 1990. He turned to *Open All Hours* writer Roy Clarke for a remarkable monologue in the BBC's *Single Voices* series. David played the title role in *The Chemist*. David described it as a sort of love story.

'It's about this man who adores his wife. She is promiscuous and it is driving him crazy. He has to talk to someone about it, so he finds himself telling his story to a video camera in the place where he works. It's very funny and very sad and I suppose that's what love is all about.'

David took the sensitive script and turned in a masterly, immensely moving performance with never a hint of Del-Boy. His character was Vernon Duxley, a husband opening his heart to the camera after a traumatic weekend. His cheating wife Marlene is making love with the local golf club chairman in their bed while he is making up his prescriptions.

'Vernon was a right plonker, a real wally,' said David. 'It was a marvellous part I had to get to grips with. A real challenge to be the only one on screen. It had a nice twist. Usually it's men having the affairs all over the place, but this time the man was being slighted. I enjoyed the change. If you are going to play the same jokey parts all the time it can get boring. If I looked like Robert Redford, which I don't, I hasten to add, I could play romantic leads.'

There was nothing very romantic about David's other straight role as the father of a youngster facing the death penalty for drug-running in Malaysia in Michael Wall's *Amongst Barbarians*. It was a powerful piece and the anti-drug message was very important to David. He confessed his own naïveté about drugs when he recalled being passed a cigarette at a showbiz party and thinking his hosts must be rather short of funds to be forced to share smokes. A more street-wise friend explained that he had just been offered a cannabis reefer.

David is concerned at the dreadful damage caused by drugs, particularly to young people. He was pleased to take part in *Amongst Barbarians* and said, 'It was a story which had to be told. If it saves just one person from a drugs death, it will have done something very important.'

DARLING

For David Jason, the most important aspect of the stunning success of *The Darling Buds of May* was not just the way Yorkshire Television's glossy adaptation of the H E Bates novels swept straight to the top of the television ratings and stayed there. The unprecedented audience bonanza, the international sales and the video which followed were all pleasing enough but definitely secondary to David's main reaction.

'I was overwhelmed and enormously heartened that such a simple family story with no sex, no violence and no bad language could attract more viewers than all those dreadful action adventures of the time like *The A Team* or *Miami Vice* where people get blown away in just about every scene,' said David.

'Of course, when Vernon Lawrence at Yorkshire TV sent me the H E Bates books and approached me about the idea, I realised straight away that it could make a marvellous nostalgic series set in the 1950s, a time of almost total innocence. I knew Pop Larkin was potentially a great character to play, and I also knew, in spite of what people might think, that he could be completely different from Del.

'*The Darling Buds of May* also appealed to me because it seemed to be the kind of television that is hardly seen any more. A series about a wonderful fictional family that real-life families could sit and enjoy together without any fear of embarrassment. Wholesome fun seems to have become, sadly, a little unfashionable these days and *Darling Buds* seemed to be doing something to reverse that trend.

'What stunned me was the response. Every episode going out as the most popular programme of the week ahead of *Coronation Street* and *EastEnders* was unbelievable. But maybe it meant that my views on television are not so far out of step with the public's.

'It was so refreshing that people didn't get killed or blasted to bits, women are not attacked or raped. The Larkins are actually all pretty nice people, being, on the whole, jolly decent to each other. The books were lovely and charming and, happily, I think we managed to capture much of that naïve and lyrical appeal on the screen.

'They are such simple stories that I suppose I am still surprised that they became so popular. To be honest, not that much happens. In the nicest possible way, there is not that much in it but maybe an enjoyable, undemanding hour that brings the family together round the telly somehow caught the national mood of the moment.

"I was very pleased because when you think programmes like *The A Team*, which is supposed to be a children's programme, seemed to rely for popularity on scenes where people get cheerfully blown to bits and the good guys all laugh and drive away, then something like *Darling Buds* which depends on a nice story well told certainly deserves its place on the screen.

'A lot of the fans of *Darling Buds* seemed to be young people, which both delighted and surprised me. I always knew teenagers identified with Del but I got so many kids yelling, "Hey, perfick!" at me and enthusing about Pop Larkin that I knew *Darling Buds* had clicked with them, too.'

Vernon Lawrence, Yorkshire TV's ebullient entertain-ment boss who co-produced *The Darling Buds of May* with Richard Bates, the nephew of H E Bates, must take much of the credit for David being cast as Pop Larkin because Richard originally wanted Bob Hoskins to be the star.

A roly-poly book-keeper's son, Hoskins was indeed an obvious and good choice. His proven acting ability allied to his barrel shape and crew-cut, a pugnacious manner and a cheerful cockney mateyness would no doubt have breathed much life into Pop Larkin. But just at the time *The Darling Buds of May* project was gathering momentum, Hoskins was riding high as a film star. Impressive roles in gangster movies were having him hailed in Hollywood circles as 'the new James Cagney'.

Hoskins had first impressed the Hollywood movie moguls in 1984 as an Irish-American loser in *The Cotton Club*, then as a timid Jewish-American screenwriter from Brooklyn in *Sweet Liberty*. Playing a heavy in the British gangster movie *The Long Good Friday* and *Mona Lisa* had made Hollywood further sit up and take notice.

A role in Steven Spielberg's *Who Framed Roger Rabbit?* further added to Hoskins's credentials as a movie star and by the time *The Darling Buds of May* was seriously under discussion at Yorkshire TV, Hoskins was being discussed in Hollywood as a co-star in a new movie with Cher.

In principle, Vernon Lawrence had nothing against Hoskins. He felt he would make a fine Pop Larkin. But Vernon was looking ahead and could see that Hoskins' very success in the movies counted against him for this particular TV project. Vernon was looking not for just one series of *Darling Buds* but two, possibly three. With a flourishing film career and big movie offers coming in, Hoskins was thought unlikely to give Yorkshire TV more than one series.

Vernon felt David Jason was ideal for Pop Larkin. He emphasised to Richard Bates that David had attributes which Hoskins did not have. David had a lovable quality while Hoskins' image had been built on tough gangster roles.

It took Vernon five weeks, but finally he brought Richard Bates round to his way of thinking. David took only ten days before making up his mind to play Pop Larkin. *The Darling Buds of May* was launched on British Television on 5 April 1991 and almost 17 million viewers switched on. Vernon Lawrence breathed a sigh of relief. He had gambled £3m of the company's cash on his hunch that the popular novels would success-fully translate to the screen.

'It had nostalgia, something we all love,' said Vernon. 'It is wonderfully English. Better still, it's rural English. It's about a family who live the way we secretly all love to live, never paying the income tax, never bothering about modern fads like dieting.

'It's about a little man who pits himself against bureaucracy and wins, and who breaks through all the class barriers of the period – he deals in junk, but hob-nobs with brigadiers and the lord of the manor. It's good, clean fun. And it's got that very, very important ingredient, a genuine star – David Jason.'

David's remarkable popular appeal certainly transformed a promising idea into a sure-fire hit. And he threw himself enthusiastically into the production with his usual professionalism and chirpy good humour.

He chose a typically individual way of establishing a good relationship with ample actress Pam Ferris who played Ma Larkin. Pam added two stone to her size 14 figure by packing in the pasta, but even then had to wear masses of rubber padding to fill the role of 16-stone Ma Larkin.

David knew that one of their early scenes was troubling Pam, and considering the two of them were scheduled to spend an afternoon splashing about in the bath together while eating a huge fry-up, he could quite understand her concern. So he put on some of his diving gear including flippers, snorkel and face mask, and marched on to the set announcing, "I'm ready for the bath scene. Are you ready, Pam?" When she had stopped laughing, Pam found that all her nerves had quite disappeared.

Recording went swimmingly but David insisted, 'Underneath all those bubbles and water I did actually have my clothes on. I wouldn't recommend sitting in hot water for two hours. It makes your skin look like a prune.'

The partnership between the two of them was the foundation of the show's success. David chose Pam to play his wife and is convinced he made the right decision. He said, 'Pam is an excellent actress. We have a very warm relationship because she is an extremely nice person so it was easier for us to behave as lovers. I think if we hadn't got on, that warmth you feel between Ma and Pop Larkin would not have been there.

'It's something that is very difficult to fake. When you have a really deep passionate relationship it shows in your body language. What appealed to me about Pam was her warmth and her sense of fun. Like all couples who get on well together, we laugh at the same things.

'Pop Larkin loves creeping up behind her when she is reaching up into a cupboard – he sees it all there and he dives in for a big cuddle. She responds and it looks as if they are having a bit of passion. There is nothing overtly sexual but their relationship is strong and I thought that was something refreshing to see on TV. For my money, there is too much sex and violence and not enough old-fashioned family entertainment.'

The role certainly called for versatility. David had to milk a cow, handle a horse, drive a lorry, row a boat and for one scene he had to eat no fewer than seven cooked breakfasts before the director was satisfied. Fortunately, he has always loved his food, although he felt that seven breakfasts at a single sitting was rather pushing it.

'When they brought in the cow, the director said to me breezily, "Do you know how to milk a cow, David?" When I simply answered, "Yes, I can do that for you," he was stunned. But at one time or another in my life, I have been called upon to turn my hand to most things. With cows you have to be a bit careful though. If you get in their way, it's tough luck.'

When the cow arrived she was quite happy to be milked by David but less enthusiastic about the television crew's lights. 'She kept turning away from them and pinning me against the wall,' he said. 'And when a cow wants to move around, she is a big heavy animal and you can't do a lot to stop her. In the end, I just had to get out of there. She was a nice cow but I didn't want to get hurt.

'The truck was a bit of a poser, too. Apart from anything else, it was left-hand drive, 50 years old and had a crash gearbox, which means you have to double de-clutch. They introduced me to it about three minutes before I had to drive it. But I managed to get it going without any fuss – just like Pop Larkin!'

As work on the series continued, the cast began to realise that they were working on something special. Pam Ferris said, 'People mistake David for Del-Boy but that means they don't realise Del-Boy is a brilliant artistic creation of his. In *Darling Buds*, people believe Pop Larkin is him. He is a very talented actor and great fun to work with. The first time I met him I gave him a peck on the cheek and said, "That's the first of many."'

Pam and David both found that they piled on the pounds

as life with the Larkins revolved very much round eating. David packed on an extra one-and-a-half stone and went on a diet while Pam expanded up to 14 stone. She said, 'The Larkins are such powerful characters. They're so pro-life. They're into giving, loving, making love, eating and being generous – with themselves. And they spend so much time eating. They start the day with a huge breakfast, then there's a mid-morning sandwich snack, a proper cooked lunch, high tea of ham off the bone or kippers, followed by a full hot supper, finished off with cocktails.

'We both ate so much while filming. We couldn't cheat with just a tiny scrap of food on the end of a fork, we had to shovel it in just like the Larkins. Once we did a scene where David and I were eating chocolate and pickled onions in bed.

'Then, on yet another day, we re-shot the same scene eating kippers. I never want to see another kipper in my life. And that scene was eventually cut.'

Pop and Ma Larkin certainly captured the affection of the nation. When the video version of the series was rushed into the shops it sold £1m worth of copies in the first four days and H E Bates classic novels staged a sudden revival in sales. The truth of their relationship of course was that although they lived so happily together with their huge family, they were never actually married. Although he was blissfully content with his Ma, Pop somehow never quite managed to make it official.

This cheerfully unmarried condition mirrored David's happy and long established real-life relationship with Myfanwy Talog, the attractive Welsh actress who shared his life until her sad death from cancer at the age of 49 in March 1995, made all the more tragic because twice Myfanwy thought she had beaten the disease.

Born in Caerwys, Clwyd, the daughter of a school attendance officer and a bus conductor, Myfanwy's career began in the late 1960s and was really launched with the huge success of *Ryan and Ronnie*, a comedy double act on Welsh and English television in the early 1970s.

After that, Myfanwy appeared in many of the long-running Welsh television series of the 1970s and 1980s, and in the latter half of the 1980s she became a national institution in S4C's soap opera *Dinas* in which she played Cynthia Doyle, a characteristically salt-of-the-earth Welsh woman.

Myfanwy was well established in the BBC Wales studios when she and David first met when David was on tour in a play in South Wales in the mid 1970s. He was immediately smitten by Myfanwy's striking blue eyes, natural red hair, handsome appearance and sense of fun and thereafter she and David remained very close.

Myfanwy was credited by David's friends for the tasteful decoration which transformed the stylish country home set in an acre of land which the couple shared in Wendover, near Aylesbury. Friends felt she could have had a second career as an interior decorator and, at home with David, she was always a vivacious hostess. Although Myfanwy worked a lot in her native Wales and David's work commitments meant he was frequently away from home, they were as close to being married as is possible without the certificate.

Certainly, Myfanwy was a great favourite with David's mother, Olwen, who often referred to her as the 'daughter-in-law'. Olwen was especially pleased her youngest son had fallen for a Welsh girl and Olwen made it clear she would have been very happy if Myfanwy had become David's wife.

Olwen fretted about her younger son. 'He has everything in his career,' she said as *Darling Buds* took David to a new pinnacle of popularity. 'But I'm worried that will be all he has. He might end up missing out on the honey in life. He's always worked terribly hard, even now he doesn't need to. When he was older he told me he wanted to concentrate on his career and didn't have time to settle down. Now he's gone to the top of his career he still won't marry and have children. I'd be very happy if he'd settle down with Myfanwy, but I've given up expecting him to do that. He won't hear about marrying.'

David and Myfanwy frequently visited his mother who, until her death, still lived in a humble council flat not far from the Lodge Lane home which was demolished to make room for a car park some 25 years ago.

David had suggested a home in the country for his mother in her twilight years but she was fiercely independent and preferred to stay near her old friends. As she began to age, David said, 'I would like to help her more, but what can you do?'

Although Olwen could not understand why David did not marry, David was reluctant to change the status quo. He said, 'If you have been living with somebody and you suddenly get married, then statistically quite often that ends in disaster. Maybe the reason is that you are near to breaking up and you feel insecure and decide to get married and that brings it to a head.' David did not want to risk it.

David has been irritated by ludicrous suggestions his unmarried status could indicate he is gay. 'Just because I'm not married doesn't mean I'm a woofter,' he said. 'Not that it has got anything to do with anyone else what I am in that department. I happen to prefer women but there are lots of people of all persuasions. I just don't think it's important, or anyone's else's business.

'There are so many showbiz people who are bent or lesbian or whatever, but what the hell does it matter? How does that affect anybody's ability to be a good actor?'

As a young actor, David once said in an interview that marriage was like '... throwing yourself in the river when you only want a drink'.

But as his relationship with Myfanwy continued to

blossom, he said, 'That was a flip remark that has come back to haunt me. I really am not against marriage but I'm fine as I am. Call us "constant companions". We are very happy with the way things are. We are both busy so we do not see that much of each other, but that suits us fine. This arrangement works for us. It's nice, it's refreshing. It means that when we get together, we have got things to talk about. It is something to look forward to.'

As David was happy to declare publicly that Myfanwy was 'the great love of my life', there were certainly times when Myfanwy wished she was Mrs Jason. More than once, she was heard to chide David over the breakfast table as she read descriptions of herself in the morning newspapers as 'David Jason's constant companion'. That press tag did no justice to the love, devotion and stability Myfanwy provided for David in his acting career.

David, for his part, gave Myfanwy unstinting support in 'the great fight' as Myfanwy called her battle against cancer, which began when she discovered a lump in her breast while on holiday abroad in 1990. 'My initial thought was, "This is the end,"' she said.

Myfanwy was warned that a malignant growth, which she and David nicknamed 'the Alien', could mean her losing her breast. David insisted on being with her when she went into hospital for exploratory surgery.

Myfanwy recalled: 'We told the surgeon: "We trust you utterly. Just do what you have to do."' The tumour was removed and her breast saved, and three years later Myfanwy was back on stage and, she said, '... feeling fantastic.' But the disease was to take a fatal grip.

Throughout her brave five-year battle, Myfanwy worked alongside charities, talking about her illness and trying to remove some of the stigma surrounding it.

After undergoing surgery and radiotherapy, Myfanwy

later spoke of her ordeal and how it had brought her even closer to David. 'We faced everything together, right from when I first found out,' she said. 'It improved our relationship and it strengthened what we had between us.'

David frequently broke away from filming commitments to be with Myfanwy and hold her hand as she was wheeled in for treatment. 'David has been a tower of strength,' she said at a time when she thought her cancer was in remission. 'I cannot stress enough how important it is to have the support of loved ones. David made all the difference.'

On the occasions when she was not with David, Myfanwy had lived in a small cottage in the village of Taff Wells six miles north of Cardiff. But not long before Myfanwy became seriously ill for the last time, David bought the lovely old house near Chequers with its lake and its swimming pool not far from the house that had been his home for so long.

A friend said, 'That house was bought for Myfanwy. David was devoted to her. I think, in his way, he felt guilty they never married. But nobody gets that close to David. They never have and as he gets older he becomes even more reluctant to open up to anyone. He loved Myfanwy as much as he's able to love anyone. But while some people were convinced he'd wed her, when it became obvious how ill she was, I knew he wouldn't. David is very, very single-minded. He is kind and considerate and funny and all the rest, but nothing deflects him from where he wants to go. He and Myfanwy lived apart for much of their 18-year relationship. She had her life and career in Wales and he liked his own space to himself from time to time.'

Myfanwy adored their new home and, ill and weak as she was, gained much pleasure from watching David roll up his sleeves to tackle some of the renovations or busy himself in the garden.

The £500,000 house was set in several acres of land which,

as David was soon to discover, backed on to Chequers, the Tudor mansion and estate which is the official country residence of the Prime Minister. At the time, it was John Major. Tory-voting David was delighted.

It was early in 1995 when David was filming new episodes of the detective series *A Touch of Frost* when Myfanwy's condition seriously deteriorated. Frequently, he drove the 200 miles from Yorkshire to be with her as the end drew near and he was at her bedside at the Florence Nightingale Hospice, Stoke Mandeville, when she died.

'It is with great sadness and with a heavy heart that I have to announce that after a five-year courageous, noble fight of so many battles against the dreadful disease of cancer, Myfanwy has finally lost the war,' David announced in a statement.

'I would like to thank everyone for all their kind concern and thoughts in this dreadfully sad moment in my life.'

David was devastated. He threw himself into his work and five weeks after Myfanwy's death he was back in front of the cameras filming new episodes of *A Touch of Frost*.

'Her death left a gap I had to fill,' he later explained. 'I did it by working. It was my salvation, but it was difficult. Some days I didn't want to go to work. But I had to. It helped concentrate the mind that I was really working 24 hours a day because, when I wasn't filming, I was learning lines.

'Those six months before Myfanwy's death and the three to four months afterwards were really painful.'

Gradually, after Myfanwy's death the friendship between David and Myfanwy's aged father Glyn grew stronger as they reached out to each other and shared their grief. Myfanwy's father knew how happy David Jason had made his daughter and they spent the second anniversary of her death together. David and Myfanwy tried to keep the seriousness of her condition from her family until towards the end.

That Christmas, David had to face up to the festivities

without Myfanwy for the first time in 18 years and he turned to brother Arthur for comfort. Arthur and his family and sister June joined him at his home in Buckinghamshire.

Ten months on from the tragedy as a new series of *A Touch of Frost* hit the screen, David still could not bring himself to speak openly about Myfanwy's death and the disease that had struck her down.

'I find it hard to talk about it,' he confessed. 'Yet I know it would help if I was a bit more outgoing. It would help me and help the campaign against this dreadful disease.'

Although David and Myfanwy would have made loving parents, David did not regret their lack of children. 'Sometimes, when you see your friends' kids, you think they're lovely, those kids. But I've got to be honest; I've never been a person who has craved for the company of my own children,' he said before Myfanwy's death.

But David always showed a paternal side. David rescued a stray mongrel dog he found in his garden one night. He and Myfanwy were enjoying dinner at home with friends and family when David's cousin went outside to fetch something from her car. Suddenly, David and Myfanwy heard her screaming and they rushed outside to find her shouting that something in the darkness had licked her hand.

David grabbed a torch and soon spotted a frightened and injured labrador-sheepdog cross bitch furiously scavanging for food in the garden. It was too scared to approach them and David dashed into the house for some warm milk and some food. In the morning, the food had gone but the dog was still there. David got in touch with the owners who said they didn't want the dog back and so he and Myfanwy decided to keep her.

One of its back legs was badly injured and, one day, while David was working on *Only Fools and Horses*, he received a telephone call from Myfanwy to say that the vet had advised that the leg had to be amputated or the dog would have to be

Winning double: David Jason and Nicholas Lyndhurst.

Laughtermakers: David with Les Dawson, Des O'Conner, Bruce Forsyth and Ruby Wax.

David with Sue Bond in *White Cargo*.

David and Gill Hinchcliffe arrive at London's Grosnevor House Hotel for the BAFTA TV awards. © *uppa.co.uk*

New Trotter trio: David and Nicholas Lyndhurst as Del and Rodney with Buster Merryfield who joined *Only Fools and Horses* as Uncle Albert.

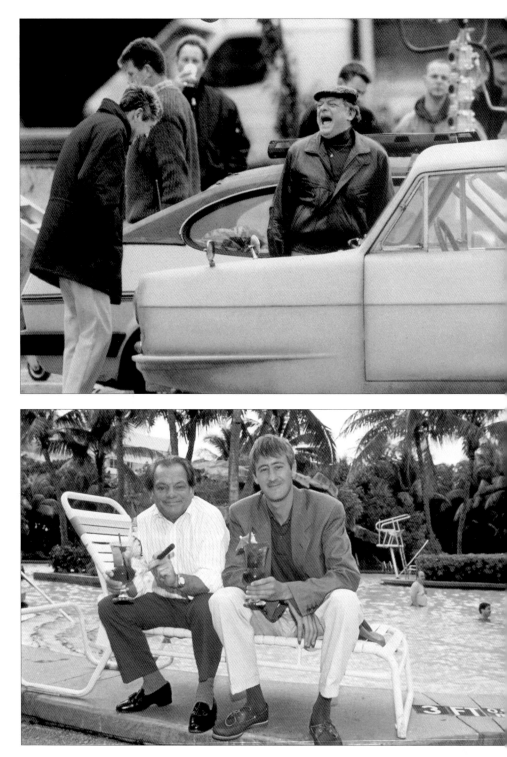

Top: Fun on set. David enjoys a big laugh with Nicholas Lyndhurst during filming of *Only Fools and Horses*.

Below: David with Nicholas Lyndhurst in Florida for the *Only Fools and Horses* special *Miami Twice*.

A knees-up for David with his *Darling Buds of May* daughter Mariette
(Catherine Zeta Jones).

Capturing the affection of the nation as Pop Larkin in *The Darling Buds of May.*

Top: *The Darling Buds of May* cast with the owners of the house where the series was filmed.

Below: As Pop Larkin in *The Darling Buds of May*, which was never bettered in the ratings.

David with his screen wife Gwen Taylor in *A Bit of a Do*.

David with his long-time love, actress Myfanwy Talog, who tragically died of cancer.

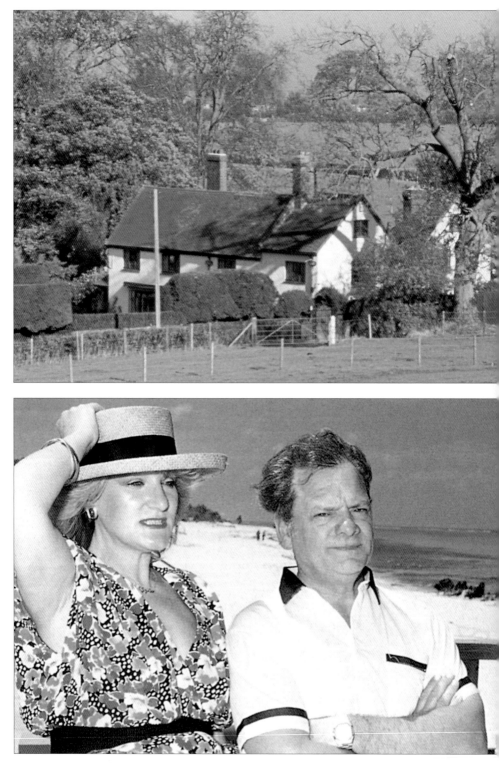

Top: David's beautiful country home in Buckinghamshire.

Below: On holiday in Florida with Myfanwy Talog, the actress who shared his life for so long.

The face of a winner. David with a coveted BAFTA award.

Posing outside Buckingham Palace after receiving his knighthood from Queen Elizabeth II, the ever modest Sir David Jason said he was 'delighted and humbled'.

Portrait of a TV detective: Jack Frost.

Top: David Jason and Ronnie Barker shortly after Barker presented his old friend with a BAFTA lifetime acheivement award.

Below: David and Gillian Hinchcliffe celebrate after the investiture ceremony in which he was presented with his knighthood.

© *Empic*

put down. The poor animal could not walk for weeks after the operation and David carried her with him everywhere, gently cradling her in his arms. David had already christened the dog 'Peg', so that seemed highly suitable and she became an integral member of the household. Friends or David's mum babysat the dog when both David and Myfanwy were away together and Peg managed to get around just fine with a single back leg.

The business of acting does not come easily. David is a perfectionist and if he can't quite capture a role, it worries him enormously. He still remembers his only panto appearance, in Newcastle in 1986, when he felt he had not quite got his character right. He suffered terrible stomach cramps and the doctor told him it was colon trouble. But once the panto opened and the audience started laughing, the pain went away. 'I felt I was not good enough for the audience,' said David.

He no longer stays in hotels when working away on location because he is such a light sleeper he found himself staying awake making sure everyone had come back in.

'Even if I went to bed at 10.00pm at night, I could not sleep because I was counting all the people. Knowing that 502 was not back, I could not get to sleep until he came in.

'Then someone would put the telly on or have a shower,' he said. 'Now, I try to rent a house if I'm away from home.'

Many times, David tried to persuade his mother to move into a luxury home near him but she preferred to stay near her friends and lived in Finchley until she died. David said, 'We are a very independent family, like a lot of families that lived through the war. My mother was defiant, a very proud lady, so it was difficult to do anything for her. She was wonderful, bless her cotton socks. She had a tremendous spirit. What can you do with someone who is independent and wants to be on their own? I could suggest whatever I like, and she'd go, "No, I'm all right."'

David fiercely protects his private life, and he loves his

exotic holidays where he can remain happily anonymous. Well, for most of the time that is true but when he and Myfanwy were thousands of miles from home on the Cayman Islands, he thought he had completely escaped because the mainly American tourists had never clapped eyes on Del-Boy. 'But the fellow who ran the diving school was a Welshman. He recognised me right away. I told him, "Don't say anything," but he let it out to this American woman who I was. She was amazed I did the voice to *Dangermouse*.'

That was enough to accord him the instant celebrity status he was struggling so desperately to avoid. 'They all went potty,' he recalls.

'I'd just been diving and they rushed up demanding my autograph. I could have throttled the woman. There I was, thousands of miles from home, thinking I was totally incognito and I suddenly become famous for being a cartoon!'

It's a long way from Lodge Lane, Finchley, to the Cayman Islands and it's a route that David Jason's single-minded determination to make it as an actor has helped him to travel.

But he never forgets his humble origins. He recalls once seeing a pineapple in a greengrocer's priced at a time when pineapples were a real luxury at 13s 6d. 'I wondered who could possibly spend that amount of money on a single fruit. It was more than my mother paid in rent on our little terraced house.'

Now he could afford to fill his conservatory with pineapples, David, in fact, lives sensibly and simply and never flaunts his hard-earned wealth. 'I am not an extravagant man,' he said. 'I'm not for the boat in the marina and the helicopter in the Home Counties.'

He is well aware that an actor with his popular appeal in America would be a multi-millionaire and he is also a victim of his own remarkable ability to make the difficult business of acting look desperately easy.

David said, 'People say to me, "Wow, it must be wonderful, I wouldn't mind your job. It must be great to be famous."

'You would be surprised at the number of people who sit around watching a piece of filming, watching me do something, and when we go for another take they say, "You're not going to do it again, are you?"

'Then, after they have been there for two or three hours, they will say, "Isn't this boring? It would drive me up the wall." And they have only been there for three hours. Then you realise they are the sort of people who couldn't handle it anyway. They want what they think they want, which is the "fame", if you like. And that is supposed to be pleasant but, in fact, it is very hard to handle.

'They want a lot of money, and to swan around in swimming pools like Larry Hagman and have 10,000 acres in Beverly Hills and a Rolls-Royce and all that. I'm sorry, but that happens in America. It does not happen here.

'They also have the idea that once you have that "fame", it is a panacea, a sort of magic fairy that has come and all your troubles will be solved. They think being famous must be like being in heaven, that you are like a God walking on clouds with nobody touching you because you have money and you have fame and everybody bows and it is wonderful. But it ain't like that.

'It is very difficult to say to people that what you put in right at the very beginning, in anything, not just in acting, affects your reward at the end. Reap as ye shall sow, I suppose.

'I did not go into the theatre thinking one day I want to be rich and famous. I knew 99.9 per cent of the people who want to be actors never even make a decent living at it. The people who go in really believing in themselves, and really wanting to do it, perhaps a small percentage of them make it and turn that corner into being successful.

'I became an actor because I wanted my work to be recognised, not because I wanted to be famous. I know I have a high profile and I am delighted to do good work that is popular, but I don't enjoy the endless recognition.'

David believes that the best comedy actors do not get the recognition and the critical acclaim that their dramatic counterparts inspire. He said, 'Nicholas Lyndhurst once showed me something written in a newspaper. Some Page Three girl had said, "I want to get into acting. I want to start off in comedy and then get into real acting." That's the sort of attitude that gets quite a long way up my nose.'

David worries about his business more than most actors. He is frustrated that his awards and his colossal comedy success have not brought film offers.

'If I were in America in my situation, I think I would have had real film chances, like Danny de Vito from *Taxi* or Alan Alda from *M*A*S*H*. If you're a success in TV over there, they make movies with you and finally you become an international movie star. Who have we got? Bob Hoskins had to fight his bollocks off to get a film that he really believed in, *The Long Good Friday*, and that gave him status, but why do we have to go to America to become international stars? We should be able to do it ourselves.' But the fame side of the success he could cheerfully live without.

'People say to me, "Go on, you love it, really." Well no, I don't. When I was struggling, it was a different ball game, because it was all part of the aggression of wanting to succeed. I couldn't get my face in the paper if I killed someone in those days. Now I still find it hard to come to terms with people finding my life interesting.

'Ronnie Barker is the man in my business who has inspired most of my respect. I understood and agreed with the way he got out of the business. He did not want to dribble on for ever and neither do I. I haven't reached it yet but I will know when the time to go has come.'

There are moments, David concedes, when he really does seriously wonder what his life has come to. These questioning moments usually occur when he is filming at night, usually in some deep discomfort due to the elements.

One such moment occurred during the making of *The Bullion Boys*, a one-off film David made when he returned briefly to the BBC after his *Darling Buds of May* triumph.

'There I was making *The Bullion Boys*,' he recalled, 'standing in the rain, drenched to the skin, freezing cold, at four in the morning on a January night in Liverpool. That's when I questioned what I was doing with my life. I bet they don't do this to Tom Cruise, I told myself. All he seems to do is put his tongue down Nicole Kidman's throat or fly around in an aeroplane.'

The Bullion Boys was a film based on a true story about a bunch of Liverpool dockers who seize a golden chance to get rich. The film was set in 1940 at a time when the German armies are on the march and England is under threat of invasion. To safeguard the country's gold reserves, a top-secret plan is drawn up to move the priceless cargo from the Bank of England to a bank in Liverpool. Only a handful of policemen, a group of senior bank officials and a gang of dockers have been told about the bullion transfer. But it gives dockers leader Billy Mac, played by David Jason, a chance to hatch an ingenious plan to 'sample' the cargo.

His scheme involves a clever 'interruption' to the conveyor belt rolling the bars of gold to the Liverpool vaults which allows the dockers to replace the genuine gold bars with fake replicas.

The role was picked out by David's agent from the dozens of scripts which regularly arrive on her desk for him. She insisted that he read it and David was instantly hooked by the story.

'It was such a good yarn,' he said. 'That's what attracted me to it. It was a good once-upon-a-time *Boy's Own* adventure story. What also attracted me to *The Bullion Boys* was the brains of Billy Mac in working out an ingenious way to get the gold right from under the noses of the guards. It was nothing short of sheer genius.

'I also felt that this kind of film had been missing for a while. When I was a lad, I'd spent so much time in the cinema I'd seen all those old British B movies that this country used to do so very well, and I felt *The Bullion Boys* had all the values to be an entertaining film in the old-fashioned sense.'

Much as he loved the script and the whole tone and ingenuity of the story, David could see no way he could take the role of Billy Mac. He was simply too busy with the final episodes of *Darling Buds of May*, a first series of *A Touch of Frost* and an *Only Fools and Horses* Christmas Special.

'I reluctantly told the BBC it was impossible,' he said. 'I said I'd love to do it but I just couldn't fit it in. But I also told them I knew how annoyed I'd be when I eventually saw *The Bullion Boys* with someone else starring in it, knowing it could have been me. That's when they came back and said that if I was that interested in playing Billy Mac, would I be prepared to film it the following year? When I said "Yes," they said they would be prepared to wait for me – which was wonderful.' *The Bullion Boys* was duly postponed for a year to accommodate him.

David had plenty of time to think about the role and one challenge he was patently going to have to face was producing a convincing Liverpool accent. He had never played a Liverpudlian before and he went so far as to ask the director whether it was essential for Billy Mac to be a Liverpudlian, hoping the answer would not be in the affirmative.

'I asked if it was necessary for Billy to be a Scouser and he replied it was,' said David. 'So I asked once again if he'd really prefer him to be Scouse and he said "Yes". He wasn't getting my signals at all and so I knew that it was going to be a toughie to get the accent right. I knew I simply had to learn to speak Scouse.

'It's a very difficult accent to do and I didn't suppose for a minute that I was going to be able to fool real Scousers, but I wanted to get my accent near enough. It was important to me that Billy should sound from that area.'

To that end, David sought out London voice coach Jo Washington who, besides giving him a few lessons, also furnished him with audio tapes, pages of notes, and instructions on sounds for him to reproduce to help him towards a Liverpool accent. With typical dedication, David took them all with him when he managed to snatch some precious time away with Myfanwy in Miami before filming of *The Bullion Boys* began.

He spent much of the Florida holiday uttering Scouse encouraged by Myfanwy. Coming from north Wales, Myfanwy was familiar with the Liverpool accent. She had encountered it many times while living on the north coast of Wales where it's possible to look across to Liverpool.

It was while he was in Miami with Myfanwy that the news became official that David had been awarded the OBE.

He had, of course, been notified of the honour long before, but he had obeyed to the letter the instruction to keep it a secret. He had not told a soul, not even his mother or Myfanwy.

On the day he knew the announcement would be made to the media back in England, David had arranged for himself and Myfanwy to have a convivial lunch with friends. Naturally, he was itching to share his joy with Myfanwy and he devised a neat way of finally letting her in on his secret. Excusing himself from the lunch table, he put in a telephone call to his secretary back in London who excitedly offered her congratulations and confirmed that his OBE was now headline news.

'I came back to the table,' he recalled, 'and I decided that what I would do was write down my address to give to Myfanwy to pass on to our friends at the table. I duly wrote it down on a piece of paper, gave it to Myfanwy and, as she glanced at it, I took it back from her and said, "Hang on, there's something missing." She looked at what I'd written and asked what. That's when I wrote the initials OBE after my name and handed it back to her. She did a double-take. She was absolutely stunned.'

When the penny dropped, Myfanwy flung her arms round a beaming David and she whooped for joy. Their lunch guests sprang to their feet and joined in with back-slaps and handshakes. The waiter was quickly summoned to bring champagne.

'After all the euphoria and the champagne had been consumed, I got up from the table to phone my mum,' said David. 'I was very excited when I called her up and asked her if she'd heard the news.

'And can you believe what she said, she said, "Yes, I have. I suppose it'll cost money now for me to speak to you. What I want to know is, when are you coming round to mend my cooker?" I was phoning her from the other side of the world about my OBE and all Mum wanted to know was when I was going to fix her cooker! Actually, it was wonderful because it brought me straight back down to earth.'

Miami had become something of a favourite resort for David and Myfanwy after he had flown there to film a feature-length Christmas Special for *Only Fools and Horses* called *Miami Twice* in which he played two roles – Del and a Mafia boss.

In Florida for *Miami Twice*, David had been given the star treatment and had been chauffeured around in a huge limousine. With Press photographers desperate for pictures of Peckham's favourite son filming abroad, Myfanwy, who had accompanied him, travelled some distance behind in an Espace so she and David were not photographed together.

If David was brought down to earth by his mum asking for her cooker to be mended, back in England filming *The Bullion Boys* it was down to earth with a real bump. Rarely off-screen, David was sometimes working 16 hours a day. It was a gruelling schedule.

'The glamour of films doesn't really exist any more,' said David after completing the scene in which he found himself soaked and cold at 4.00am. 'They're trying to make films in a shorter time and extend the working day.'

As Billy Mac, the moustache he had grown for *A Touch of Frost* was shaved off and his hair dyed black under the cap he wore for much of the film.

'I had to keep on colouring it,' said David 'and, of course, there were times when it was neither fish nor fowl and I'd go into a restaurant and hear people saying, "Look! Doesn't he dye his hair badly?" I felt like putting a notice round my neck saying, "I'm sorry my hair's like this. I'm growing it out for my next character. It's part of my job."'

At least he had the satisfaction of ultimately knowing it was all worthwhile. *The Bullion Boys* attracted an audience of 14 million and a good reaction from the critics.

The closing scenes of *The Bullion Boys* called for David to play Billy as an 85-year-old grandfather. The make-up department transformed him into a frail figure with wisps of white hair. He was just as convincing an octogenarian as the old men Dithers and Blanco he had played on TV years before.

'But this time, it was murder sitting in a make-up chair at five in the morning for four hours and just being able to drink through a straw,' said David. 'I didn't like seeing myself in the mirror aged 85. It made me think I'd not long to go now ...'

FROST

David Jason has always enjoyed a good working relationship with Yorkshire Television. He got on well straight away with David Reynolds who directed him in *A Bit of a Do*. When they met for the very first time for lunch at Reynolds's home, the two men hit it off instantly. Reynolds had an old mongrel which David took an immediate liking to during a pre-lunch stroll in the garden.

On their walk, David noticed that an area of the garden was sopping wet and Reynolds was embarrassed to explain that a drain was blocked and he was getting someone round to fix it. 'Don't worry about that,' said David and promptly took off his jacket, rolled up his sleeves, got down on his hands and knees and quickly cleared it. Reynolds was extremely grateful though somewhat taken aback. He and Yorkshire Television were hoping to conclude a multi-million pound deal to create a brand-new series and here was his potential star on his hands and knees with his arm up a drainpipe. But, in the end, he signed the deal for hundreds of thousands of pounds and fixed the drains for nothing.

Reynolds, and indeed the crews David worked with at Yorkshire TV, found him to be wonderfully professional in his work, an actor who talked not just to the bosses but everyone on the team to make sure everybody was happy.

They discovered that he made no ridiculous demands and, for their part, Yorkshire TV paid him handsomely, provided him with a cottage and a car and generally looked after him very well.

It was during his run of successes with Yorkshire TV that the ITV company offered David an exclusive deal to leave the BBC to come and work solely for Yorkshire. The offer would have made David an instant millionaire but Yorkshire felt they could justify such a fortune because of the output they were getting from him.

David turned it down, largely because he did not want to be tied down and also because of loyalty to John Sullivan who still had more episodes of *Only Fools and Horses* up his sleeve. As it transpired, he chose to stay with Yorkshire because of the quality of scripts and directors for his next project *A Touch of Frost*. Even so, David was unprepared for events which led to his taking on the role of detective Jack Frost based on the best-selling novels by R.D. Wingfield.

'Basically, it was a touch of me being head-hunted,' David later recalled with undisguised satisfaction. 'Yorkshire TV took me out to lunch while I was working on *Darling Buds* and said, "What would you like to do? How do you see your future progressing?" I was amazed. My knife and fork dropped on to the plate and I nearly choked on the decent wine they had bought.

'It took me completely by surprise. It was the first time anything like that had ever happened to me. Although it's probably quite normal in America, it's not normal in this country to ask an actor what he wants to do. Usually, the project comes first and then the actor is offered it. But here *they* were asking *me* what I wanted to do.

'Throughout the lunch, we talked about various ideas and I explained I'd always liked detective series. I watch the *Starsky and Hutch* and *Cagney and Lacey*-type of series but for me they have never been as interesting as *Inspector Morse*, the *Wexford* series, and *Taggart* and *Columbo*. I like the sort of detective who unravels the mystery, not the ones who go around blowing people away.

'During the lunch, I said I felt there was an area which British TV had been missing out on – a copper who was a bit off-the-wall, a bit odd, a down-to-earth detective who had more than one job to do, perhaps three or four like most coppers do. I felt there was room for a detective who has to deal with the cut and thrust of life and the dross and the terrible things that happen, a man who is overworked but has a sense of humour, a man who has a sense of sympathy for the victims for a change and isn't just out to beat up the crook. So Yorkshire TV said, "Right, leave it to us."

'*Frost* was just one of three books Yorkshire came up with and as soon as I'd read it, I said, "That's the one. Get me *Frost*!" I knew it would be a tremendous challenge but one of the reasons I wanted the challenge of taking on a major dramatic role like Frost was that it had never been offered to me before. *Porterhouse Blue* had done a great deal for me but after that I was never offered those parts again. Basically, I went back into the comedy box and once you are in the comedy box it's very difficult to be taken seriously. When I read the first *Frost* script, I thought, "Bloody hell, this is good."'

Indeed, much of the enormous success of *Frost* was down to the excellent scripts, by award-winning writer Richard Harris. He had worked with David Jason and producer

Richard Bates many times before, most notably on *Darling Buds of May*. Bates and co-producer Vernon Lawrence asked Harris to write the key pilot episode. The production team was delighted by the result, but Rodney Wingfield, the author of the original book in which Frost first appeared, was not so happy. 'He slammed me for, in his opinion, ruining his book,' recalls Richard Harris, who nevertheless went on to write the first ten hours of *Frost* and contributed a great deal to the high quality of the series. Harris only stopped writing *Frost* because he was commissioned to write his own series, *Outside Edge*.

Only a handful of top British actors have been considered certainties when it comes to delivering big ITV audiences consistently. Most drama chiefs would place the late John Thaw, Dennis Waterman, George Cole, James Bolam and Sean Bean in this category. Given a script of quality, sound production values and an able and accomplished director, these stars are reckoned to be bankers that guarantee solid audiences.

Now, due to the remarkable ratings success of *A Touch of Frost*, David Jason is the most bankable of them all. He tops the lot. Since *Open All Hours*, Jason's name has only ever been associated with success while even the much acclaimed John Thaw had the blot of *A Year in Provence* on his CV.

But when David signed to play Detective Inspector Jack Frost in a brand new police drama series for Yorkshire TV, it still represented something of a risk. His acting credentials were deeply rooted in comedy but, ironically, it was a scene from an episode of *Only Fools and Horses* which convinced everyone at Yorkshire TV of David's capabilities as a serious actor.

It was the scene at the hospital when Raquel is giving birth to Del's baby. One moment he prompts a big laugh by grabbing Raquel's oxygen mask to gulp in a huge lungful of air for himself before rushing out of the delivery room to tell Rodney and Uncle Albert, "It's a baby!" – having completely forgotten to discover whether it is a boy or a girl. The next moment he stands by a window cradling his son in his arms and movingly talks to the sleeping infant and promises him a secure future.

'It was exciting to see such a great comedy actor as David become a great tragedian,' Vernon Lawrence observed. 'When you look at him in something like that birth scene in *Only Fools and Horses*, he makes you cry. Such talent is amazing.'

A Touch of Frost producer Don Leaver was of the same opinion. 'When we first started, we knew David as a serious actor from *Porterhouse Blue*,' he said. 'And although it was comedy, the sequences where Raquel was having her baby in *Only Fools and Horses* really showed his range. We knew he had a lot to bring to the role of *Frost*.'

As Yorkshire TV supremo, Vernon's instinct was that David would comfortably manage the sharp change in direction which the role of Frost clearly required.

In the first episodes, Frost would be a detective investigating such crimes as multiple murders, violent armed robbery and the poisoning of a football star – a stark contrast with Del-Boy's petty schemes and scams and Pop Larkin's golden-hearted, what's-mine-is-yours way of life.

Vernon felt sure Jason's huge following would warm to him. The dark nature of the crimes Frost was set to investigate would be offset by viewers seeing David playing Frost as an unperturbable cop who was still a caring, compassionate man who retained his humour and his humility after years of seeing the worst of human nature. Vernon's gut reaction and intuition told him David's fans would empathise with him as Frost and the show would be a success.

'I knew how good David was,' he explained. 'I was confident of David. I knew the story was good but what I wasn't confident of was whether we would take David's entire audience with us. That's what concerned me.'

To banish those doubts, Yorkshire TV decided to commission a survey to discover the public's likely reaction. The survey quizzed 3,000 people after the following introduction: 'A Touch of Frost is a new thriller series featuring David Jason as never seen before, starring as a hard-nosed detective faced with the roughest back-street crimes. Jack Frost is an intuitive Detective Inspector yet he is by no means a model policeman. Rash, sloppy and disorganised, he has a healthy disregard for the rules but always cracks the case despite unorthodox methods.'

The survey posed a number of questions about the popularity of detective series in general, the Frost books in particular, and the public's perception and appreciation of Jason as an actor. Happily for Yorkshire, the results proved to be highly encouraging.

Only 2 per cent polled said they would not watch A Touch of Frost. Of those who said they would watch, 58 per cent said their main reason for tuning in would be David Jason and 38 per cent said it would be because they enjoyed whodunnits. Even Yorkshire TV's proposed Sunday night slot for A Touch of Frost met with firm approval.

The fact that Frost would not have a regular woman in his life – Frost's wife was to die of cancer in the opening episode – also won plenty of backing. Asked if it was important that David Jason's character had a girlfriend or a wife, a total of 84 per cent said 'No'.

The survey held only one cautionary note for Yorkshire TV. A total of 78 per cent stated they most associated David with comedy roles and only three per cent with serious roles.

Intensive research and analysis before the launch of a major TV series is common practice in American television. But it was only the second time Yorkshire TV had ever used such a survey to back up its programme plans.

'It's something that all self-opinionated TV producers and

directors naturally go against,' said Vernon. 'In our arrogant way – and you have to be to do the job in the first place – we all think our gut reaction and intuition tells us what the public wants. But because of the incredible costs of programme making, we are forced into making sure we are going along the right lines.

'By and large, an awful lot of what we had felt all along about the project was vindicated by the research. The only thing we did from the findings was to shorten part one of the first episode by five minutes and put it into part two. Some felt it was a bit long and concentration started to flag.'

As the opening two-hour film was to cost £3m with a further three shows costing another £3m, the £10,000 spent on the research seemed a trifling sum to pay.

Fortified by such favourable statistics, Yorkshire TV felt more confident than ever that they were on to a winner with Jason and *A Touch of Frost*. But as the launch date approached, Yorkshire mounted an expensive, carefully targeted advertising campaign in the Press.

Vernon explained, 'We had two sets of people we thought would watch the show – the Jason addicts and the people who love programmes like *Inspector Morse* and *Taggart*. We were therefore trying to attract people who weren't Jason addicts and others who might not watch the show because it's not a genre they love.

'Our biggest problem was to convert the audience into accepting David in something they had never seen him in before, playing a detective in an opening episode in which his wife dies of cancer, where there are murders, and a prostitute's daughter is abducted.'

Naturally, David himself was as anxious as anybody to find out whether the public would warm to him as a detective.

'Taking on *Frost* in the first place was quite frightening for me,' he confided. 'The challenge was to convince people of my worth as a serious actor. It would have been very easy to do just comedy and avoid the risk of projects like *Frost*. But then what would have happened if I'd stayed where I was and the audience had tired of comedy from me?'

He was genuinely and openly relieved when early previews of *Frost* indicated he had little to fear. After the first two-hour film had been shown to a private audience, he was jubilant. 'Some people said they thought I could never do this sort of thing,' he said. 'But those who have seen *Frost* confessed that they forgot about me after the first few minutes and they got drawn into the story.'

That two-hour opening film of *A Touch of Frost* was screened on 6 December 1992, and pulled in the incredible audience of nearly 18 million, an audience share of 73% of people watching TV at the time. It was way beyond Yorkshire TV's expectations and the first series reached an average audience of 16 million.

David was overjoyed and had only one tiny quibble. 'We haven't been quite as faithful to the book as I would have liked,' he said. 'Frost is painted a bit darker in the books. He's much more anti-Establishment. But what works in literary terms does not necessarily work on TV unfortunately.

'I've had one or two criticisms, but then life wouldn't be any fun if we were all the same, would it? What's nice is that a lot of people have appreciated the efforts that went into the change of image.

'Sometimes the police are painted badly on television, and I hope *Frost* redresses the balance the other way to a degree. He's a rather old-fashioned policeman, a policeman like we want them all to be. He's honest, he cares, he has no time for the criminal but believes the victim should be cared for. I enjoy playing Frost, not least because he's got a lovely sense of humour and that's fun to get across. You'd imagine with his lonely personal life he'd be a bit depressing. But not a bit. There are lots of facets to him. I admire him because he's opinionated and because he's totally dedicated which is one of the reasons he's lonely at times.'

The role of Frost proved a physical challenge for David, quite apart from asking him to achieve a major change of direction. While filming the final episodes of *The Darling Buds of May*, he had piled on the pounds. For a small man, he was now considerably bulky and he knew it.

'I realised that wouldn't look right for Frost,' he said. 'Frost would look lean and hungry. On my TV set at home I had a picture of myself in my dinner jacket at an awards ceremony and I remember putting on the same dinner jacket after not wearing it for a year and thinking I'd better have a button moved. When I later saw photos of myself, I realised it wasn't the button's fault. I was like the Michelin man. I was huge.

'During the filming of *The Darling Buds of May*, I was eating 24 hours a day. The problem was that the food on the set was real and one morning we were filming two different episodes. Spread over the two shows were five scenes which all took place at breakfast which I had to eat with great gusto. So that morning I had no less than five breakfasts.

'It finally got to the point where I felt I couldn't take bacon and eggs any more and I asked for fish instead. I had to tuck into a huge cod and for different camera angles I had to eat it several times. In the afternoon, for tea we had huge slices of bread, ham and cheese, even though we weren't hungry. I just went up like a balloon.

'For *Frost* I knew I had to put myself on a strict, mainly fish diet. I cut out biscuits and toast and anything in-between meals and, when I was hungry, I'd just eat a couple of apples or an orange instead of tucking into a sandwich. Because I'm naturally a slim man, it fell away quite quickly. I lost a stone and a quarter on this strict diet and, although it was hard, I'm glad I did it.'

David also chose to set a personal example about cigarette smoking in *A Touch of Frost*.

'Frost is a chain-smoker in the books and that was very much part of his character,' he says. 'But I felt we should be socially aware and mindful that a lot of people were trying to give it up. So I told Yorkshire TV I wasn't going to chain-smoke on screen. For a start, I'd fall over dead – although I do smoke a bit, maybe a few cigarettes in the evening, but none during the day. What I asked was, "Do we need this socially?" It's not a good idea any more to smoke. So we hit on the idea of making Frost a smoker who is giving up the habit. That way, the idea was there all the time, but I didn't actually chain-smoke.

'I had to smoke a couple of cigarettes, but mainly I was lighting up and being told to stub it out. I feel I must set an example. It's the same with swearing on TV. I always ask: "Do we need it?" I want more people to watch me, not less. That means families watching and I believe you can be real on TV without resorting to the language of the gutter. I don't like going past a bus stop and hearing loads of kids aged seven or eight effing and blinding.

'When I was a kid, I used to get a whack if I said the word "bloody". And if we were standing at a bus stop being a bit rowdy, we'd get a clip round the ear from a man who'd say, "Cut that out, there's ladies present." We might have pulled a face behind the man's back but we certainly shut up.

'So, if I don't like swearing, why should I encourage people to do it? I feel the question as far as TV goes should be "Can we avoid it? Do we need it?" People may say, "Ah yes, but people swear in real life." Yes, they do. But do you like it?'

Eschewing the sex and violence which has often been so fashionable in TV cop shows, *A Touch of Frost* captured that crucial audience and prospered beyond everyone's hopes at Yorkshire TV.

But after the remarkable ratings for the three 1996 Christmas episodes of *Only Fools and Horses* when Del and Rodney did finally become millionaires, Yorkshire Television executives could be forgiven for some anxiety as they prepared to launch their final series of *A Touch of Frost* just six weeks later. Would David's triumphant return as Del-Boy over Christmas have harmed the public's perception of him as Jack Frost, they wondered. After all, a staggering 23.4 million viewers had watched the final episode with the first two of the three pulling in over 22 million each. These were the sort of figures that had not been seen since the early 1970s, in the days when there were only three television channels. Once again, the image of David Jason as Del-Boy had been stamped firmly in the nation's mind.

But if producer Martyn Auty had any real fears for his new batch of four two-hour dramas, they were quickly dispelled when the first episode, *Penny for the Guy*, was screened on ITV on 9 February 1997. It was a strong storyline centred on a major case of kidnapping, following the discovery of the body of a young boy dumped in a shop doorway. Frost knows he is dealing with a cool customer capable of amputating a child's little finger. But he comes close to losing his own cool when he realises he's got his man but doesn't have a scrap of evidence.

Once again, David and Frost delivered. An audience of 16 million viewers tuned in, a staggeringly high rating considering the alternative BBC attraction ranged against *Frost* was the popular drama *Ballykissangel*. David's return to the *Frost* beat thus decimated the BBC's traditional dominance of the Sunday night ratings and that set the tone for another compelling series in which Frost investigated child abuse, juvenile murder and kidnapping, armed robbery and an apparent suicide.

The new series featured two adaptations from the original *Frost* book. Both were written by Malcolm Bradbury whose writing connections with David dated back to *Porterhouse*

Blue. 'Although Malcolm hadn't done much detective drama, he took to the genre like a duck to water,' said Auty. 'And his name helped us attract top directors.'

For his part, Malcolm Bradbury appreciated the challenge. 'I enjoyed adapting the two episodes because Frost is a very strong character,' he said. 'I have favourites like Agatha Christie, Edgar Wallace and Reginald Hill who created *Dalziel and Pascoe*. The best always have that well-defined central character, so you are writing about an individual who is also a policeman. So, for that reason, you can put *Frost* in the same league as *Inspector Morse*.'

For devotees of *A Touch of Frost*, there were several changes to savour. A little more was revealed of Frost the man, as he became involved with three women, although not at the same time.

The last time viewers had witnessed Frost living over a curry house after his home had burned down. Now viewers saw him staying with, indeed in bed with, ex-good time girl Kitty (Gwyneth Powell) before moving on to another woman.

The four episodes also saw Frost working out of a new police station. Yorkshire TV already had the building but designed a new set from scratch to reflect the modern look. Despite a new canteen, however, Frost was still seen munching on his fast-food snacks, especially his old favourites, bacon sandwiches. Frost was also given a computer – but mistook it for a microwave and left a pork pie on top.

As in previous series, Frost also found himself working with new colleagues and had to deal with his prickly relationship with DS Liz Maud, played by Susannah Doyle. Two faces new to *Frost* – but not to David – included Gwyneth Strong and Arthur White, David's brother. Gwyneth had, of course, played Rodney's wife Cassandra in *Only Fools and Horses*, and now she was cast as a high-flying plain clothes officer D S Bailey, who gave Frost an uncomfortable interrogation.

'I enjoyed that scene immensely,' Gwyneth enthused. 'After so many years as Cassandra, it felt like I had the power on my side for a change.'

David was pleased to say that he felt the new series achieved the high quality viewers had come to expect. 'It's difficult to be inventive and meet those standards we have set ourselves,' he said. 'We avoid being predictable by being a little more off-the-wall in the cases Frost has to investigate.'

In one important scene, David had to be filmed wading into a river in the middle of winter. 'It's one of the perks of the job,' he joked. But there were other moments to treasure.

'We had a massive demolition caterpillar truck on location to film a house being knocked down and I got to drive it between shooting. It was really fantastic, but knocking down a brick wall is not as easy as you might think.

'Then I went up in a helicopter when we were filming at the end of the pier at Blackpool. Some guys running joyrides offered to take me up for a spin. I told the director and producer and they went white.

'Earlier in the year, I'd managed to fly a Harrier Jump -Jet. They reach speeds of 500 knots and it was a totally exhilarating experience. It was the ultimate ride.'

David and his brother Arthur shared some excellent comic scenes in the last series of *A Touch of Frost*. Arthur played quirky collator Ernie Trigg, the copper in charge of the station files and the source on endless meticulously ordered information who became one of Jack Frost's closer confidants. The brothers worked wonderfully well together and it gave Arthur the chance to move, for a moment, out of the shadow of his more famous younger brother.

Arthur said, 'In the early days, people would say to Dave, "Aren't you Arthur White's brother?" Now it's the other way round, of course.'

Although the brothers shared a bedroom as youngsters, they were not close as teenagers. Arthur is very cautious about talking publicly about his relationship with his brother but he did try to describe his feelings.

'Being an elder brother by seven years makes one hell of a difference. For example, when David was still at school, I was preparing to go in the Army to do my National Service. By the time I came back, he had changed and so had I. So our early beginnings of getting to know each other as brothers were interrupted and never quite matured until later. I remember the days of the Blitz and parts of peoples' bodies landing on our roof. David and I used to share a crystal set.

'I remember when I had become an actor, my wife Joy and I had a party and David, still an electrician, was invited and said to Joy, "They are bloody theatricals, no one wants to talk to me." And apart from us, no one did, except my old friend Edna Dore who spoke at great length to him. She was a great help in changing his mind about "bloody theatricals". Gawd bless her, we still say.

'We share a mutual respect of each other's work, and a brotherly bond of love. I introduced him into the theatre, getting him his first job. And my first advice as he finished work was "No, I'm not introducing you into the world of TV." At the time I was co-starring in *Crane*, *Orlando*, *A Place to Hide*, etc. I said to him, "Go out into rep and learn like I had to." He did! And the rest, as they say ...

'We have worked a lot together in the early days of his TV work. In fact, we did a commercial together where I played a ventriloquist and David played the dummy. It came from larking about down the Green Room Actor's Club I had introduced him to. I shoved my hand up his jacket after someone had said, "Who's working him?" Our natural inborn sense of comedy and timing and David's ability to become a vent doll had them in stitches. We even went around some clubs hoping we would make a good sideline with the act.

'I have very fond memories of our days when we were out of work, spent taking my wife's Mini to bits and putting it back together, jugs of cheap wine afterwards with Joy's superb dinners. We'd have theatre chat around the table, and play games of Monopoly. We watched the first moonwalk with my son Russell. David got him up to see history even though he was only one year old. I am vastly proud of his achievements.'

On 2 March 1997, ITV screened the emotional finale to *A Touch of Frost*. David had millions of viewers dewy-eyed as he shed genuine tears on screen as Frost grieved over the death of a woman friend. The scene was all the more moving because the nation knew he was drawing on the harrowing personal experience of watching his beloved Myfanwy Talog's own decline towards death.

'It was an incredibly difficult scene to do,' said David, 'the hardest I've ever done.'

FAME

David Jason will go to any lengths to get away from
it all. When the pressures of fame and constant
recognition build up too much, he loves to escape high into
the clouds or deep into the ocean. Autograph hunters and
nosy journalists are left a long way behind because action
man David's idea of relaxation is following one of his two
favourite dangerous sports – flying a glider hundreds of
feet above the ground or scuba diving off the remote
Cayman Islands.

He is honest enough to accept that the perilous nature of
both pastimes is part of the appeal. 'I suppose the edge of
danger is quite attractive,' he says frankly.

'But that is part of the challenge. I am a very physical person
and I get an indescribably warm feeling doing things that are a
real physical challenge. I am not a big one for just lying on a
beach sizzling in the sun for hours on end. I think I would get
pretty bored with that pretty soon. I can't play ball games very

well, I can't hit a tennis, golf or snooker ball. But I do love to get involved with something physically demanding.'

That enthusiasm for a challenge has brought David into real life-threatening danger in both air and sea.

He learned to fly a glider at the London Gliding Club in Dunstable, Bedfordshire, where he shared the hire-purchase payments on a glider with a few close friends. It took him six months' practise and training before he made his first solo flight. David always found it very exhilarating until the day he took off in completely the wrong mood.

'I was flying with not the right attitude of mind. I went up when I had had a row with somebody and because the row was more on my mind than flying the aircraft, when I came into land my mind was not really on the job. And I really messed the landing up. I did a ground loop and ripped the bottom out of the aeroplane. It was a very hairy moment. I thought, "This is it, I've had it. What a bloody stupid way to go!"

'I was coming in far too fast. And there was a cross wind and I was just coming in too quickly and got it all wrong. If a wing touches the ground – which you must never do – it's all right if you are travelling really slowly, but if you are moving at quite a high speed then you can go into a ground loop. The whole plane spins and does a somersault. My wing tip hit the ground and the plane went right over and I thought I was a goner. I was terrified. It was not a very pleasant experience.

'Amazingly, I was not injured. I couldn't believe I had got out of it without a scratch. I was all right but I ripped the bottom out of this aeroplane, and I was very very shocked. It put me off flying for a bit. It made me wonder what I was doing up there for a while. "Why do I do this?" I thought. But it is all part of the challenge.'

David is also a qualified and experienced diver after becoming interested in the sport when he saw an under-water film on television at the age of 18. During his several spells of summer seasons at Bournemouth, he startled the rest of the cast by arriving on the packed beach complete with scuba equipment.

'They fell about in hysterics when I began getting into my rubber wet-suit, pulling on the flippers and mask,' recalls David. But when he returned from the sea with a dozen tasty mullet '... their expressions changed to hunger.'

But there was no mullet on the menu much more recently when David spent a week in the Cayman Islands and encountered a crisis 100 feet down.

'Two years ago, I went to the Caymans and completed a dive-master course. It was a full, concentrated week and I dived every day and when I had finished diving at four o'clock I went back to study the diving manuals and took all the tests. I spent seven solid days diving and studying. It was really a way of switching off and I wanted to be better at diving than I was, that's why I enrolled for the course.

'The problem happened on my first dive. Would you believe it? It would have to happen on the very first one. One of the things you have to do to qualify as a dive master is to conduct a dive, supervise other divers. You start by briefing them on board the ship, take them through the dive and then bring them all safely to the surface. Instructors watch you at every stage.

'I gave the initial briefing and provided the dive plan which was to do a 20-minute dive to 100 feet below the surface and then carefully come up. You always ensure that you have more than enough air to get safely through the exercise. You make sure you are never on what they call the "high profile" for decompression. You need a safety margin.

'And to make sure you don't come up too fast, you always get all the people on the dive into a decompression spot. You make a three-minute safety stop at 15 feet for total insurance. And one of the things you insist on, if you are in charge of the dive, is that the others do not go below you.

'Anyway, it was my responsibility to control everything. And I was watching one of the guys on the dive – half your experience is you are taught to observe people carefully, and try to make nervous people feel calm – and he is putting weights into his life-jacket. So I went up to this guy and said, "Do you really need all those weights?" He said he had about 12 pounds.

'That's heavy and he had not got a wet-suit on. He was putting all these weights in his life-jacket. I felt I might have trouble with this guy unless I was careful.

'So, anyway, we all got in the water and swam down to 100 feet and I am in charge of five people on my first dive. Suddenly, I see this guy below me and he is down to 110 feet and sinking. I went down and motioned to him to go up and he went up. Then, when I turned round again, he started to go down again. I motioned to the others to stay where they were. And this guy is going down to 120 feet. I kept waving at him to get up but he kept constantly sinking down again.

'Soon, we needed to go back up and all this messing about meant I was beginning to run short of air. I was very unhappy with him because all the time I spent chasing after him meant I was pushing the limit of my decompression time. I was really not very happy because every time I went down for him meant that my profile was getting higher, which might mean another decompression stop which I wanted to avoid.

'Eventually, we are just about to return to the surface and this bloody guy signals that he is running low on air. I went over to him again and saw his dial was right on the red for danger. He was supposed to have told me, the man in charge, long before, so I could have aborted the dive safely. He has exhausted a lot of his air inflating the device to keep bringing himself up.

'So I signal to everyone to go up and we all get to the decompression stop. And there is a hang bar at six feet which is another slight safety measure. This guy should still have been all right. But he goes to the hang bar and he signals he is completely out of air. I am starting to worry a bit now, and I looked at these two instructors just floating there watching me with their arms crossed. And they didn't do anything. They turned their backs. I was really panicking then because I had to share the last of my air from my mask with this guy. I had to calm him down and put my mask in his face. Somehow, I got him up to the steps and on board. But it was all I needed on my very first test.

'I was quite polite to this guy afterwards when he said he was all right. I told him he must remember the rules. But when we got back to the shore the two instructors came up to me and said, "Well, you have learned something today. But you were far too easy on that guy who ran out of air. You should have given him a really big bollocking. That guy endangered his own life but he also endangered yours. If anyone ever does that again, you must give them a real dressing down."

'But that is what you take on when you start diving. If you want the responsibility of being a dive master that is what it is all about.'

It can take David Jason anything up to 20 minutes to do the simplest of shopping. He can spend five minutes choosing a shirt, perhaps, and another 15 politely having to put up with other shoppers slapping him on the back, asking for autographs, enquiring after Rodney, or pleading with him to just come over and say a quick hello to the wife.

The extraordinary mateyness with which the general public regards Derek Trotter, plus the genuine affection they have for David's other well-known characters, such as Granville and Pop Larkin, means that, all too often, his life is not his own.

Recently, at a party a fellow guest was asking David to do something for a charity and when David said he was sorry but he simply could not fit it in, the man's wife grabbed David in a headlock and would not let go.

There was even an occasion when David was followed into a gentleman's lavatory by a fan who attempted to shake his hand while it was otherwise engaged.

If you spot David at a restaurant, it's more than likely his back will be to the entrance. If he faces the majority of diners there is every chance his meal will be constantly interrupted by strangers just wanting to say hello.

Top showbiz writer and author Gareth Pearce was astonished at the reaction of fellow diners while lunching with David at L'Etoile restaurant in Charlotte Street in 1988 when he was enjoying unparallelled success in *Only Fools and Horses*. This was a smart restaurant where the lunch bill came to £68 a head.

'Two men separately came over with their table napkins and asked David to autograph them,' Pearce recalls.

'They had actually taken the trouble to buy the napkins from the manager of the restaurant just so they could get David's autograph. Also, while we were there, a bubbly woman from Inverness staying at the Meridian Hotel in Piccadilly for a couple of days, rushed up and greeted David like a long-lost friend. She was a complete stranger to him. Then, when we left the restaurant, a pretty girl raced up to David in the street and planted a kiss on his cheek. The popularity of the man was, and is, astonishing.'

Pearce's lunch with David took place just 17 days before Christmas and, looking ahead to the festivities, David commented, 'I want to go home, lock the door, sit in front of the TV and relax. I can understand people who want to have drinks and parties. For me, that can happen any time during the year. I want to be able to turn off at Christmas.

'I shall be going to see my brother and sister in Brighton. They might have a few people round, which is great if I know them. But if I don't, I have to start talking again about all the things I do.'

Fame does not rest easily on David's shoulders. 'I'd love to do the work I do and have the benefit of being able to go to a restaurant or pub or anywhere and be totally anonymous like everyone else,' he says. 'The fame, the intrusion, the lack of privacy is very odd. It's just something I don't enjoy.

'People think they'd enjoy it. They think it would be wonderful to be recognised. But it's not.'

The days when David felt able to use public transport have long gone. 'If you get trapped on a train, you're public property,' he points out. 'I had a nasty experience when I was working in Hammersmith and travelled by Underground from my flat. I met a wally who attacked me for nothing. He was a coloured lad – quite smart – but he had a big chip on his shoulder.

'He saw me at 9.30am and started to have a go and push me about. I had a big bag with me containing my cheque book, wallet, and lots of personal stuff, and I thought that if I put it down he'd have a partner somewhere who was going to whip it away. But if I was to whack him one, there was no way I could hit him with a bag around my shoulder.

'So I had to take this rather humiliating experience. He didn't hit me. He just knocked my hat off. There were all these people looking. It can happen to anybody but I thought, "Oh, do I need this in my life? Do I need to go to rehearsals like this? No, dammit, I'll either go by taxi or by car."'

David was not so lucky the night he went to the aid of a girl he saw being attacked in London's Soho. He had been dining with a friend and while his friend went ahead to find a taxi, David saw a woman being punched by a man across the street. There was another man egging the thug on but, bravely, David decided to intervene.

'I went over and said, "Can I mediate?" which was a really

stupid thing to do but I was afraid and I thought that by trying to be reasonably nice they'd be reasonably nice back.

'Unfortunately, the two guys, who had their backs to me, took offence and I got really badly beaten up. I said, "Excuse me, is there some problem?" and I don't remember much after that except my head ringing and, in total shock, I realised I was being hit. I got seven shades beaten out of me.'

One of the thugs punched David so hard in the face that he fell backwards into a wall some yards away. Then they put the boot in.

'I remember falling on the floor and thinking that I was really going to sort the problem out,' he says. 'And then I passed out.'

The thugs continued to beat David senseless until his friend reappeared with a taxi and dragged David away by his jacket collar and into the cab.

'He bundled me into a taxi and the last thing I remember before passing out was seeing one of the blokes hitting the woman again as we drove past. We went back to my friend's flat and each time I had a bath I discovered more bruises. I was a real mess. I should probably have gone to hospital.

'Strange as it sounds,' he reflects, 'I thought I could make people stop hitting each other and talk. It was very naïve and it's made me think about going to the rescue of damsels ever since. I'm not one of the world's natural fighters – I'm just too busy trying to survive.'

Just before *The Darling Buds of May* brought David a whole new wave of affection from the general public, he admitted, 'I hardly go out at all. It's not bad where I live because they've got used to me. But I still don't go out very much socially to pubs, only because it does create an interest.

'People do want to come and talk to you and buy you a drink and I can't blame them for that. They want to know what's going on with Rodney and when we are coming back on TV. You can never really relax wherever you sit. People come up and are usually very nice but you can never get away from yourself.

'So what I tend to do is to go and see friends and go round to dinner with them or stay in. I watch an awful lot of television. I mess about with my motorbikes. I only do it because I know what's going to happen if I go anywhere.'

The constant attention of the fans has become a particular burden for David to bear when he goes shopping.

'I have to steel myself,' he admitted. 'If I want to go and buy a pair of shoes, I think, "Do I really need these shoes or this tie?" I tend not to buy clothes.

"I don't want to go and buy anything, so I save it all up until I think I have to go. I know what's going to happen. It's not much fun when people shout at you in the street. Again, you can't blame them.

'I find it a bit of a strain to keep having to explain to people what I'm doing and what Ronnie Barker or Nick Lyndhurst is like. It makes you very tired. So I found that I was staying in more and more. But in order to stay in, I needed something to do.'

To this end, David has developed a hobby he can enjoy at home – restoring motorbikes and old fairground machines. The outbuildings at his Buckinghamshire home are a treasure trove of old machines of all descriptions and his frequent partner in grime is Brian Cosgrove. Whenever David Jason is in the north of England, he stays at Brian Cosgrove's home near Manchester.

Brian says, 'My wife always laughingly refers to herself as his northern landlady. I think he first stayed when he was in a play in Wilmslow, and he would come back late at night and Angela would cook him meat and two veg and we would sit and talk until one or two in the morning as he eased down after his performance.

'We do share an interest in old machines, but we also have an understanding not to talk about it too much. We do both enjoy that sort of do-it-yourself small engineering, but once a thing like that gets talked about too much and written about too much in magazines and people ask you about it, then it somehow takes the edge off it.

'But it is one of those things where you get your old clothes on and get covered in oil and have a darn good time "being normal". You get back to the time when you were a young fellow before you had done anything and there is something very nice about that, something very relaxing, and something very private that I am reluctant to spoil. We just want to enjoy it.'

The two men have worked together on a variety of old machines, from aged fairground sideshows to vintage motorcycles.

'It is nice facing little challenges of whatever we are working on rather than the big challenges of everyday life,' Brian says. 'We work well together because David is very good mechanically and I bring the artistic side to it. And we each have our own way of solving problems, whatever we are working on. I do it in an artistic way but David has a great engineering talent.

'He is particularly good with old motorbikes. He can take them to bits and put them together again with great ease. But if you put together two chaps with those different approaches it works well. And we just love to work together, we each enjoy what the other guy does. It gives us both feedback. We are forever saying, "It's great what you've done there, terrific." It happens in such a little way but it is important. It's like telling a keen gardener what a smashing garden he has produced. The lift we both get from it is important. It is one of life's little pleasures and we both prize and protect it.'

Brian's love for machines encompassed everything from

pin-ball to penny slot. But there was one fairground machine in particular which fascinated David called *Marvo The Mystic* which featured a doll with a cone in his hand. When a penny was inserted in the slot, the eyes went up and down, the wand was waved and, with the help of a cone, he could make things disappear.

David was so enthralled by this machine that he went on and on at Brian asking him how much he wanted for it. Finally, Cosgrove said: 'If you really want it so much, why don't we make one? We'll take it to bits and build it again.'

The next time David was in Manchester, he and Cosgrove went down into Cosgrove's cellar and took the Marvo machine apart.

'For the next two years, we re-built it,' David says proudly. 'Twice I was on tour and I used to stay with Brian working on *Marvo The Mystic*. Brian is a great artist whereas, as he says, I tend to concentrate on the mechanical side. I'm a great one for mechanical things. I suppose it's because I was an electrician and I was taught engineering.'

If fame has made David somewhat reclusive, those who work with him say they have never seen him get angry with fans, however rudely they might have been interrupting his life.

Writer David Nobbs travelled on a train with David from London to Leeds and witnessed a stream of well-wishers and fans who all wanted to ask about Rodney or to call him a plonker or a dipstick for the 400th time that morning. The breakfast that David was trying to eat was cold by the time they arrived. As they got off the train, Nobbs remarked that such attention must be difficult to deal with. Nobbs said, 'David just looked at me and said, "Well, those people are the reason why I am not still an electrician."'

His fan mail appears to cover all ages and two fan letters in particular stick in David's mind. The first followed the episode in which Rodney got married and Del-Boy was left all on his own at the reception. It was a wonderful, bitter-sweet moment and soon afterwards David received a letter from a woman who said that after seeing this scene her three-year-old daughter had not been able to get to sleep and had ended up crying all night and that the only thing she wanted in the world was for Del to go and live with her. It was not the first time David had been aware that *Only Fools and Horses* is watched by people of all ages.

The second letter that David has never forgotten came from a woman who wrote to him to say that every appearance he made on TV had a strange effect on her cat. The cat "loves you," ran the letter. What tickled David pink was that, to prove it, the woman had enclosed a photograph of her moggy gazing adoringly at the TV with David on the screen!

MARCH

In the very first series of *A Touch of Frost*, Frost's screen wife had died of cancer and subsequent series revealed that, after years of loneliness, Frost had enjoyed a love-life brightened by occasional passionate flings.

The parallels in David's own life were apparent for all to see when by October 1996, 18 months after Myfanwy had died, there was a new woman in his life. She was former Yorkshire TV assistant Gill Hinchcliffe who first emerged at David's side, happily basking in his reflected glory, at London's Royal Albert Hall where David received a standing ovation as he accepted a Special Recognition award at the National Television Awards presentation.

Gill, who had joined Yorkshire TV as a secretary and had steadily worked her way up, had first met David when he was making *A Bit of a Do* and they had subsequently worked together on *A Touch of Frost*. A long-serving Yorkshire TV employee noted, 'Gill often used to be in the bar with her boyfriend who was much older than she was. We thought he was her father but he was pretty unhappy at the suggestion and was always very protective. Gill always liked older men. She said she felt more comfortable with them than 'boys', as she called them, of her own age. Nothing sparked between them until long after Myfanwy's death, we could all see it happening on the production. It wasn't at all sudden, they just gradually seemed to be spending a lot of time with each other. Gill was totally smitten. David can be quite charismatic and very, very funny.

'At first she was quite in awe of him. Anyone who has seen him act knows what an incredible talent he has and wherever he goes, even though he's a little guy, he just has this amazing presence. When he comes into a room, if he's in the mood, he can completely dominate any occasion.

'Gill told a pal they were really good friends for quite a long time before they became lovers. He was very respectful and old-fashioned even. There were lots of bouquets of flowers and candle-lit dinners for two. I guess Gill's warmth and David's loneliness was the start of it. Everyone in the crew was delighted when they got together, they make a lovely couple.'

Gill, an attractive 37-year-old blonde, and David looked radiantly happy arm-in-arm at the star-studded party after the awards. Even The Spice Girls were momentarily ignored by photographers as they jostled each other for pictures of David Jason with the new woman in his life who, it was noted, bore some resemblance to Myfanwy with her sparkling eyes, ready smile and cropped hair.

Taking Gill to the awards was a very public statement by David that he had found love again and that he now did not care who knew it. Nor, it seemed, did Gill's mother.

'They are meant for each other. They make a wonderful pair and they are very much in love,' said Mrs. Hinchcliffe at her home at Mirfield, West Yorkshire.

Gill's mother had been impressed with David when Gill brought him home to tea one day. 'He's a wonderful man, very considerate and charming,' she said. 'And she's a wonderful girl who deserves happiness. She's not extrovert or bubbly – just very nice. Gillian is very grown up and knows what she is doing. Her romance with David was certainly no surprise to us.'

Unlike Myfanwy, Gill had observed David's work at close quarters during her time at Yorkshire TV and she was very aware of the effort he always put in and the strain he had been under to continue with *A Touch of Frost* while trying to come to terms with his grief over Myfanwy. Gill saw the way he worried away at his lines to get them absolutely perfect and how he found it difficult to wind down after a performance.

Gill also understood that she had become a soft shoulder for him to rely on. But it was not until David and Gill flew out to the Montreux TV festival as guests of the BBC in the spring of 1997 that he was able to reveal the extent of Gill's influence in his life.

'She's great,' he said. 'People are always asking me to do things all the time and I find it hard to relax. But she shields me from all of that pressure. She takes all my phonecalls and keeps me relaxed so that I have to do the minimum of work. It's so nice to have someone as lovely as her who is so caring and loving, especially after what I've been through.'

Gill has been a calming influence and when she and David flew off for a romantic holiday on the Caribbean island of Providenciales, David was able to see 1997 stretching ahead of him with no TV projects firmed up. He was physically and mentally exhausted and it was his first real carefree holiday for many years. During their sun-filled fortnight at a luxurious £2,000-a-night villa overlooking the sea, David did little more strenuous than swim, snorkel and hire a four-wheel-drive Suzuki to see the local sites on the island which covers only 28 square miles. On secluded beaches they lovingly held hands as they strode into the sea. But even behind dark glasses, and by now sporting a small grey beard, he still found his fame had followed him to such a remote setting. Emerging one day from a frolic in the sea with Gill, a young British holiday-maker looked up and exclaimed to his parents, 'Look, it's Del-Boy! What are you doing here, you dipstick?'

As Christmas 1996 approached, David had made plans to spend the festivities with Gill at his 18th-century farmhouse. It was a joyous occasion, so different from the year before when he was still mourning Myfanwy's loss.

Together, they both sat down to watch the last episodes of *Only Fools and Horses*. Just a few months before, David's loyal fans had voted him Favourite Situation Comedy Performer at the BBC's Auntie's All-Time Greats Awards ceremony, celebrating the Corporation's 60th birthday.

That award was another treasured moment in a remarkable year for David. It was a year in which he had found new love and rounded off *Only Fools and Horses*, the TV series which had enthralled, entertained, and endeared him to the nation.

Four months later, Gill was with him glowing with pride again as her famous lover received yet another standing ovation when David scored a double triumph at the BAFTA Awards. He won the Best TV Comedy Performance award for the *Only Fools and Horses* Christmas Special and the show itself was named Best TV Comedy.

'Lovely jubbly,' said David as he collected his award.

His career seemed to be going from strength to strength.

Scouring the ocean depths in a bathysphere with glamorous actress Linda Hamilton in a big screen movie would appeal to most men. Given David's love of the undersea world and his ambition to break into movies, he was understandably excited when he found himself in line to play an eccentric Englishman in just such an adventure movie alongside Linda, known to millions of moviegoers from *Terminator* and *Terminator II*.

Hollywood, it seemed, was perhaps beckoning David at last. But the movie industry is littered with projects which never get off the ground and this opportunity for David to step into big time films was destined tantalisingly to pass him by.

David had liked the synopsis and was definitely interested but before he could get to read a script the project abruptly fell from his grasp through no fault of his own. Linda Hamilton, actress wife of *Titanic* director James Cameron, was snapped up for another film. 'She pulled out and the film project collapsed like a pack of cards,' David reflected ruefully.

But as 1997 drew to a close, David had plenty to cheer him. He had been named Top TV Actor at the British Comedy Awards, and at the prestigious National Television Awards in London he was crowned the undisputed king of British TV when he scooped three top gongs.

He pipped big names including Rowan Atkinson and Harry Enfield to be voted Most Popular Comedy Performer for his Del Boy role in *Only Fools and Horses*.

He also picked up the Most Popular Comedy Programme award for the show's Christmas Special the previous year. No mean achievement considering the stiff opposition from *Birds of a Feather*, *Friends*, and *Men Behaving Badly*.

But best of all, he was named Most Popular Actor for *A Touch of Frost* and took the award ahead of American idol George Clooney in the hospital drama *ER*, Robson Green, and Ross Kemp of *EastEnders*.

It was a triple triumph greeted with thunderous applause at London's Albert Hall.

David was clearly overwhelmed as he stepped up to collect his awards sporting the bushy beard he had grown for his new TV role of a British spy in *March In Windy City* which was scheduled to be shown in the spring of 1998.

The heartiest cheer was reserved for David when he went up to receive the programme award with his *Only*

Fools co-stars Nicholas Lyndhurst and Buster Merryfield. 'I am going to miss it more than anything,' said David of the now-ended sitcom.

David had topped off his year by giving TV viewers a remarkable insight into the underwater world he so enjoys in a new Yorkshire TV documentary series *David Jason In His Element*.

Instead of Linda Hamilton, David's companions in the deep and dangerous waters off Florida and the Bahamas turned out to be sharks, dolphins, stingrays and a sick turtle which he helped nurture back to life and return to the sea with its health fully restored.

David's courage simply had to be admired when he was seen scuba-diving in the Caribbean with man-eating sharks swimming menacingly around him.

As one brushed against his leg, David's instructor had to warn David not to move.

'It was an exhilarating experience but not one that I want to repeat too often,' he said when he came up for air. 'It was scary. The sharks were hungry and I was glad I hadn't cut myself shaving that morning

'I was aware that if anything went wrong, I wouldn't have stood much of a chance. There were 50 or 60 sharks around me and I knew if one of them accidentally happened to hit me or draw blood, then I wouldn't be here now."

For once, *David Jason In His Element* gave everyone just a glimpse of the man behind all the characters he plays. Underwater he seemed most thoroughly at ease. Clearly David saw plunging to the ocean depths as a generally peaceful occupation, especially since he had given up flying lessons. He had imagined at first that flying would help him unwind but admitted it used to stress him out because handling an aeroplane can be a high pressure experience.

Back on dry land in *David Jason In His Element* he appeared uneasy having to be just himself for the cameras as he wandered around harbourside bars, sampled raw conch, and talked to the locals. For once there was no dramatic character for him to hide behind or immerse himself in, just an inviting ocean.

On March 25, 1998, David Jason faced one of the toughest challenges of his illustrious acting career. After Del Boy, Pop Larkin and Jack Frost, he now had to persuade British television viewers that he could slip convincingly into a new role playing Steven March, a former MI5 operative lured back into action in Chicago after falling on impecunious times.

March in Windy City, a two-hour thriller made by Yorkshire Television, had been eagerly awaited, not least because it seemed fated never to happen. It had taken four years to bring the film finally to the screen and it was completed only after the project had been temporarily abandoned for two years.

So it was with relief all round that ITV was able to clear its schedules on a Wednesday night to present David in his new guise sporting a grey beard and natty tweed suits as a British secret agent and assassin.

He played March as an eccentric operative who had been the victim of compulsory retirement but was now desperately required back in action after a Russian Mafioso named Dimitri Petrovsky had re-surfaced in Chicago.

Alarmingly, Petrovsky had re-invented himself as an on-the-level businessman Dan Paterson who had become a naturalised American citizen and was now running for Senate office.

With the very real threat of a Russian gangster operating in the top corridors of American power, security chiefs decided that this danger must be 'taken out'. March, who has good reason for exacting his revenge on the Russian, is invited to be the assassin with the bait of a fee of $50,000 dollars from MI6. Bored with his civilian life and hard up, how can he refuse?

Arriving in Chicago, March is assigned two detectives – Joe

Riggs and Grace Wallace – as 'babysitters', although they are kept in the dark as to the real reason for March's mission.

He manages to lure Petrovsky into a trap but then discovers that the Mafia man's daughter has been kidnapped by the FBI and it becomes hard for March and the police to tell who are the good guys or the bad guys.

The idea for *March In Windy City* was first broached over a dinner between David and Geoff McQueen who shared a mutual admiration for each other's work.

It was McQueen who had created the popular comedy-drama series *Stay Lucky* for Yorkshire TV back in 1989 and David had a high opinion of his writing talents. McQueen, for his part, pronounced himself a huge fan of David's and the convivial dinner ended with the two men agreeing they should work together.

McQueen went away and enthusiastically began drafting an outline for a story a about a British agent brought out of retirement for one last mission in America. But, quite suddenly, McQueen died, and all thoughts of developing the project were instantly abandoned.

It was some two years later before the possibility of reviving it was seriously mooted once more. Both David and David Reynolds, his great friend at Yorkshire TV, felt that to complete the project would be a tribute to McQueen.

'If we hadn't started working on it again when we did, then it would have definitely gone on for ever,' Reynolds reflects. 'It would have lost its freshness and we wouldn't have had the same enthusiasm.'

David Jason was so enamoured with the project that he decided that the time was right to have even more input into his television work by taking on, for the first time, the additional onus of Executive Producer, joining forces with Reynolds.

Thomas Ellice was approached to write a script. Importantly for David who likes to have a tried and trusted team around him, Ellice was known to David, not only as a quality writer, but as the husband of actress Jan Francis who had starred in McQueen's hugely popular Yorkshire TV comedy-drama series *Stay Lucky*.

David knew the couple socially and had been grateful for their warm hospitality while filming *The Darling Buds of May*. On several occasions, they had welcomed David into their picturesque home overlooking a village green deep in the Kent countryside just a few miles from the *Darling Buds of May* film locations.

Gradually the idea of *March In Windy City* was fleshed out.

Everyone agreed that it was too soon after *A Touch of Frost* for David to play another policeman but portraying a spy was a very different proposition.

'We came up with the idea of Steven March as a spy because James Bond is the wrong sort of spy because he actually looks like a spy,' Reynolds explained. 'We felt it would be cleverer if a spy was someone who looked like David.'

Anxious as he was to spread his wings as an Executive Producer, David saw great merit in setting the film abroad, thus exploring a different culture in the story.

New York was an option but the choice narrowed to Chicago.

'It was a different backdrop, while still obviously American,' said Reynolds, and producer Martin Auty felt he could capitalise on Chicago's visually exciting skyline. On the downside, as the accountants were soon aware, Chicago is one of the few US cities which still maintains a 6 per cent entertainment tax. The tax payment they had to stump up would have allowed the crew another two days' shooting.

With David firmly and enthusiastically in place to star as March, the hunt was on for an actor of sufficient stature in the eyes of American audiences to take the role of the Russian Mafioso Dimitri Petrovsky who resurfaces in Chicago.

Auty spoke with a number of actors in the USA, but he felt

none of them was totally suitable. Then he had a flash of inspiration. He remembered that David McCallum, perhaps best known as Ilya Kuryakin in the Sixties spoof spy series *The Man From UNCLE*, lived in New York. Not only did McCallum have star quality and a solid reputation as an actor, but Chicago for him would be just an easy plane hop away. Crucially, while David Jason was not a name that would automatically register with American audiences, David McCallum's would.

Equally important for Auty was that he had worked with McCallum on another Yorkshire TV series *Heartbeat* three years earlier and the two men had got on well both professionally and personally.

Born in Glasgow, McCallum had first gone to Hollywood in 1962 to play Judas in the film *The Greatest Story Ever Told* and had lived in America almost permanently ever since. But he had retained a British passport and had comfortably managed to work fruitfully as an actor on both sides of the Atlantic. Auty decided to try for him and, once he had read the script, McCallum needed no persuading to join *March In Windy City* as second billing to David.

Auty was especially pleased to discover how easily McCallum slipped into the role the minute he arrived on set. That was underlined when they filmed a political rally at which McCallum's *alter ego*, Dan Paterson, had to make a speech. Senate election campaign posters bearing McCallum's photograph had been erected at strategic points around Chicago and they looked authentic enough for locals to declare he would get their vote. 'He looks like a reliable guy,' was the verdict they offered to a delighted Auty.

Paul Bates, an accomplished Los Angeles-based actor, and local Chicago actress Kate Goehring, completed the major castings as detectives Joe Riggs and Grace Wallace.

Neither Bates nor Kate, who had appeared in the popular American hospital series *ER* and in the TV version of *The*

Untouchables, knew anything about David Jason, but they quickly warmed to his professional approach.

David preferred to make an apartment his base in Chicago rather than stay at a hotel. It proved the right choice. As filming progressed he was surprised to find himself recognised on the Chicago streets, not just by the odd British tourist, but by the locals. Despite David's bushy beard, they spotted him as the star of *A Touch of Frost* which was regularly screened in Chicago on cable TV as *Mystery Movie of the Week*.

On one occasion, as the cameras rolled under Chicago's elevated rail track, David found himself button-holed by an inquisitive stranger requesting some advice on how to get into showbusiness.

Despite meticulous preparation and co-operation from the local police and authorities, the four-week shoot was not entirely uneventful.

Kate Goehring cut open a finger on a model cowboy in an important scene but managed to carry on filming for four hours before going off to hospital at midnight. There, she had three stitches inserted in a deep gash before going straight back to work.

Frustratingly, nearly one whole day was lost to rain when a vital car chase was scheduled to be filmed. The rain made the surface so slippery it was deemed too dangerous to attempt the stunt they had planned.

On other days, temperatures soared over 100 degrees Fahrenheit. Taking into account the high humidity, filming was stiflingly hot for the British contingent.

Throughout the four weeks of filming in Chicago, a policeman was assigned to the unit to ease the production's passage through the city. Auty conceded that the eventual filming of the crucial car chase could not have been achieved without the help of the police.

However, the most worrying moment on location came

one night when David was filming at a graveyard on the edge of Southside, a known Chicago gangland area and a notorious troublespot.

Proceedings were suddenly interrupted by what sounded to David at first like cars backfiring. Chillingly, it rapidly dawned on him and everyone else that it was gunfire.

'It's a gunfight round the corner,' was the nonchalant confirmation by one of the Americans working on the production.

The reaction of the British was very different. Fearing they were an easy and obvious target under the huge lights focussed upon them, they huddled nervously together.

'We all tried to be very cool, calm and English,' David later recounted, 'but it was terrifying. We were lit up like targets. We heard a shootout with the police before we got out of there.'

Eventually, the danger passed but Auty recalls being advised by the police officer attached to the production to drive home without stopping, even for a red light.

'He said it was going to get hot in that area,' Auty recalls. 'That night, it really felt like Al Capone's Chicago.'

But, generally, alarms were few and far between and there was a feeling of satisfaction in a job well done as the final day's shooting began. Then, suddenly, during a break in filming at a disused warehouse, everyone became uncomfortably aware of some urgent activity a few blocks away. It transpired there had been an armed bank robbery and police were laying siege.

Production on the last day's filming of *March In Windy City* was temporarily held up to allow police cars with their sirens wailing to flash past while overhead the sky was swiftly filled with helicopters bearing TV camera crews homing in on the hot news story of the day.

'It's amazing,' said David with a shake of the head. 'We're down here filming the imaginary while the real thing is happening just a few hundred yards away.'

Filming did have its lighter moments. 'Everyone fell about laughing early in the shoot when I mentioned that I could do with a fag,' David recalled with a chuckle. 'On that side of the Atlantic, a fag does not mean a cigarette!'

As the day of transmission neared for *March In Windy City*, David admitted he was apprehensive as to how his portrayal of March would be received.

'I wanted to stick my neck out,' he said. 'But people assume that I don't get worried about taking on a new project because people have generally liked what I've done before. In fact the opposite is true. You become a victim of your own success. You don't want people saying: "He was good then but he's terrible now. He should have just stuck to that." But I believe in living dangerously. You have to keep moving on.'

David had been so worried about taking on the challenge of a new character that he had spent sleepless nights phoning the director and producer for reassurance.

'With every new role, you take a risk you are going to fall flat on your face,' he said.

Another daunting aspect of playing March was that, for the first time, David was playing a character who looked like David Jason.

'I didn't have any make-up or wigs or dye in my hair to transform me,' he explained. 'I just went on as I was and it actually made me more nervous bcause I had nothing to hide behind.'

He did, however, give March a full, grey beard. It's David's normal practice to grow one when on holiday and he decided that a beard would add to Steven March's character and reflect another aspect of March's old-fashioned, military background.

One personal trait David brought to his portrayal of March was the spy being naturally good with his hands. Like David, March had a penchant for making models and repairing toys and it was a convenient cover for March's spying activities to pose as a collector of automata.

The very real anxieties David experiences whenever he creates a new character for his adoring public were put into perspective when David paid a nostalgic visit to the north London theatre group, The Incognitos, who had first fired his enthusiasm for acting some 40 years earlier.

It brought back to him the days when he was happy simply to be an actor, even if it had meant trawling modest bed and breakfast digs to take small parts in theatre productions.

'It was there at The Incognitos I had all my dreams about what I wanted to do,' said David. 'When I walked in the door again, all the years fell away and I met all these young kids who were just like I was. It took me right back to how I was. All I wanted to do was act.'

David was keen to stress the simplicity of those early days compared with the pressures of making a film for TV in Chicago when you are both Executive Producer and the star.

In ratings terms, *March In Windy City* was a success, pulling in nearly 12 million viewers. But the reviews were mixed and, in some cases, savage, thus posing a serious question mark over whether Steven March's exploits could be stretched into a series.

By the time of transmission, David was already embarked on filming further episodes of *A Touch of Frost*. But the dream of a big break into films was still apparent.

'Anthony Hopkins is my hero,' he declared, 'I'd love to have the sort of career that he has. I'd be happy just doing the parts he'd turned down.'

And the future?

'I should feel elated at everything I've achieved, but I don't really,' David remarked in an interview before the screening of *March In Windy City*. 'Something inside me pushes me on to do more.'

FINALE

The real David Jason is a complex personality. The towering talent that has transformed his life comes with a large slice of insecurity and a strange reluctance to open up even to his closest friends.

Richard Harris, the acclaimed playwright who penned *Stepping Out* and *Outside Edge*, was a very good friend to David when they were young men. The couple were introduced by David's friend and business partner Malcolm Taylor and met in Edinburgh when David starred, with Virginia Stride, in Richard's farce *Albert and Virginia* that was produced at the Arts Theatre. Richard recalls, 'David was very energetic and very good in the play. When we met we were both totally unknown and both beginners. He had just finished working as an electrician and was starting out as an actor. He was a very funny guy and a great mimic but never in my wildest dreams did I imagine he would go on to such fame and fortune.

'For a time, we were pretty close, going on holiday several times to Corfu, me and my wife, Malcolm and his wife and David. We always had an enormous laugh. David always seemed very easy-going. Gradually, we drifted apart over the years but I always watched his rise and rise with interest. Then he got *No Sex Please – We're British* and I could see him building a nice career.

'Then, years later, I saw David again when I was asked initially to write the television adaptation of *The Darling Buds of May* and then *A Touch of Frost*. It was interesting work and I was delighted to do it, thinking that it would be nice to renew my old friendship. But when we met again it was almost as if he didn't know me. During all the time we were working on the same projects, I don't think David and I exchanged more than ten words. He had changed. There was no reaching out. We never had a drink together and we never had a meal together. I thought it was strange. I think he has become very, very private. I thought we were friends from way back and, while I did not particularly want to wallow in nostalgia, I did have lots of happy recollections of laughs we had enjoyed together. But he did not seem to want to take a single step down memory lane.

'Malcolm Taylor arranged for us all to get together and have dinner one night but it turned out to be a rather dismal evening. David was very unforthcoming. I think, perhaps, he has got to the position in life where he thinks everyone is after something from him. David just did not want to know. He certainly did not want to have any of those "Do you remember the time we all did so and so?" conversations. It was very strange because we had lots of laughs when we were younger. Good God, many a time he slept on my floor when he didn't have tuppence, but he didn't seem to want to open up on that at all.

'I loved adapting *A Touch of Frost* for television and David seemed to enjoying playing the role. I did the first ten hours of *Frost* but he never once said to me that he thought the scripts were any good. People might think he landed me the work, but that's not the way it was. I was surprised he wanted to forget the old days. He obviously liked working on my writing because he told other people so, but he certainly never found time to tell me, which would have been nice but there we are. I wrote the first five episodes of *Frost*, that is ten hours of television.

'When David won his awards, I dropped him a note saying "Well done" but I never got anything in return. Make of that what you will ... I hadn't spoken to him for about 20 years in between. I was very disappointed to renew an acquaintance with someone with whom I was fairly close, only to find there was no desire from him to remember those days.

'He has always kept himself very much to himself and he does so even more now. I don't think he is very comfortable with being a star. It must be terribly difficult. I think he is haunted with anxiety about when he is going to make the wrong move. Let's face it, these days you've only got to say the name David Jason and you've got a successful television series. He has not had a flop recently. He had all his flops when he was young. He had lots of chances. *Only Fools and Horses* is a marvellous creation and his other work is tremendous. *Porterhouse Blue* was terrific.

'As a young man, he was very determined to do well. We had a lot of laughs and a lot of fun but there was also a very dark side to him. He used to get incredibly frustrated when he didn't get the breaks. He had a lot of insecurity inside him, as much as any creative person I've known. Now he is very protective of his privacy. I was just disappointed he was protective with me, an old mate. Fame is a funny thing. It must be very, very hard being that famous.

'David is extremely talented. He was wonderful in *A Touch*

of Frost. There was one particular scene that took my breath away. I wrote the scene and the director directed it but there was just something about the way that David played it that surprised us both. He was brilliant. He just had this look that told you everything that only a great actor can convey. The face tells you everything. He is a very human actor, that humanity is very evident. It's in his face. Both the comic and the sad side are so very real and he shares that with the audience. And he burns with this incredible energy. It's almost impossible not to watch him. He has come an awful long way from being a Finchley electrician. But he always was a solitary sort of chap. Now he's even more so.'

Virginia Stride, the actress who starred with David in *Albert and Virginia* now lives only a few miles from David's mansion. She'd like to renew their old friendship, too.

'David was so alive, he was great to work with,' said Virginia. 'When I realised we lived so close, I thought it would be nice to get in touch for old times' sake and I wondered if he might open our village garden fête, but his brother Arthur warned me off. He said David was a recluse these days, so I didn't bother any more.'

The story of the relentless rise and rise of David Jason does have its sad side. As a boy and a young man, there is no doubt that David was the life and soul of any occasion. His clowning and mimicry and love of life shone through his early years, but it also obscured the steely determination underneath.

A friend who was close to David as a young man said, 'Once we had had too much to drink and he suddenly opened up and said how much it meant to him getting on in life and making a name for himself as an actor. I had my ambitions, too, and agreed. But he gripped my arm and his eyes burned into me as he said, "You don't understand. My brother didn't make it. My twin, I mean. So it's all down to me. I must make it. I just have to."

'I didn't think anything of it. I didn't even know that David's twin brother had died. Then another pal warned me not to mention it. He said, "It's the one thing that really gets to him. He feels it's like part of him died so he has to try that much harder at everything."'

The sociable fun of David's early years are a complete contrast to his life now. He lives in splendid isolation in his mansion, with Tony Blair as his neighbour and Special Branch as his local neighbourhood watch. And it's only at home that he feels really happy. He is very, very careful about who he lets into his domain. Close colleagues and trusted friends, such as Nicholas Lyndhurst, come to dinner. But the house was really bought for Myfanwy. It's a fabulous place with a lake, a swimming pool and he has a tractor and acres of land. She loved the space and the scope it provided for her flair for decoration. But after she died, David found it very difficult to be there on his own. Memories of Myfanwy were in every room and David threw himself into work to try to buy some time and space between him and his tragedy. Now his relationship with Gill has blossomed, friends say somehow the great house feels happy again.

But David's favourite times are not when hosting glittering dinner parties. Instead, he much prefers the moments spent tinkering in his garage with something mechanical. One of the keys to the success of his love for Gill is that she loves to see him absorbed in his work. He is a very practical man. And she sits for hours watching him with a spanner or screwdriver in hand dismantling some old engine, his mind relaxed and blissfully happy to be in a world where there are no autograph hunters yelling, 'Oi you plonker!'

Gill will even help to scrub all the carbon off a corroded part. They love gardening together and doing anything practical. He is not an intellectual, he's a man who prefers to do things with his hands rather than his brain. He loves to switch off and forget the ceaseless pressure of being Britain's number-one television personality and maintaining his appeal. At the end of the day, he is a jobbing artisan, it's just that instead of making a few quid a day as an electrician, he makes a few thousand as an actor. But he is haunted by the fear that it might all dry up.

Much of his insecurity is rooted in the knowledge that he is not really quite sure why he is so immensely popular and successful. He knows he can act most thespians off the screen, but there is also an undefinable 'X' factor which makes the public switch on to whatever he does on television.

It is certainly not money that drives Jason. Several times in his career, he has turned his back on the most lucrative options. And a senior TV executive who has negotiated with David on a string of projects, insists he is a joy to deal with.

'He is probably only about number five in the league of top British actor earners behind Waterman and Bolam. But he is number one in terms of audience attraction. If I had a script that I wanted to turn into a successful drama or comedy, then I'd go for David first, second and third.' And the people in charge of British television rate David as a second Chaplin, a comic genius who delivers fabulous performances and enormous audiences every time.

But the rewards are enormous. The son of the fish porter who still grumbles about being ripped off when he bought a bicycle from a neighbour as a teenager is now a millionaire many times over. But there is a former leading man who will always be grateful to Jason's unselfishness. The actor, who agreed to talk to the authors on condition his identity was not revealed, said: 'I'd just done a 13-part series for the BBC and we had all been approached about a second run. I'd taken out a huge mortgage on a house on the strength of it and then suddenly I was hit by a wave of really bad asthma attacks. I'd had asthma as a child but this was much worse. It was a nightmare. One minute I was on top of the word and then next minute I was out of work and unemployable at the job I loved.

'I've not worked as an actor since. But just when I was really on my beam ends I was helped out by a large cheque from David Jason. I was absolutely stunned. I didn't know him that well. We'd only worked together once. But someone told him about my problems and without saying a word he had this cheque hand delivered to my house. It meant I could keep the bank at bay while I sold the house again and it made all the difference in the world to me and my family. And I know other people he's helped as well, but he always does it quietly. The last thing he'd want to get is a reputation as a soft touch. But when people say he's tight it makes me very angry. David Jason is a gent in my book, always will be.'

David certainly makes regular large contributions to a string of more conventional charities, but always insists so far as possible on anonymity. But then he can afford it. For the last series of *A Touch of Frost* he was paid £106,000 a film. The accountants at Yorkshire TV considered it money well spent when the show swept towards the top of the TV ratings. And that £106,000 will quickly be doubled by the 100 per cent repeat fee for the second screening. After that repeats are paid in a slowly declining but still lucrative scale.

Even the penny-pinching BBC were made to pay handsomely for the sensationally successful three part swansong for *Only Fools and Horses*. David's ability to earn the Corporation a runaway win in the 1996 Christmas ratings battle earned him £69,000 for each of the three hilarious films. With lucrative video sales, occasional voice overs, and the re-runs of *The Darling Buds of May* on UK Gold, David Jason is by anybody's standards a very rich man. But apart from his home and his beloved car, he insists 'I was brought up to respect money and I'm not going to change. I drive a Jaguar because it is comfortable and I do a lot of miles. It's not a status symbol.

And I live in the country because I like it. I love holidays so I spend a bit on them but I never spend just for spending's sake.' Money has certainly never been the driving force behind any of David's decisions, he turned down £500,000 to advertise Typhoo tea without giving the offer a second thought.

David is very generous professionally. He always sets out to try to inspire a team atmosphere on all of his shows and he is much more likely to spend his off-duty moments laughing with the crew or his fellow actors than closeted away in his caravan.

But David is incredibly shy of commitment. He never married Myfanwy, even though he knew it would, more than anything, have made her and his mother very happy. When ITV offered him a fantastic £1m deal to sign up to work for them exclusively, he refused. He certainly did not want to shut the door on Del, but he is also very wary of anyone taking control of his life. A friend said, 'His insecurity is frightening. I tried to get him to relax once. I said, "David, you're a millionaire. You're the most popular actor in the country. You've got a lovely lady in your life. Why on earth can't you just lie back and enjoy life from time to time?" He looked at me as if I was talking Russian. He is a driven man and there's no changing him now.'

David agonises that his colossal comedy success has masked his dramatic achievement. Although he loves playing Del Trotter, he is always incensed if people or newspapers confuse him with the character.

'Why do they call me David 'Del-Boy' Jason?' he raves. 'You never hear anyone talking about Alec *'Bridge Over the River Kwai'* Guinness.'

But however he feels about the public's perception of his acting, David Jason has saved his best production until pretty late in his career. He was 60 years old when he learned that girlfriend Gill Hinchcliffe was expecting their baby and David freely admits that he received the news with a mixture of joy and concern.

'I think I almost fainted,' joked David afterwards. 'When I regained consciousness a month later I felt pleased. But for that first month I was not here. I was unconscious. Whether you can say it was pleasure or horror, I don't remember. But it did actually frighten me a bit. It is a brave new world.'

David and Gill were delighted to become expectant parents but they were unable to keep the news a secret for long. A change in David's busy working schedule revealed the couple's secret and the actor realised that his life was about to change comprehensively. He was honest about his fears at the prospect: 'I suppose I am happy and proud. But I don't really know. I have very mixed emotions about it all. Having spent most of my life enjoying my work and being away and all that, suddenly I have this complete change of lifestyle looming.' He did not know whether he was coming or going but he welcomed the prospect of a new experience with open arms.

And when Sophie Mae arrived on February 26, 2001 David and Gill's lives changed forever. Close friends insist the couple make perfect parents. They are wise and mature enough to savour every moment of their daughter's precious early days. And a fellow actor told the authors: 'David has been so dedicated to his craft for so long that sometimes he has neglected his private life. But now he is making up for lost time. He is totally besotted by Sophie Mae.'

Indeed David, who was 61 by the time of the birth, admitted to Michael Parkinson that: 'when she arrived it was quite an emotional moment.' But he joked that: 'You believe all the stories about "Ooh, you'll never sleep again. This is the end of sleep. You'll be sleep deprived. You'll never work again. You'll be dead by the end of the year." And like any proud new dad he joked that Sophie Mae was really: 'A little fart machine. She was two or three days old and milk was going in one end and hanging about a bit and then she went [David blows an enormous raspberry]. How on earth does she know how to do this at two days old? She makes a red face like I do.'

But more seriously David revealed why he had waited so long to have a child. Until now his career had always come first. 'I didn't actually wait, it was thrust upon me. My life has been in reverse. It wasn't fame and it wasn't money I was after but I always wanted to succeed. The only way I could do that was to try with every job to be better than I was in the last one and to learn. Because of that I needed to be footloose and fancy free. I needed to go where the work was. As soon as things started to get heavy with a relationship, I'm afraid that I was one of those who would be off, gone. Only because I knew for me I couldn't be responsible for a family and the silly work I was doing in this business you have to have what they call an idiotic determination to succeed.'

Since Sophie Mae's birth David has scaled back his workload considerably, but he has still found time to work on projects close to his heart. For Christmas 2001 he delivered two presents to his faithful fans – a starring role in *Micawber* on ITV1 and the revival after five years of Only Fools and Horses on BBC1. He might have winced at the scheduling but they were two projects from the prolific word processor of John Sullivan that delighted huge armchair audiences.

Jason was to have played Micawber in the BBC's dramatisation of David Copperfield two years earlier but writer Sullivan clashed with the drama department and the actor loyally withdrew. Sullivan, who had loved the book since childhood, was able to refloat the re-focussed four parter on the rival channel and David Jason was delighted to take on the demanding title role. 'Playing Micawber is what I originally became an actor for,' he said. *A Touch of Frost* was continuing but David admitted: 'I don't enjoy playing Frost so much as I used to because I've done everything with him.'

Enormous effort went into adapting Dickens famous character but David warned viewers not to expect some kind of historical Del Boy. And when the shows arrived on the screen Micawber was quite different from fast talking Mr Trotter. But both succeeded as usual and David Jason was again the face of Christmas present.

Since then viewers have seen David Jason in more Frost adventures and in a highly personal story called The Quest, which was screened on ITV at Easter 2002. It was based on David's early experiences as an intrepid motorcyclist which are featured earlier in this book. David worked for long hours with a writer drafting out a drama based on a particular trip up north with two young pals all desperate to lose their virginity. David recruited Roy Hudd and Hywel Bennett to play his friends as they are now and three young actors (Greg Faulkner, Jim Sturgess and Max Wrottesley) to play the younger versions. David said: 'I was looking for something in a drawer when I came across some old photographs of me and my two mates. It brought back memories and I started to think about our experiences then and what has happened in the years since.'

In the TV drama the sex-hungry threesome had all sorts of scrapes with women in their desperate bid to make love for the first time, but David explained that although the script was inspired by his own experiences it was not autobiographical. He really did go up north with some friends on motorbikes looking for Nirvana. And they had a scruffy caravan on the edge of Lake Windermere. 'That's the same and one of the lads really did find romance,' said David. 'But the rest is fiction and an examination of friendship in a vastly different age. Things were more innocent in the Fifties. The expectation of enjoyment was simple. You made your own pleasure. I hope that nostalgic feeling comes across.' David also directed the piece and it was a charming film.

For the future David cheerfully admits that he intends to become even more selective about his work as he is finding it increasingly hard to drag himself away from his family. 'It is getting more and more difficult to pull myself away from home to work,' he said. 'But the only answer is to say no to work and not do any more. I would be happy to be paid to stay at home.'

FAREWELL, FROST

By the time he celebrated his 68th birthday in February 2008, David was seriously starting to wonder whether the time had come for Inspector Jack Frost to call it a day. After 15 years the TV series was as popular as ever, he was thoroughly comfortable in Frost's shoes, and he still had enough of an appetite for the character and enough confidence in the quality of the programmes that he would have happily gone on making the show indefinitely.

But he was also becoming increasingly aware that the years had caught up with Frost. The fact was that retirement from the police force was permissible at 50 and compulsory by the age of 60, and he had come to realise by the time a new batch of *Frost* programmes hit the screen, he would be nearly 70. It was nevertheless still something of a surprise when he announced at a London press conference in September 2008 that he was quitting as Frost.

'It's time to move on,' he declared. 'Frost is getting a little long in the tooth – it's time for him to hang up his coat and scarf. We thought we've got to draw a line in the sand somewhere and if it's not this year, it will be next so we took the decision that Frost, unfortunately, would be leaving the force.'

There was, however, some good news for *Frost* fans: three new episodes were to be screened that autumn before David would film a final two-parter to be screened in 2010. To preserve utmost secrecy as to how Frost would bow out, it was planned to film three different endings.

'I thoroughly enjoy playing Jack Frost,' David stressed. 'He's been a huge part of my acting life after more than 40 episodes and I'll give him a dramatic and fitting send-off, whichever ending we decide to screen.' He added there would not be a dry eye in the house when the Inspector solved his last case. But how would Frost bow out? That was the question everyone was asking.

'Perhaps he just retires gracefully, gets the gold watch and walks away from Denton nick, tears all round. He just hangs up his hat,' David enigmatically suggested.

The final two-parter, titled 'If Dogs Run', followed Frost's battle to convict Gerry Berland, a dangerous criminal masquerading as a successful businessman. After being tipped off to an illegal dogfight by RSPCA officer Christine Moorhead, Frost attempted a raid. The story also saw the detective investigate a series of homicides, which seemed to mirror crimes that he had failed to solve more than 16 years before. He then faced a race against time to stop the copycat killer from striking again.

Over 15 series, DI Frost had been held hostage, kicked, shot at, attacked, spat at, held at gunpoint on top of a building and had his home vandalised. Now it was time for him to go and on 5 April 2010, David bade a sad farewell to the TV hero he had played for 18 years and Jack Frost disappeared from our screens for good.

As the scheduled broadcast of the final episode approached, there was much speculation as to whether Frost would literally be killed off. Would he come to a grisly end, or would he exchange retirement from Denton for contentment with his RSPCA officer love Christine Moorhead, played by Phyllis Logan? Only David and ITV executive producer David Reynolds were in the know. Not even the rest of the cast were allowed in on the secret.

It turned out to be something of a happy ending when Frost did indeed finally find love. But his wedding day to case witness Christine was ruined by her vengeful ex-husband driving his car into the groom's party as they arrived at the church, in the process killing Frost's long-time friend and colleague DS Toolan, played by John Lyons. Frost is among the injured, but he survives.

It proved to be an emotional episode, estimated to have been seen by 10 million viewers. Fittingly, Frost had found love again after tragically losing his wife in the opening episode of the first series. The final episode was no less emotional. 'On the last day of filming there were moments in the script when I had to find tears,' recalled David. 'And let's just say those tears weren't hard to find. I think everyone on set had the feeling something really special, which had been a big part of all our lives, was coming to an end.'

It was indeed the end of an era – for David, for ITV and for one of television's best-loved detectives. Right from the very first read-through in a hired room in London, David had always believed *A Touch of Frost* to be something out of the ordinary. R.D. Wingfield's books had immediately impressed him with their imaginative invention and never failed to set him thinking as to the who and why a certain crime had been committed.

'On top of that I could see that Jack was a character we could work on,' he explained. 'When we met Frost, his wife

273

was dying from cancer so the first episode was pretty dark. That suited me because I wanted to show the public that, even though I was known for comedy roles like Del Boy and Pa Larkin, I could go for the jugular, too, and explore the dark side. It was a very bleak start in the first episode with his wife dying of cancer.' But when 18 million viewers tuned in to see Frost's debut, the massive audience meant his long-term TV future was assured, as was his development as a character.

'Later, though, as the years have gone by, we developed Jack so that there was also a lighter side to him,' added David. 'We introduced a lot of funny moments into the script, too – little quirks and tics, like Jack's hatred of paperwork and love of snacking. He's the only copper on TV that'll eat a bacon sandwich while looking at a corpse! What I always loved about Jack was he bent and broke the rules, but he always got his man. And he never lost sight of being a human being.'

It was David who chose for the happy ending to be Frost's finale, but the alternate ending was later posted by ITV on the internet. The six-minute finale also showed the wedding crash, but this time everyone just has minor injuries. However, when DI Frost is taken to hospital, he is seen to clutch at his chest and goes into cardiac arrest. It was left to his fiancée to turn off the life support machine after doctors tell her he is brain-dead. The episode ended with a funeral, in which Frost was given full police honours.

MOURNING FOR A GENIUS

On 23 April 2011, David was devastated by the death of his close friend and *Only Fools and Horses'* creator and writer, John Sullivan. John had died at the relatively young age of 64 in a private hospital in Surrey, where he had been in intensive care for eight weeks battling viral pneumonia.

David was deeply saddened at the loss of a true friend. At first theirs had been a warm working relationship on *Only Fools and Horses*, but it had rapidly developed into a firm and lasting close friendship. The two men had great respect for each other and, of course, their success was closely allied. Their stars had risen together and the bond remained strong throughout, although latterly David had not seen quite so much of John as he would have liked because Sullivan chose to spend much of his time living in Majorca.

In tribute, David said: 'We have lost our country's greatest comedy writer but he leaves us a great legacy, the gift of laughter. My thoughts at this time are with his lovely family.

He was a man of great compassion, a great writer and a lovely fella.'

The BBC's head of comedy, Mark Freeland, added: 'No one understood what made us laugh and cry better than John Sullivan. He was the Dickens of our generation. Simply the best, most natural, most heartfelt comedy writer of our time.'

And actor Robert Lindsay, who starred in Sullivan's first TV success, *Citizen Smith*, said: 'He was probably the best sitcom writer of his generation.'

At this terrible moment of grief for David, the thought would not have been further from his mind that there would never be any more episodes of *Only Fools and Horses*, but it was nonetheless an inescapable fact. It was inconceivable that any other writer could pick up the reins or would even dare try to prolong the adventures of the Trotters, such was the quality of Sullivan's scripts.

Before he was taken ill, John Sullivan had achieved more TV success with *The Green Green Grass* (2005–09), a spin-off featuring the *Only Fools and Horses* characters, Boycie and his wife Marlene, enjoying a new life in the country. And viewers had also been able to enjoy another Sullivan-penned series, *Rock & Chips* (2010–), a prequel to *Only Fools and Horses*, which focused on the adventures of a teenaged Del Trotter (played by James Buckley), in Peckham in the Sixties.

Of course there was no role for David in *Rock & Chips*, but ever since the screening of the final episode of *Only Fools and Horses*, devoted fans of Del Boy retained such affection for his characterisation that they always harboured the hope that he would one day resume the role in yet another series in some form or other. It would have been a difficult task to revive the show, given there would be no Uncle Albert, following the death of actor Buster Merryfield, and Boycie and Marlene had moved away from Peckham. Sullivan's death put an end to any thoughts of an *Only Fool and Horses'* sequel, though.

At the end of the year, nine months after John's death, it emerged that *Only Fools and Horses* had been the most-watched programme of the decade. Statistics showed that 21.3 million viewers (74 per cent of the available audience) watched the BBC1 special in 2001, which aired on Christmas Day. This festive episode followed the Trotter family as they try and recoup their lost millions after a bad investment.

Such is the lasting popularity of *Only Fools and Horses* that DVD box sets continue to sell in sizeable quantities, repeats on the UK TV channel Gold still pull in substantial and committed audiences, while devotees ensure the annual fans' convention, the Only Fools and Horses Appreciation Society, is never less than enthusiastically well attended.

In recent times, fans have also been able to find an episode or two to watch on their televisions almost every day of the week. Indeed, Del Boy's followers proved devoted enough to prompt Gold to select 40 of the show's greatest moments and ask viewers to vote for their all-time favourite clips. They were astonished to find no less than 35,000 votes were cast – which produced a special programme counting down the most popular clips in reverse order, with a string of celebrities adding their comments. Among the famous fans queuing up to chuckle over the clips and add their comments were Sir Jimmy Savile, Sir Trevor McDonald, former BBC chairman Michael Grade, actresses Linda Robson and Sally Lindsay, football manager Ron Atkinson, comedy actress Helen Lederer, celebrity chef Gary Rhodes and comedy writer Barry Cryer. The line-up was indicative of Del Boy's broad appeal.

At number 10 was Trigger's claim that he had owned his road sweeper's broom for 20 years before announcing the broom had required 17 new heads and 14 new handles over that time! Number 9 was the sequence in which Rodney tries to solve the riddle as to why Trigger always mistakenly called him Dave, followed at 8 by the episode where Del turns impresario when he puts on a cabaret night for local villain, Eugene McCarthy. Unfortunately for Del, Tony Angelino, the singing dustman he has hired, turns out to be not only a terrible vocalist but to have a speech impediment to boot, in which he doesn't know his r's from his elbow!

Grandad's truly 'offal' Christmas turkey cooking was voted in at number 7. And at number 6 was the wonderful moment when Del and Rodney sit quietly in their three-wheel van, then whoop with joyous delirium on the realisation that a long-lost watch has brought them £6 million at auction after 16 years of poverty.

'It was always the plan to make them millionaires,' commented John Sullivan. 'And it was the first time ever that it got a standing ovation from the studio audience. It choked me up a bit that they'd got everything they'd ever dreamed of.'

'The Jolly Boys' Outing' came in at number 5, an episode in which Del and his mates take a coach trip to Margate. A pivotal moment came when the coach's faulty radio, bought from Trotters Independent Traders, turns out to be a fire hazard and no special effect is spared as the coach is consumed in a gigantic fireball.

Number 4 featured the episode in which Del receives a consignment of dolls, not of the toy variety but more of the adult type to be found in a sex shop. The clip sees Del and Rodney investigate a squeaking sound in their sitting room only to be startled by the sight of a self-inflating plastic female popping up from behind their bar.

John Sullivan's ingenious idea of Del and Rodney unwittingly preventing a mugging on their way to a fancy dress party was voted number 3. Dressed as Batman and Robin, they emerge through the south London mist, causing the would-be muggers to scatter at the extraordinary sight of the Caped Crusader and his assistant running towards them.

Runner-up was the episode in which Del offers his services

as a chandelier cleaner to Lady Ridgemere. The clip has Del and Rodney on ladders, holding a blanket ready to catch one of two chandeliers to be released by Granddad from the floor above, but he releases the nut from the bolt holding the wrong chandelier and it crashes to the floor, smashed to smithereens.

John Sullivan revealed he had based the scene on the true story of a similar mishap that had befallen his father and resulted in several men being given the sack.

Somewhat predictably the all-time greatest moment from *Only Fools and Horses*, as voted for by Gold's viewers, turned out to be David's remarkable pratfall through the upraised bar flap when he and Trigger ditch the Nag's Head for a night and go 'on the pull' at a trendy wine bar. This episode required exceptional agility from David to fall rigidly sideways and to top it off so cleverly by scrambling upright again, shaken and somewhat dishevelled but managing to have clung onto his wine glass – still partially filled. 'David did it live – it was a little gem and it took the audience by surprise,' enthused the episode's producer Gareth Gwenlan. 'He's a great physical comedian.'

During the countdown, John Sullivan revealed that originally Trigger was not included in this particular scene. Roger Lloyd-Pack (who played Trigger) happened to be in a nearby rehearsal room at North Acton working on another project at the time. 'When he said he was not that busy and could make himself available if need be, I went into the office and re-wrote the scene,' John recalled. 'We then got a mattress and practised it for the rest of the week.' Trigger's bewildered spin around, wondering how Del could have suddenly and so totally disappeared, adds the final touch of comedy to the scene.

The bar flap fall was also based in truth. John said: 'I actually saw it happen many years prior to that in the George pub at Balham, where I lived. I saw a guy lean away from the flap to get a light from a friend's lighter. Then the barman came out and left the flap up, and the guy fell through it.

'I told David about it and we wanted so badly to use it in the show but we couldn't in the Nag's Head because Del knew every inch of it and would never be fool enough to do it. We had to wait to do it somewhere where he was a stranger and the opportunity came when he went to the wine bar.'

Sullivan chose this special *Only Fools and Horses'* Top 40 moments programme to sheepishly own up to how it came about that he found himself writing, singing and recording the show's familiar theme song. Originally, he had hoped Cockney duo Chas and Dave would sing and record it but they were busy riding the crest of a wave, thanks to their big hit 'Ain't No Pleasing You' and were thought to be unavailable. Sullivan reluctantly decided to offer to sing it himself but only after he had sunk nine pints of beer as Dutch courage to try and steady his nerves.

In a separate poll by Gold to find Britain's most memorable Christmas TV moment, *Only Fools and Horses'* Batman and Robin scene came out on top, beating animated shows *Wallace & Gromit: The Wrong Trousers* and *The Snowman* into second and third places respectively, as well as triumphing over *Morecambe and Wise* and *The Office*.

The popularity of both the pratfall scene and the chandelier disaster is reflected on the internet, where several versions of varying lengths have found their way onto YouTube, where they have received many millions of hits between them. Universal access to these classic clips via the internet is thought to have partly contributed to the decision by American TV to re-make and adapt *Only Fools and Horses* for US viewers. The show had been successfully adapted for various European TV versions but now the Americans, too wanted to have a stab at making their own.

When the plans were announced, however, David

suggested an American remake would be an extremely difficult task. 'They can do brilliant comedy [in America] but I don't see that they can bring off *Fools and Horses*,' he told *BBC News*.

He was far from alone in voicing the opinion that the original London setting and language was so essential to the show's success that an Americanisation of John Sullivan's creation was nigh on impossible. 'I don't see that it will travel across the pond,' David was quoted as saying. 'It might work, but you've got to change it so much that, in the change, in order to Americanise it, do you lose the whole concept of the piece? It's London-based and it took quite a long time for the rest of the country to catch up with the phrases. I have no idea what the American equivalent of "plonker" is, for example. Or "dipstick."'

Plans for the US version happened to emerge in the summer of 2011, just as Gold launched celebrations for the 30th anniversary of *Only Fools and Horses*. The actual anniversary was 8 September 2011, but to mark the milestone Gold threw a party a fortnight earlier to announce they would be screening three episodes every single night through the month of September and promised devotees they would get to see every episode ever made.

Amusingly, the party venue was a replica of Del Boy's Peckham high-rise flat in Nelson Mandela House, complete with dizzily busy swirling carpet, jazzy wallpaper and well-stocked bar. Among the celebrities who attended the event was Rolling Stone Ronnie Wood, who professed to be an avid fan as he took a close look at the yellow three-wheel van on display for the occasion.

In an imaginative gimmick, Gold offered fans the chance to spend the night in the London SE15 flat for the 1981 price of £18 a night. Fittingly for such an iconic comedy series, it was all done with a good-hearted sense of fun.

As David Jason moved on to other projects he was able to reflect on the 30 years of *Only Fools and Horses* and say: 'We always had a laugh. It was probably the most enjoyable experience I've had over the years. The scripts made you fall about laughing even before you started. It was just a joy to go into work.'

All the fun of making the series came flooding back when he bought his daughter Sophie the *Only Fools and Horses'* DVD box set and he was able to sit down and watch the series with her. David clearly felt she was ready at the age of 10 to enjoy and appreciate her father's antics as Del Boy Trotter.

'I don't really like watching myself as I get haunted by the bits I've done wrong,' he confided, 'but, to be honest, it feels like I'm watching a different person when I see Del Boy now.'

DURING THE WAR...

David Jason has given television viewers many memorable moments down the years but when he looks back over his TV career, there is one moment that he particularly treasures and savours, and it's one of which he is immensely proud.

It's not a scene from *Only Fools and Horses*, nor is it a dramatic confrontation with a criminal in *Inspector Frost*. In fact, it's the moment when David appeared in front of millions of viewers in the cockpit of a World War II Spitfire as it performed a barrel roll of honour, flying high up in the sky above the white cliffs of Dover.

David took to the skies above the English Channel for *David Jason: Battle of Britain* (2010), a documentary to mark the 70th anniversary of the remarkable, and unlikely, World War II victory, which despite overwhelming odds RAF pilots managed to pull off against German planes – 4,000 German bombers and fighters massed against a mere 600 RAF fighters.

'Never in the field of human conflict was so much owed by so many to so few,' was Prime Minister Winston Churchill's tribute in a wartime speech to the courage of the 'few' British pilots as they fought the pivotal air battle in 1940 with the German Luftwaffe, while Britain braced itself for invasion.

David was thrilled to be allowed to fly the Spitfire with a trainer sitting in front of him, but wisely handed over control of the aircraft for the barrel roll – 'a kind of ecstatic, airborne dance of victory,' as he described the ritual performed by pilots as they returned safely home after engaging the enemy. His elation was there for all to see and he later admitted: 'There are not too many things in life that have reduced me to tears but this was one of them. I felt humbled and so proud of those men who fought for us in our darkest hour – it's an experience that will never leave me.'

David was just a six-month-old baby when the Battle of Britain ensued but he confessed that making the documentary was nonetheless an intensely personal journey. He could recall the air raid shelter in the garden of his family's north London home and the importance of switching off lights to preserve the Blackout to confuse enemy bombers on their way to London targets.

Moreover, tales of his father's experiences in the Reserves had left a lasting impression. As a boy he had listened with awe as Arthur White described how he and his fellow local Reservists mounted an ack-ack gun on the top of a nearby gasometer to fire at German bombers but, as his dad would tell him with a chuckle, they did so without real bullets because genuine ammunition was required elsewhere.

As a keen flier himself and a patron of the RAF Benevolent Fund, the TV project fitted David perfectly. He had become interested in flying after his wife Gill had given him a flying lesson as a present but by the time he came to make the Battle of Britain documentary, he had flown only helicopters. He had even bought his own chopper, a Robinson R44, which he uses to fly to film locations or to business meetings.

Sitting at the controls of a Spitfire was therefore an extra-special thrill, not least for the fact that the old RAF machine he was piloting had flown 300 combat hours during World War II and had shot down the first enemy plane during D-Day.

While he expressed the utmost admiration for the Battle of Britain pilots, David was keen to explore and to accord due praise to the less well-sung efforts of the engineers and all the back-up organisations which helped keep the planes air- and combat-worthy.

The documentary offered a new and revealing slant on the legendary courage of 'the few' and the following year he was delighted to figure equally prominently in another wartime programme. In *David Jason's Great Escapes* (2011), he took another trip back in time to relive some of the true stories of prisoner-of-war escapes. 'Like most of us who grew up in the 1950s, I was a huge fan of films that celebrated wartime escapes, where plotting Germans were outwitted by the heroic antics of plucky young Brits,' he said.

He started his journey at the supposedly escape-proof Colditz, a 16th-century castle in Germany, to see the most ambitious escape tunnel ever dug there. Colditz sits on a rock with seven-foot thick walls and terraces with 250-foot plunges down to the surrounding river. 'When you see how this castle is constructed, it's almost unimaginable to think of men digging tunnels here,' David observed.

Later, travelling with two surviving prisoners of war to hear their stories, David went to Poland to visit the site on which once stood Stalag Luft III, the notorious prison on which the famous Steve McQueen film *The Great Escape* (1963) was based. On learning the escape tunnel was desperately narrow, David crawled through a replica to experience the same claustrophobic conditions for himself.

He also learned from Ken Rees, the last-known British survivor of The Great Escape, details of the evening on which the daring mission took place and the terrifying moment he became trapped in the tunnel. Out of the 200 men attempting to escape, only 76 made it out of the tunnel before being spotted by guards. Ken was the 77th man and was still inside. He says: 'It was my turn to disappear and a guard came along, and I think he noticed the hole or something and fired in the air, and we knew we'd been found and it was all over.' Ken remained in Colditz until, on Hitler's orders, he and other prisoners were forced to make a terrible 1000-mile march out of Stalag Luft III to Bremen towards the end of the war.

David also visited the train station where the escapees bought their tickets to freedom. Unfortunately, only three man evaded capture and 50 of those caught were shot on Hitler's orders. As his journey came to an end, he reflected: 'I shan't forget in a hurry the courage and dignity of the veterans I met on my travels – all of them united by one thing, their passionate desire for freedom.'

As before, this second wartime documentary made for interesting, and popular, viewing. And there was no doubting his sincerity when David said: 'I suppose that I just grew up knowing, in a very vivid way, that if it hadn't been for the men who fought in the Second World War, we'd all be living in a very different world now.'

The two documentaries added a fresh dimension to his career, which took yet another new turn when he made his directorial debut (for no fee) on a short film titled *All the Way Up* (2010). It was the tale of a man intent on having an affair, whose life changes when he steps into a lift.

All the Way Up went on to win six awards (including Best Director for David) at the Angel Film Festival in Monaco. This is a festival celebrating non-violent films and in addition to his Best Director gong, he was also presented with the Angel

Lifetime Achievement Award. It was an especially gratifying accolade for the actor, given his long-held beliefs in wholesome entertainment.

'One of the things I've been fortunate enough to do is to work in TV and films that have the Angel ideology,' he said in his acceptance speech. 'All my comedies and dramas have been for entertainment, or at least I've tried to make it that way.'

It was this philosophy that persuaded him to take a jump back into comedy for the first time for many years – in a new, family-friendly BBC series called *The Royal Bodyguard*.

HUBBLE AND STRIFE

E ver since the end of *Only Fools and Horses*, David had been on the lookout for a chance to return to TV comedy. Over the years, a number of scripts had come his way, but none of them had ever quite suited. Either the timing was wrong due to his *Frost* commitments, or the role on offer always fell some way short of being the perfect fit. Out of the blue, the BBC came looking for him again, though.

When Danny Cohen was appointed as the new controller of BBC1 in 2010, among his top priorities was to try and woo David Jason back to the BBC. He duly invited the actor to lunch, during which he asked him to return to BBC screens if there was a project that caught his interest. Cohen subsequently sent David three scripts, one of which was a very visual comedy called *The Royal Bodyguard* (2011).

The central role of a bumbling soldier mistakenly promoted above his station appealed to David enormously. He would play Captain Guy Hubble, an ex-Guardsman and head of security at Buckingham Palace car park, who is surprisingly appointed as royal bodyguard after saving the Queen's life in an act of bravery on the day of the State Opening of Parliament. But it is a promotion too far and hapless Hubble proves utterly incompetent – and yet seemingly indestructible.

David saw *The Royal Bodyguard* as 'a lovely piece of fun,' a traditional, broad-appeal sitcom and a feel-good series, which the whole family could sit down and safely watch together. He told *BBC News*: 'I do think there is more of a space for this old-fashioned type of comedy. There is enough out there that's what they call edgy, and quite hard-hitting and modern and fashionable. There's nothing wrong with that – it's fine, but you can't have a diet of just potatoes. You've got to have meat and two veg. I think we haven't been catering enough for families in general. And I think the BBC have taken that on board and are trying to redress the balance.'

As usual, he threw himself whole-heartedly into the role and insisted on performing his own stunts as much as possible. For his pains, he was dumped in mud and puddles; he swung on pipes, jumped down a chimney and was pulled into tanks of water. One scene even saw him hanging from a balcony in his underwear.

'The humour is quite visual,' he commented, 'and we tried to make it so no one would be worried about sitting there with their kids or grandmas.'

In hard-hitting interviews prior to the Christmas launch of *The Royal Bodyguard*, David accused modern comedy of being obsessed with swearing and breaking taboos, and he branded TV talent shows voyeuristic and cruel. He said he was concerned at the increasing need to protect his young daughter from bad language and violence when the television was on in his home.

The first episode of *The Royal Bodyguard* went out on Boxing Day, 2011, and initially attracted a highly creditable audience of 8 million but somewhat ominously, 1.5 million had switched off by the end of the half-hour episode.

Many viewers took to the social networking site Twitter to voice their disappointment and their criticism of the script David had been given and the improbable premise. Others complained the comedy was all too contrived and even the *Radio Times*, which traditionally supports the BBC, acknowledged the adverse reaction, saying: 'Oh dear, we are not getting many complimentary tweets about *The Royal Bodyguard*. Can't remember the last time we had a Twitter reaction like this.'

Over the ensuing weeks, audiences continued to fall away and had all but halved by the time the last episode went out on 30 January 2012. David eventually admitted the show had not been the hoped-for success and told *BBC News*: 'You can't get it right all the time. We tried, we had a good go, we enjoyed doing it and yeah, perhaps I think we didn't quite bring it off and it came in for quite a lot of harsh criticism.

'But there you are,' he added cheerfully. 'If you don't put your head above the parapet, you won't get it shot off – you've got to do that occasionally.'

Undaunted, David quickly embarked on another comedy – but this time as director. He took the helm on a pilot for a new BBC sitcom called *Pearly Gates* about a firm of undertakers with hopes it would become a series.

And, intriguingly, with *Only Fools and Horses* destined for a US remake, David has also been quietly exploring the possibilities of a British version of the hit American sitcom *Everybody Loves Raymond*. He revealed it was a show he had always enjoyed and said: 'I've always thought it needs a wider audience. I could never understand why they didn't put it out at prime time because it's so goof. And so I said, "Why don't we do an English version?" So watch this space it could happen...'

TV CREDITS

MAJOR TV ROLES

DO NOT ADJUST YOUR SET (Rediffusion/Thames)
FIRST BROADCAST: 26 December 1967
SYNOPSIS: Subtitled *The Fairly Pointless Show*, this was a zany
comedy revue aimed at children written by Michael Palin,
Terry Jones and Eric Idle with music by The Bonzo Dog Doo-Dah
Band. David Jason and Denise Coffey starred in the show in a
pastiche spy serial called *Captain Fantastic.*

HARK AT BARKER (London Weekend Television)
FIRST BROADCAST: 11 April 1969; Series II 1970.
SYNOPSIS: Ronnie Barker as Lord Rustless, a titled old lecher
enjoying his life in his stately mansion. David Jason played his
gardener Dithers with Josephine Tewson as his secretary Mildred,
Mary Baxter as the cook, and Moira Foot as Effie the maid.
PRODUCER: Humphrey Barclay

WRITERS: Included Peter Caulfield, Bernard McKenna, Bill Oddie and Gerald Wiley (Ronnie Barker)

TWO D'S AND A DOG (Thames TV)
FIRST BROADCAST: July 5, 1970
SYNOPSIS: Children's series about Dorry Charles (Denise Coffey) who is left broke when her father dies. Her only friend is Dingle Bell (David Jason), her late father's chauffeur and a dog called Fido Dog. WRITTEN by Jan Butlin, the series followed the fortunes of Dorry and Dingle as they looked for work and enough money to survive.
PRODUCER: Daphne Shadwell

PORRIDGE (BBC)
FIRST BROADCAST: 5 September 1974
SYNOPSIS: The shifting fortunes of prisoner Norman Stanley Fletcher (Ronnie Barker) serving a five-year sentence in Slade Prison for robbery. Other regulars included Fletcher's cell-mate Lennie Godber (Richard Beckinsale), Chief Officer Mackay (Fulton Mackay), Warden Barrowclough (Brian Wilde) and prisoner Blanco Webb (David Jason) in jail for the murder of his wife. Jason's three starring episodes were *No Peace for the Wicked* (1975), *Happy Release* (1975) and *Pardon Me* (1977).
PRODUCER: Syd Lotterby

THE TOP-SECRET LIFE OF EDGAR BRIGGS
(London Weekend Television)
FIRST BROADCAST: 15 September 1974
SYNOPSIS: By a clerical error, hapless Edgar Briggs (David Jason) is transferred to Counter Espionage at the Ministry of Defence. Appointed Assistant to the Commander (Noel Coleman), he manages to achieve remarkable results despite his stupidity and his total unsuitability for the job. His astounded colleagues were Michael Stainton as Buxton, Mark Eden as Spencer, and Elizabeth Counsell as Cathy. Edgar Briggs's wife Jennifer was played by Barbara Angell.
PRODUCER: Humphrey Barclay

OPEN ALL HOURS (BBC)
FIRST BROADCAST: 20 February 1976, BBC 2; Series IV ended 1985.
SYNOPSIS: Roy Clarke's stories about stammering shopkeeper
Arkwright (Ronnie Barker) whose three aims in life were to extract
as much money as possible from the customers at his corner shop
in Yorkshire, to make his nephew and assistant Granville (David
Jason) work as hard as possible, and to lust after nurse Gladys
Emmanuel (Lynda Baron) who lived across the road. Other regulars
included customers Mrs Featherstone (Stephanie Cole) and Mavis
(Maggie Ollerenshaw).
PRODUCER: Sydney Lotterby

LUCKY FELLER (London Weekend Television)
FIRST BROADCAST: 2 September 1976
SYNOPSIS: Series about shy Shorty Mepstead (David Jason) who
ran a small plumbing business with his brother Randy (Peter
Armitage). Shorty's girlfriend Kath (Cheryl Hall) gradually coaxes
him out of his shyness but she also has affections for his brother.
WRITER: Terence Frisby

A SHARP INTAKE OF BREATH (ATV)
FIRST BROADCAST: 20 February 1978. Three further series.
SYNOPSIS: Stories based on the efforts of Peter Barnes (David
Jason) and his wife Sheila (Jacqueline Clarke) to understand and
beat 'the system'. Peter's belief in freedom of choice often involved
an innocent third party being dragged into his escapades. Regular
cast members included Alun Armstrong and Richard Wilson.
PRODUCERS: Les Chatfield and Stuart Allen
WRITERS: Ronnie Taylor and Vince Powell

HIS LORDSHIP ENTERTAINS (BBC)
FIRST BROADCAST: 5 June 1979
SYNOPSIS: Sequel to *Hark at Barker* with Ronnie Barker as Lord
Rustless whose stately home has been turned into a hotel. The cast

293

again included David Jason as Dithers the gardener, Mary Baxter as the cook, Josephine Tewson as the secretary and Frank Gatliff as Badger the butler.
PRODUCER: Harold Snoad

ONLY FOOLS AND HORSES (BBC)
FIRST BROADCAST: 8 September 1981
SYNOPSIS: The adventures of the male members of the Trotter family; street trader Derek or 'Del-Boy' (David Jason), his much younger brother Rodney (Nicholas Lyndhurst), and Grandad (Lennard Pearce). Buster Merryfield joined as Uncle Albert after the death of Pearce in 1983. Other regulars included barman Mike (Ken Macdonald), spiv Boycie (John Challis), Boycie's wife Marlene (Sue Holderness), road sweeper Trigger (Roger Lloyd-Pack), Rodney's wife Cassandra (Gwnyeth Strong), and Del's girlfriend Raquel (Tessa Peake-Jones).
PRODUCERS: Ray Butt, Gareth Gwenlan

SERIES 1: 8 September – 13 October 1981 (30 minutes each)
1. *Big Brother*
2. *Go West, Young Man*
3. *Cash and Carry*
4. *The Second Time Around*
5. *A Slow Boat to Chingford*
6. *The Russians Are Coming*
7. *Christmas Crackers* – Christmas Special, 28 December 1981 (35 minutes)

SERIES II: 21 October – 2 December 1982 (30 minutes each)
8. *The Long Legs of the Law*
9. *Ashes To Ashes*
10. *A Losing Streak*
11. *No Greater Love*
12. *The Yellow Peril*

13. *It Never Rains*

14. *A Touch of Glass*

15. *Diamonds Are For Heather* – Christmas Special, 30 December 1982 (30 minutes)

SERIES III: 10 November – 22 December 1983 (30 minutes each)

16. *Homesick*

17. *Healthy Competition*

18. *Friday the 14th*

19. *Yesterday Never Comes*

20. *May the Force Be with You*

21. *Wanted*

22. *Who's a Pretty Boy*

Mini Episode Special 1983: *Christmas Trees* (11 minutes)

23. *Thicker Than Water* – Christmas Special, 25 December 1983 (30 minutes)

SERIES IV: 21 February – 4 April 1985 (30 minutes each)

24. *Happy Return*

25. *Strained Relations*

26. *Hole in One*

27. *It's Only Rock 'n' Roll*

28. *Sleeping Dogs Lie*

29. *Watching the Girls Go By*

30. *As One Door Closes*

31. *To Hull and Back* – Christmas Special, 25 December 1985 (90 minutes)

SERIES V: 31 August – 5 October 1986 (30 minutes)

32. *From Prussia with Love*

33. *The Miracle of Peckham*

34. *The Longest Night*

35. *Tea for Three*

36. *Video Nasty*
37. *Who Wants to be a Millionaire?* Royal Variety Live
    Performance 1986: *The Dulane Club* (5 minutes)
38. *A Royal Flush* – Christmas Special, 25 December 1986
    (75 minutes)
39. *The Frog's Legacy* – Christmas Special, 25 December 1987
    (75 minutes)
40. *Dates* - Christmas Special, 25 December 1988
    (80 minutes)

Series VI: 8 January – 12 February 1989 (50 minutes)
41. *Yuppy Love*
42. *Danger UXD*
43. *Chain Gang*
44. *The Unlucky Winner Is....*
45. *Sickness and Wealth*
46. *Little Problems*
47. *The Jolly Boys' Outing* - Christmas Special, 25 December
    1989 (85 minutes)
48. *Rodney Come Home* – Christmas Special, 25 December 1990
    (75 minutes)

SERIES VII: 30 December 1990 – 3 February 1991
(50 minutes each)
49. *The Sky's the Limit*
50. *The Chance of a Lunchtime*
51. *Stage Fright*
52. *The Class of '62*
53. *He Ain't Heavy, He's My Uncle*
54. *Three Men, a Woman and a Baby*
55. *Miami Twice* Christmas Special: *The American Dream*
    24 December 1991 (50 minutes)
56. *Oh to be in England*: Christmas Special, 25 December 1991.
    (90 minutes)

57. *Mother Nature's Son* – Christmas Special, 25 December 1992 (65 minutes)

58. *Fatal Extraction* – Christmas Special, 25 December 1993 (90 minutes)

59. *Heroes and Villains* – Christmas Special, 25 December 1996 (60 minutes)

60. *Modern Men* – Christmas Special, 27 December 1996 (60 minutes)

61. *Time On Our Hands* – Christmas Special, 29 December 1996 (60 minutes)

62. *Comic Relief Special*, March 1997 (10 minutes)

63. *If They Could See Us Now* – Christmas Special, 25 December 2001 (71 minutes)

64. *Strangers on the Shore*, 25 December 2002 (75 minutes)

65. *Sleepless in Peckham*, 25 December 2003 (75 minutes)

PORTERHOUSE BLUE (C4)
FIRST BROADCAST: 3 June 1987
SYNOPSIS: Adapted from the Tom Sharpe novel, David Jason starred as head porter Skullion at Porterhouse, the most archaic and reactionary of Cambridge colleges. The arrival of a new Master (Ian Richardson) signals the end of Skullion's 45 years in service.
PRODUCER: Brian Eastman
DIRECTOR: Robert Knights

A BIT OF A DO (Yorkshire TV)
FIRST BROADCAST: 13 January 1989. Series II: 20 October 1989.
SYNOPSIS: Adapted by David Nobbs from his own novel about two Yorkshire families in a town where everyone seems to know everyone else's business. The series followed the lives, loves, marriages and deaths in the two families, the snobbish Rodenhursts and the inferior Simcocks.
Main cast: Ted Simcock (David Jason) and his wife Rita (Gwen Taylor) and their sons Elvis (Wayne Foskett) and Paul

(David Thewlis). The Rodenhursts were dentist Laurence
(Paul Chapman) and his wife Liz (Nicola Pagett), their son
Simon (Nigel Hastings) and daughter Jenny (Sarah-Jane Holm).
PRODUCERS: Robert Banks-Stewart, Peter Norris, Simon Lewis.

SINGLE VOICES: THE CHEMIST (BBC)
FIRST BROADCAST: 22 April 1990
SYNOPSIS: Monologue with David Jason as Vernon Duxley, a
husband opening his heart to a video camera about his personal life
after a traumatic weekend.
WRITER: Roy Clarke

AMONGST BARBARIANS (BBC)
FIRST BROADCAST: 11 July 1990
SYNOPSIS: David Jason starred as the father of one of two
young men facing the death penalty for smuggling heroin in
Malaysia.

THE DARLING BUDS OF MAY (Yorkshire TV)
FIRST BROADCAST: 1 April 1991
SYNOPSIS: The happy-go-lucky lives of the warm-hearted
Larkin family living in the Kent countryside, adapted from
the novels of H. E. Bates. The family included Pop Larkin
(David Jason) Ma (Pam Ferris), their daughter Mariette
(Catherine Zeta-Jones) and her husband Charley (Philip Franks).
PRODUCERS: Robert Banks-Stewart, Peter Norris, Simon Lewis.

THE BULLION BOYS (BBC)
FIRST BROADCAST: 24 October 1993
SYNOPSIS: Based on a true story set in 1940 when Britain's gold
reserves were transferred for safety to Liverpool as the German
armies marched through Europe. The top-secret operation is
known only to a handful of security men, top bank officials and a
group of Liverpool dockers who handle the move. Dockers' leader

Billy Mac (David Jason) hatches an ingenious plan to steal some of the gold bars from under the noses of the guards.
PRODUCER: Christopher Morahan

A TOUCH OF FROST (Yorkshire TV)
FIRST BROADCAST: 6 December 1992
SYNOPSIS: Thriller series with David Jason starring as hard-nosed detective Jack Frost faced with the roughest back-street crimes. An intuitive Detective Inspector, he is by no means a model policeman. Rash, sloppy and disorganised, he has a healthy disregard for the rules but always cracks the case despite unorthodox methods.

MARCH IN WINDY CITY (Yorkshire TV)
FIRST BROADCAST: 25 March 1998
SYNOPSIS: When detectives Riggs (Paul Bates) and Wallace (Kate Goehring) are told that an ex-MI5 spy is coming to Chicago, Steven March (David Jason) is not quite what they are expecting. Short, afraid of heights and a collector of old mechanical toys, he's certainly no James Bond but he does have a dry sense of humour and he's a crack shot. The Chicago cops think March is in the windy city on a lecture tour but in fact he has been brought out of retirement for a more deadly purpose – to kill Dan Patterson (David McCallum), formerly Russian Mafia man Petrovsky who is running for the US senate.

ALL THE KINGS MEN (BBC)
FIRST BROADCAST: 14 November 1999
SYNOPSIS: David Jason starred as Captain Frank Beck in this moving true story of the Sandringham company which mysteriously disappeared in action at Gallipoli in 1925.

MICAWBER (Yorkshire Television)
FIRST BROADCAST: December 2001
SYNOPSIS: Jason teemed up with *Only Fools and Horses* writer
John Sullivan to present the life of the Dickens character in the
years before he meets David Copperfield.

THE QUEST (Yorkshire TV)
FIRST BROADCAST: Easter 2002
SYNOPSIS: Based on idea by David Jason himself, *The Quest* tells
the story of three young Southern lads at large in the North of
England during the 1950s. David Jason, Roy Hudd and Hywel
Bennett played the characters' elder selves in the drama.

GHOST BOAT (Yorkshire TV)
FIRST BROADCAST: April 2006
SYNOPSIS: Jack Hardy is the sole survivor of a mysterious
submarine disaster in World War II. Now, in 1981, the ill-fated
submarine *Scorpion* has resurfaced, miraculously intact. Naval
Intelligence need Hardy's expertise to retrace the course and
mission that led to her original disappearance. But what's waiting
for them under the grey waters of the Baltic Sea turns out to be
much worse than the Russian submarines they're expecting. Before
he knows it, Hardy is fighting for his life as the forgotten events
of 1943 start to have deadly consequences for the modern-day
crew of the sub.

THE SECOND QUEST (Yorkshire TV)
FIRST BROADCAST: 5 April, 2004
DIRECTOR: David Jason
SYNOPSIS: Follow up to the 2002 slice of nostalgia about the
adventures of three young lads, Charlie, Dave and Ronno,
growing up in the Sixties. Loosely based on David's own
reminiscences of his teenage years, this sequel takes the trio to the
Isle of Man in the hope of losing their virginity. On the boat over,

the boys meet up with three of the contestants for the final of the Miss Isle of Man beauty contest. They later get mixed up in a plan by the girls to steal the Manx cat belonging to the contest's judge in revenge for him failing to keep his promise to award one of them the crown. David Jason, Roy Hudd and Hywel Bennett again play the characters' elder selves reminiscing about their holiday. Supporting cast include Les Dennis as the sleazy beauty pageant compere, and ex-Coronation Street barmaid Jennifer James as a scheming contestant.

DIAMOND GEEZER (Yorkshire TV)
FIRST BROADCAST: 20 March, 2005
SYNOPSIS: One-off drama featuring David Jason as imprisoned criminal Des Parker feigning senility while plotting an outrageous heist from behind bars. Des persuaded naïve petty criminal Phil to help him steal valuable diamonds from the possession of prison thug Benny. Caleb Ranson's sparkling script and high quality support from George Cole and Jenny Agutter ensured the production was very received and three further adventures featuring devious Des were made and screened in 2007.

THE HOGFATHER (Sky TV)
FIRST BROADCAST: 17 and 18 December, 2006
SYNOPSIS: Based on the book by Terry Pratchett, this adventure follows the residents of Discworld, a parallel universe balanced on four elephants, as they anxiously await presents to be delivered from the kindly Hogfather during the holiday of Hogwatch. But when the gift-giver mysteriously vanishes, his granddaughter tries to figure out what happened to him while Death and his manservant Albert, played by David Jason, take over his duties. David Warner, Tony Robinson and Nigel Planer co-star.

THE COLOUR OF MAGIC (Sky TV)
First broadcast: 23 and 24 March, 2008
SYNOPSIS: In an adaptation of Terry Pratchett's first two novels, David Jason plays an incompetent wizard named Ricewind as he guides a stranger called Twoflower (Sean Astin) and his magical luggage chest through the medieval-like Discworld. On their tour the pair encounter a collection of fantastical and bizarre beings including wizards and trolls, dragon lords, Druid mercenaries and the wicked wizard Trymon, played by Tim Curry. Co-stars include Jeremy Irons, Janet Suzman and Nigel Planer.

THE SHOW MUST GO ON (Five)
First broadcast: 7 June 2010
SYNOPSIS: Documentary in which David Jason helped the Argosy Players, an amateur dramatics group, to stage a performance in the West End. With his advice and encouragement, the aspiring actors from Ruislip, northwest London, had just three weeks to rehearse and prepare a one-act comedy at the Playhouse Theatre.

ALBERT'S MEMORIAL (ITV)
First broadcast: 12 September 2010
SYNOPSIS: David stars as Harry, a cabbie and war veteran, with David Warner as his friend Frank. Together, they pay a visit to their dying friend, Albert. On his death-bed Albert makes the strange request for the pair to steal his body from the mortuary and bury him in a field in Germany, where the three of them witnessed an un-revealed tragedy which bound them together.

DAVID JASON: BATTLE OF BRITAIN (ITV)
First broadcast: 12 September 2010
SYNOPSIS: Documentary marking 70 years since RAF pilots managed to pull off a most unlikely and remarkable victory against German planes in World War II. David took to the skies in a Spitfire, met pilots who shot down enemy aircraft in 1940 and

engineers who kept the British planes running for up to six scrambles a day.

COME RAIN COME SHINE (ITV)
First broadcast: 20 December 2010
SYNOPSIS: TV film with David starring as retired Cockney ex-docker Don Mitchell, a devoted family man, and Alison Steadman as his wife Dora, whose lives begin to unravel when the financial fortunes of their seemingly wealthy son take a disastrous turn for the worse.

ALL THE WAY UP (Emerald Sky Films)
First screening: 2010
SYNOPSIS: David made his non-acting directorial debut in this 17-minute comedy about a high-flying businessman with a seemingly perfect life who gives in to temptation and is about to embark on an adulterous affair with a work colleague. But, events take a different turn when he steps into an elevator at the smart Queens Hotel.

DAVID JASON'S GREAT ESCAPES (ITV)
First broadcast: 28 August 2011
SYNOPSIS: Documentary re-living some of the amazing true stories which inspired films and dramas such as *The Great Escape* and *Colditz*. David visited Colditz Castle in Germany to see the most ambitious escape tunnel ever dug there and travelled with two surviving POWs to the site in Poland of *The Great Escape*.

THE ROYAL BODYGUARD (BBC1)
First broadcast: 26 December 2011
SYNOPSIS: Comedy series with David starring as Captain Guy Hubble, an ex-guardsman who is accidently promoted to a position way above his head. Thanks to bravely saving the Queen's life on the day of the State Opening of Parliament,

Hubble is thrust from Buckingham Palace car park attendant to royal bodyguard but proves to be horribly accident-prone and a thoroughly incompetent minder to her Majesty – and yet seemingly indestructible.